The Great Surprise of the Small Transformation

The Great Surprise of the Small Transformation

The Demise of Communism and the Rise of the Private Sector in Hungary

Ákos Róna-Tas

Ann Arbor

THE UNIVERSITY OF MICHIGAN PRESS

Published in the United States of America by
The University of Michigan Press
Manufactured in the United States of America
⊗ Printed on acid-free paper

2000 1999 1998 1997 4 3 2 1

A CIP catalog record for this book is available from the British Library.

Library of Congress Cataloging-in-Publication Data

Rona-Tas, Akos.
The great surprise of the small transformation : the demise of communism and the rise of the private sector in Hungary / Ákos Róna-Tas.
p. cm.
Includes bibliographical references (p.) and index.
ISBN 0-472-10795-X
1. Hungary—Economic conditions—1945– 2. Hungary—Economic policy—1945– 3. Hungary—Politics and government—1945– 4. Hungary—Politics and government—1945–1989. 5. Post-communism—Hungary. I. Title.
HC300.24.R66 1997
338.9439—dc21 96-54238
CIP

To Adam

Contents

Tables

Acknowledgments

If writing an academic book seems a private enterprise, it is not. The lonesome author is a myth, propagated by book cover designs, catalogue entries, and copyright laws. Like any human activity, this one too is deeply embedded in a social world of people, who all, in their own ways, participated in the final outcome. To cast a fleeting glimpse at the social context of the knowledge a book represents, one has to read acknowledgments.

My colleagues in the Sociology Department at the University of California, San Diego, have provided generous intellectual stimulation. Martha Lampland, through interminable and sometimes tempestuous (but always amicable) debates, brought me around to understanding the importance of process and lived experience in sociological explanation. She has been also very generous in sharing with me her superbly proficient command of Hungarian social history. Juan Diez Medrano, Harvey Goldman, Leon Zamosc, Christena Turner, Carlos Waisman, and Jeff Weintraub helped with clarifying theoretical questions. Jeff Haydu, Gershon Shafir, Rick Biernacki, Maria Charles, and Lisa Catanzarite all read and commented on parts of the manuscript. Tim McDaniel read the work in many of its incarnations and patiently pointed out some of my small mistakes and large errors.

Anyone who reads this book will notice many of its intellectual debts without realizing their personal nature. Iván Szelényi's work has been a constant source of inspiration. His invitation to a large-scale multinational East European survey project, which he codirected with Donald J. Treiman, introduced me to an excellent research team. Working with this team was both exciting and satisfying. Without my long conversations with József Böröcz and Éva Fodor this book would be very different. The workshop organized around the survey project at the University of Californa, Los Angeles, was worth the drive, in the worst LA traffic, two hours in each direction.

Andrew G. Walder, David Stark, Iván T. Berend, Ellen Comisso, Daniel Chirot, and Victoria Bonnell have aided with valuable suggestions in different stages of writing the manuscript. I am especially grateful for Michael D. Kennedy's contribution. Exercising his gift for gentle but incisive criticism, he was always there to administer the crucial push when it was needed. I have also discussed ideas that found their way into this book with Michael Burawoy, Victor Nee, Anna Seleny, Teodor Shanin, Albert Simkus, Jadwiga Staniszkis, Anna Szemere, David Wank, and Marty Whyte. During my stay at the Juan March Institute in Madrid, Victor Perez Diaz, and, at the Freieuniversität in Berlin, Burkhard Strümpel and Florian Schramm, offered critical observations. It goes without saying that many of them will find several things to disagree with in this book.

And so will my Hungarian colleagues, who lent me their knowledge and time so generously. I have spent many hours interviewing private entrepreneurs with two Hungarian colleagues: Tibor Kuczi and Pál Schiffer. In Budapest, my manuscript was the subject of public and private debates. During those discussions I collected useful comments and criticisms from Péter Galasi, István R. Gabor, Endre Sik, György Lengyel, Teréz Laky, Anna Wessely, György Csepeli, Erzsébet Szalai, László Bruszt, Mihály Laki, Wim Swaan, Iván Major, Ferenc Moksony, Balázs Krémer, András Bozóki, Bálint Magyar, István Rév, and Éva Voszka. Tamás Kolosi and his team at the data archive, TÁRKI, made available the data sets from the 1981 and 1986 Social Stratification Surveys.

In Hungary, I could rely on the friendly assistance of archivists in the arcane world of public archives. I would also like to thank the Hungarian economic weekly, *HVG,* for letting me use its own archives and Györgyi Kocsis, whose investigative reporting on *nomenklatura* privatization was an invaluable source. Róza Hodosán helped me with obtaining legislative documents. It was my good fortune to meet Anna Székács. One of the key policymakers promoting the private sector in the 1980s, she kept all the official documents that passed across her desk at the Ministry of Finance. Besides providing me with rich and lively insights into the internal workings of the socialist state machinery in its final years, she also allowed me unlimited access to her papers.

The final form of the manuscript owes an unusually large debt to its first editor, Kathy Mooney. Her editing went far beyond policing proper grammar, spelling, and punctuation. She unsnarled tangled narratives, ferreted out faulty logic, and brought silly metaphors to justice. I express my gratitude for her dedication, expertise and kindness. Emily M. Maxon, Lida Nedilsky, Ilona Hicks, and Alya Guseva were indispensable in turning out the final product, and thanks are also due to Charles T. Myers of the University of Michigan Press for his support and professional handling of the manuscript.

My parents, while busy with their own books and articles, always found time to help me out even with the most mundane tasks. My debt to them can be compared only to the one I owe to my wife, Judit Hersko. She was always my first critic, and without her love and intellectual partnership this book would have never been written.

Finally, I want to acknowledge the largesse of the University of California, which supported my research with several Academic Senate grants.

CHAPTER 1

Introduction

With the fall of communism in 1989, the countries of Eastern Europe bid final farewell to a social order that was predictable and oppressive but also secure and centered. The daily routine of safe, if underpaid, employment in large state-owned factories and offices has been shattered. Now, with high unemployment, a shrunken work force is scattered across a myriad of small- and medium-sized enterprises. Resources have been divided up. Property previously in the control and ownership of the state has been distributed among new owners. Fragmentation of organizations and resources has gone hand in hand with fragmentation of choices. Careers so stable that they could be planned decades into the future have given way to a dazzling number of possibilities. Identities have become ambiguous. Occupational titles, once arranged by the socialist state in a solid scheme of classification covering all gainful human activities, now can be invented every day—by anyone—leaving people to wonder just what someone who introduces himself or herself as a project manager, sales representative, natural healer, or entrepreneur actually does for a living.

The clear distinction between "official" and "nonofficial" is gone. In the past, anything that emanated from an organization carried the central authorities' stamp of approval. If prices were high, if the soles of new shoes detached, or if the tableware in restaurants was unclean, there was little doubt about who was ultimately responsible for these shortcomings. The state, as the owner of shops, shoe factories, and restaurants, provided a ready target for complaints. Now that the distinction between public and private has become blurred, grievances that used to be focused on one, large, culpable entity are dispersed across a myriad of small culprits.

The splintering that has occurred in intellectual life is equally profound. By the late 1960s, the state's ideology, Marxism-Leninism, had become a hollow edifice in which few believed. Nevertheless, even in the last decades of communism, it continued to dominate discussion by setting the agenda and terms for debate. All ideas, including critical ones, had to encompass the official worldview in some measure. There were cracks in this edifice, of course, and some new notions and theories trickled through. But, since 1989, the intellectual fashions that developed in the rest of the world over the last four decades have poured in as a single deluge of incompatible ideas. The intellectual landscape has become balkanized among small factions, each vying for its own microstate on the intellectual map and sometimes, more frighteningly, on the geographical map as well.

This process of deconcentration that has been dissolving socialist society's few large structures into many small ones began decades ago. It has accelerated and taken new forms since 1989, however. This accelerated devolution of a highly centralized system that transports postcommunist societies into the postmodern era, I call the Small Transformation.

The Private Sector as a Social and Political Space

The private sector in Eastern Europe—the sum of those economic activities that were not initiated and directly controlled by the state—has emerged as part of the process of deconcentration. Its development was influenced by institutions—or rules—such as property rights and regulations determined by the state.[1] Yet, the "rules of the game" that actually prevailed in the private sector were shaped to a large extent by its players. What rules have been imposed and how they have been put into practice have depended mainly on the social composition and history of the private sector. The private sector has evolved as both a social and a political space. Under socialism,[2] its social composition depended on its relationship with the state sector, and its political weight depended on its social composition. This interdependence persists and is clearly discernible in the recent efforts of various postcommunist societies to create strong private sectors. Governments facing similar economic problems involving the private sector have opted for different institutional solutions, and similar institutional solutions have given rise to very different private sector practices.

This book chronicles the development of the Hungarian private sector from the beginning of Communist rule until 1994 with a view of the entire region. I present two broad, interrelated arguments: the first seeks to explain why communism fell and to show how the development of the private sector was strongly implicated in the collapse. The second argument attempts to account for the course post-Communist privatization has taken. The two arguments are linked by a wider social process: the devolution of the one-nation-one-factory model.

Why Communism Collapsed

The end of communism was first perceived as a perplexing, great surprise (Kuran 1991, 1995; Lipset and Bence 1994; Domański 1994; Draper 1992), a miracle that defied human comprehension. Soon, however, an immense post hoc literature developed in which a wide variety of factors were identified as causes of the collapse. These explanations typically stress one or more of the following elements as key: world market pressures, military challenges, economic inefficiency, cynicism about official ideology, corruption, elite fragmentation, the development of self-organizing autonomous spheres in society, and intellectual dissent. Undoubtedly, most of these forces did contribute to the collapse. Still, it is ironic that before the fall of communism many of these same factors were held up as proof of the stability of the system. Withstanding world market pressure and military challenge, muddling through with an inefficient economy, being able to do without ideological mobilization, allowing pluralism inside the Communist Party, letting civil society grow, and even affording a small measure of intellectual opposition all were noted by various observers. Rather than being viewed as detrimental, before 1990 most were touted as signs of an increasingly confident socialist regime. A credible explanation of the collapse requires, first, a theory of social order in state socialism that accounts for how the system reproduced itself over several decades. Second, the processes through which the many previously noted causes worked to undo this social order must be specified.

Theories of the Communist Social Order

Theories of the social order in state socialist societies were either preoccupied with the overbearing, all too visible, totalitarian state foisting itself on society or were intent on finding some hidden economic logic that reproduced class relations behind the seemingly rational transactions of economic self-interest. Totalitarian theory correctly pointed out that state socialism constituted a novel form of governing an entire society (Arendt [1951] 1973; Friedrich and Brzezinski 1956; Friedrich 1954; Friedrich, Curtis, and Barber 1969).[3] It rightly stressed the unprecedented importance of an explicit, totalizing ideology, which sought to give prescriptions for all aspects of life. It also properly noted that these systems strove to create a single hierarchy of power. Yet, while totalitarian theory might have fitted very early stages of socialism better, it underestimated the extent to which socialist states were able to create social order based on economic self-interest, and it also underestimated the depth of society's cooperation. Mobilization and public rituals, propaganda and indoctrination, physical coercion and terror, though always present, were not the primary means of maintaining social order from the early 1960s onward in Eastern and Central Europe.

Class theory recognized the importance of economic incentives in maintaining social order (Djilas 1957; Konrád and Szelényi 1979; Szelényi 1982; Wright 1985; Burawoy and Lukács 1992). Adherents of this theory contended that the ruling class in socialism governed society through its control over property and the mechanism through which the economy as a whole was coordinated. Yet class theory explains social order only if one believes that those who control property share the same interest and that economic objectives never contradict political ones. Class theory overestimated the coherence and collective rationality of the ruling class. It failed to explain how economic self-interests were molded into a coherent social order and how subordinate groups were made complicit in the system because it overlooked the Party-state leadership's not so subtle efforts to stage-manage economic interests through the central institution of social order in socialism: the system of universal state employment. The social order in the last three decades of state socialism was maintained primarily by the institution of universal state employment. Universal state employment was designed to organize society in harmony with the requirements of large-scale production and allow the Party-state to exercise power through its ownership rights rather than through coercion.

Universal state employment was the product of socialist industrialization, and it emerged as the solution to a puzzle: how to concentrate production and reduce the entire population to wage labor while not allowing a labor market to develop. It was the magnifying projection of factory code to society as a whole, turning what Marx called "the capitalist caricature" into a new mural of social order. On this immense tableau all appeared as subordinate employees under the watchful eyes of the boss, with a few vigilant secret policemen hiding in some dark corners. The picture of state socialism presented here is closest to the theory of neotraditionalism as proposed by Walder in the context of Chinese industry (Walder 1986).[4] Walder contends that the crucial feature of communist society is that it is organized according to a particular version of industrial authority. This peculiar form of authority was unique to communist societies. It emerged from a form of employment that was not primarily a market relationship (Walder 1986, 11–12). Social order was ensured by a complex, nationwide system of organized dependence whereby one's supervisors were entrusted not only with enforcing hard and productive work but also with the chores of imposing political control.[5]

Thus supplanting both totalitarian and class theories of state socialism I offer my own theory of state socialist social order that is best described as institutionalist (Nee and Stark 1989; Powell and DiMaggio 1991). It was neither the almighty state nor the power of the dominant class that kept society constantly in line. It was an institution, universal state employment, which was created by the state and maintained inequalities of power and privilege among social groups. Universal state employment was a real institution with hard boundaries. It was not purely a heuristic conceptual device invented by social scientists to comprehend a set of seemingly disparate patterns of social behavior. It was real, in the sense that it was the object of people's aspirations, fears, and rational calculations and the subject of state plans, decrees, and policies. State employment was measured, classified, and policed. It was the central fact of life for almost all adults living under communist rule. It was also unique to communism. No other authoritarian or totalitarian state sought to hire its entire populace.

This institution had an unexpected autonomy. Its gradual erosion, which led to the final collapse of state socialism, was a process that neither the state nor any privileged social group was able to prevent. Yet, if state employment had lost its ability to uphold, it was still able to outlive state socialism. State employment, shrunken by postcommunist economic policies, is still a way of life for a substantial portion of the population. Today, as the most vocal opponents of market reforms, state employees are the first to feel nostalgic about the last years of communism. They rally in defense of a system that was still able to provide them with life-long security but was already too weak to dominate their lives.

The collapse of communism became possible as the result of twin processes that undermined this social order: the erosion of universal state employment and the parallel emergence of the private sector. This book argues that the collapse of socialism marks the end of a social system developed from a coherent, modernistic vision shaped by the rapid industrialization of nineteenth-century Western Europe. This powerful ideology regarded large-scale production as inevitable, and it understood the concentration of production as the essence of historical development. Following what they believed to be the lessons of nineteenth-century capitalist industrialization, the original Great Transformation, to use Karl Polanyi's famous phrase ([1944] 1957), communist parties in the twentieth century sought to establish large-scale factory production with an emphasis on extractive and manufacturing industries. To accommodate large-scale production, they developed elaborate bureaucracies and imposed factory discipline on the entire population, forcing a separation between home and workplace that rendered fixed work hours and rigid labor routines the norm. Just as had occurred in the nineteenth century, the socialist Great Transformation generated enormous social dislocation, moving large portions of the population between geographic locations and across occupational boundaries. Despite these similarities, however, the socialist Great Transformation was not a mere replica of its predecessor, as Marxism-Leninism prescribed the complete elimination of markets and private property of any sort.

The socialist version of the Great Transformation in many respects made Fordism, the dream of a society based on and subordinated to the needs of large-scale mass production, more real than it had ever been before, but even in socialist societies Fordism did not fully succeed. It is not my contention, as various Marxist and post-Marxist critics of capitalist Fordism have claimed for capitalism, that in large-scale production lies the hidden meaning of the history of state socialism. Instead, I argue that in state socialism large-scale production developed as the object of clearly proclaimed state policies guided by an explicitly stated philosophy of history. It subordinated most aspects of social life not because it was the moving force of history but because the Party-state did everything it could to make society compatible with large-scale production. Factory production in state socialism emerged not from the invisible hand of the market but from the all too visible fist of the state.

In implementing this model, the Communist Party–state leadership followed a modernistic ideological blueprint that provided a complete and scientifically certain vision of the world, past, present and future, and one that was also uniquely comprehensive and elaborate. This grand theory of history reduced the multiplicity of individual identities to simple categories of its own design. It also drew a clear distinction between the private and the public, a distinction of both analytic and moral significance.

This ideology held that private property and small production were impediments to economic concentration, to large-scale production and, thus, to economic progress. They had to be eradicated in order to ensure an organizationally homogeneous economy based on the one-nation-one-factory model. Thus, nationalizing all production assets and turning the entire population into employees of large state companies were viewed as both an ideological necessity and a historical inevitability. Across Eastern Europe, the communist parties suppressed or eliminated the labor market and developed universal state employment, which became the pivotal institution of social order under state socialism.

Yet, even as it seemed to have triumphed, the demise of this one-nation-one-factory model had already begun. Large-scale production proved to be too inflexible to meet the full range of economic tasks, and the creation of gigantic enterprises led to additional difficulties. Starting in the 1960s, these problems began to undermine universal state employment all across Eastern Europe. This erosion took two forms: a limited private sector developed, mostly in agriculture, construction, and certain services; and managers in the state sector became more autonomous from the leadership of the Party-state. Both challenges to concentrated state ownership developed most fully in Hungary and Poland, and these were the countries to first bid farewell to communism. The collapse in both cases was a negotiated process.

Why would any sovereign political elite give up power voluntarily? Elites give up power when three conditions are met: (1) the means by which they exercise their power have eroded; (2) elite members have lost their ideological convictions; and (3) elites have reason to expect that they will be individually better off—or at least not worse—in case they have to leave power. In most Eastern European countries, only the first two conditions were present, though in varying degrees. Thus, elites had to be dislodged by means of mass demonstrations or—in the case of Romania—by armed insurrection. Only in the case of Poland and Hungary were all three conditions present, leading to a negotiated withdrawal. Elites in Poland and Hungary were willing to jettison the socialist system because, as an unanticipated consequence of earlier reforms supportive of private business, a growing part of the elite had discovered that it could prosper in the private sector, that is, that it could succeed individually outside the system of universal state employment.

The collapse of communism in the entire region occurred for a complex set of reasons, but the disintegration of universal employment took a central place among them. Some important factors, such as poor economic performance and world market pressures, as well as military competition, contributed to the collapse primarily by deepening the crisis of universal state employment. Others, such as corruption or the development of self-organizing autonomous spheres in society, were symptoms of this disintegration. Yet other causes, such as elite fragmentation and intellectual dissent became detrimental because of the frailty of social order, just as common ailments can become lethal for patients infected with HIV. Moreover, the *way* individual communist states collapsed depended on the specific historical paths this disintegration took, resulting in negotiated or forcible dislodging of the communist leadership.

Since the collapse of communism was ultimately the collapse of the communist state, most explanations focus on high politics.[6] While there are many accounts of the erosion of communist rule from below (some of them are discussed in chapter 8), few make the linkage between these wider social processes and the end of communism. Putting state employment in the center of my discussion forces me to move beyond the dichotomy of state and society centered analysis. The institution of universal state employment linked society to state power. Universal state employment evolved and then devolved in a constant tension, conflict and compromise between state and society with the driving initiative passing from the first to the second. In the early days the state was setting the course of events;

by the end, deep changes in society played the commanding role and the state was helpless. Omitting one or the other protagonist from the analysis would be akin to watching a prize fight where one of the two fighters is invisible. The one we can see would grotesquely punch in the air and would fall to the ground every now and then for no apparent reason.

The principal contribution my book seeks to make is to establish the linkage between societal and political processes. I attempt to build the bridge between the mundane everyday choices of ordinary individuals and the momentous decisions of political elites with the aid of a novel institutionalist argument. It is my deep conviction that unless our understanding of political processes is grounded in wider social currents, political change will always come as a great surprise.

Path Dependence of Privatization

The second argument this book presents is intertwined with the first. Much as the form of the communist collapse was path dependent, so too is the course privatization has taken in Eastern Europe. These countries did not begin their postcommunist transformation with a clean slate. Rather, major social forces were already firmly in place in 1990, influencing the choices of the postcommunist leadership as these men and women began the task of developing new economic institutions.

An often remarked upon irony of the postcommunist transformation is that it began as the most ambitious attempt at large-scale social engineering since the Great Transformation of the early socialist period. During the early euphoria that followed the fall of communism, there seemed to be no contradiction in savagely criticizing the hubris of socialist planning for presuming to know how to overhaul society as a whole while simultaneously presenting daring blueprints for revamping the institutions of state socialism in their entirety. Despite disagreement over particular issues, advocates of "designer capitalism," to borrow David Stark's apt phrase, shared a vision of the postcommunist era as a period involving movement between two systems. Behind languished an odious socialist system and ahead beckoned a promising capitalist one, a market economy built on private property. The central notion of this vision was the "transition," as the years following the communist collapse would be the transitional period between these two steady states. Just how far countries would progress on this road to paradise over the coming years was a matter of debate. Few doubted, however, that forward movement could represent anything other than improvement.

Understandably, the transition paradigm had a strong normative bias. New elites took over the levers of government, declaring their commitment to radical reform and new orientations toward policy making. Economists, armed with their powerful analytic tools and a clear sense of direction, offered guidance to negotiate the transition to a market economy (e.g., Lipton and Sachs 1990; Brada 1993; Åslund 1994). Their advice was that government remove the obsolete institutions of state socialism and replace them with those of a competitive market economy based on private property. They assumed that the desired abrupt change could be engineered by government if it had the resolve to carry through its plan.

This book joins a rapidly growing literature that takes a different approach. This approach sees the changes in postcommunist societies as a gradual process of uncertain direction, deeply influenced by a complex set of social, political, and cultural circumstances that developed during the last decades of communism (e.g., Bartlett 1991; Böröcz 1993; Burawoy and Krotov 1992; Comisso 1995; Levitas 1994; Murrell 1993; Offe 1995; Pelikán 1992; Poznanski 1992, 1993, 1995; Stark 1994, 1996). This approach denies that institutions emerge as responses to abstract efficiency requirements; rather it contends that institutions develop in political contests among social groups. It claims no privileged knowledge about the future. It prefers to speak of transformation rather than transition. Its interest lies less in policy prescriptions than in understanding unfolding causal processes. For example, this approach is more curious about how specific—and different—choices about privatization come to be made than in finding the form of privatization that provides the best way to a hypothetical market economy. I argue that voucher privatization and reprivatization are choices of last resort in countries where the private sector and the autonomy of managers had developed the furthest under state socialism. Hungary decided against these two options as a result of a complex interplay among its deeply indebted state, desperately seeking new sources of revenue, and its private entrepreneurs and powerful managers. The latter two groups, which had emerged in the last decade of state socialism, were eager to gain access to state property.

The collapse and its aftermath was not a revolution—that is, it was not a profound and sudden break with the past. Changes brought about by the Small Transformation dwarf in comparison with the radical ruptures that accompanied the Great Transformation of socialist industrialization during the early years of communism. Lacking revolutionary zeal and ruthlessness, postcommunist regimes are constrained to accept preexisting social structures, making the Small Transformation path dependent: earlier choices restrict later ones, forcing societies and elites into decisions they would have rejected earlier. Unintended consequences of past actions play a greater role than do intentions about future outcomes. It is not so much the future that pulls events but the past that pushes them. This devolutionary approach emphasizes the importance of the interaction between elites, which impose a particular order, and society, which, in responding to this imposition, creates a new situation, to which elites must then respond in an iterative process where previous solutions turn into new problems, often in unanticipated ways.

Since the conceptual distinction between the socialist Great Transformation leading into and the Small Transformation leading out of state socialism underpins much of the argument this book develops, a schematic contrast between the two is provided in Table 1.1.

The Hungarian Case

Using Hungary as a case study to substantiate these claims raises two types of objections. The first asks if Hungary is sufficiently similar to other communist countries to provide more general lessons. The first part of my argument asserting the crucial role of state employment in maintaining communist social order requires that Hungary be considered similar to other communist countries. As I argue at the end of chapter 4, the communist countries set out to build the same social system, and in Eastern and Central Europe they intended and achieved considerable uniformity by the 1960s.[7] While some were more successful than others in replacing ideology and coercion with the strings of state employment, state employment became a pervasive force everywhere. What was unique about Hungary was the way it reacted to the malfunctions of this system. The second part of my argument claiming that the way communism collapsed depended on the manner in which state employment disintegrated requires only the causal relationship to uphold, but it does not demand a uniform outcome because that may vary with initial conditions. The same is true for my contention that privatization is path dependent. In both cases I will present the mechanism for Hungary and call attention to certain patterns of cross-country differences.

The second type of objection points out that Hungary was strongly dependent on the Soviet Union. Why should one care about internal causal mechanisms within Hungary when all that was important had been decided in Moscow? While I don't deny the importance of the Soviet role during the communist era, there are good reasons for not being overly fixated on it. For one thing, these countries enjoyed a considerable amount of autonomy, as can be seen in the diverging paths they have taken since the 1960s. This autonomy was evident not just in early reforms in countries like Poland and Hungary but also in the stubbornness of Bulgarian, Czechoslovak, and East German leaders at a time when the Soviet Union already had decided to embark on limited reforms.

TABLE 1.1. Main Features of the Socialist Great Transformation and the Small Transformation

	Socialist Great Transformation	Small Transformation
Ideology	Totalizing ideology Strong vision of the future Clear identities	Diversity/balkanization Weak, ostensive vision of the future Ambiguity
Historical tendency	Concentration	Fragmentation
Principal course of economic change	Industrialization (extractive and manufacturing industries)	Development of services, commerce, and consumer industries
The private sector	Marginalized and traditional Clear private/public distinction Economy of the weak	Central and modern Blurred distinctions between public and private Economy of the strong
Dominant organization of production	Large companies Mass production Separation of home and workplace Rigid work hours Formal/bureaucratic relationships aided by informal ties Accumulation, large investment/consumption ratio	Diversity of size with emphasis on small businesses Short batch, customized products Reunification of home and workplace Flexible work hours Informal relationships/kinship ties aided by formal rules Decumulation, small investment/consumption ratio
Dominant patterns of ownership	Centralization of ownership rights Complete separation of ownership and control	Decentralization of ownership rights Reunification of ownership and control
Integration into the world economy	Autarchy	Globalization
Integration of labor	Universal state employment	Labor market
Social inequalities	Generated in the state sector, moderated by the private sector	Increasingly generated by the private sector, moderated by state intervention
Political organization	Strong states Weak managers, weak entrepreneurs	Weak states Strong managers, strong entrepreneurs
Type of social change	Top down Social dislocation	Bottom up Gradual, devolutionary change

Furthermore, the relationship between the Soviet Union and the rest of the Soviet bloc was more complex than the objection suggests. Events in these smaller countries also had their impact on the Soviet Union. Economic reforms in Hungary, for instance, were crucial for the Soviet leadership to reach the probably erroneous conclusion that the socialist economy was reformable and that perestroika was possible. In the early 1980s there was a heavy flow of Soviet and even Chinese reformers to Budapest, all of whom were avid readers of the Hungarian economic policy literature.[8] They clearly believed that a small country, such as Hungary, can offer some general lessons. The reason was simple: all these countries faced similar problems and were hoping to benefit from each other's experiences.

And, finally, any explanation focusing on sustained Soviet influence in the socialist era will face an impossible task in accounting for continuities between the communist and postcommunist period. Now that Moscow is no longer in the position to influence directly events in Eastern Europe it is difficult to understand, for instance, why ex-party cadres are doing so well economically and why ex-communist parties rule in much of Eastern Europe.

Method

This book has benefited from data drawn from a variety of sources. After May 1990, the archives of the Hungarian Socialist Workers' Party (HSWP) and various ministries were open to the public.[9] The HSWP's records contain valuable information about the thinking behind the top Communist leadership's policies regarding the private sector. Internal memoranda, draft laws and regulations, and verbatim transcripts of meetings were available without limitation at the time I was doing my research. I also used the archives of the Ministry of Labor (the office chiefly responsible for managing the universal system of state employment) and the Ministry of Finance (the main player promoting economic reform and the development of the private sector in the 1980s).

Some of these documents presented formidable obstacles to my commitment to rendering accurate translations for this book. Their convoluted language as often reflects the original authors' efforts to hide as it serves to reveal their positions. To render these passages into clear prose in English, while remaining faithful to the original, was difficult at best. Translating János Kádár's elliptical sentences was especially challenging. An uneducated man with no training in economics, Kádár nevertheless was the ultimate arbiter in complicated economic matters. His pronouncements were crucial, if inelegant; my translations attempt to capture both aspects.

To follow the post-1989 privatization debates, I used the minutes of the Hungarian Parliament. Here the delegates, whose deliberations were broadcast live on television, were more given to rhetorical flourishes (often infelicitous ones). These, too, are conveyed in the text with an emphasis on accuracy, even at the cost of occasional awkwardness. I supplemented the parliamentary minutes with information gathered when I gained access to certain draft laws and amendments submitted by representatives. Finally, I interviewed many of the individuals who participated in policy making both before and after 1989. All of these sources inform the discussions presented in chapters 2 through 5, 8, and 9.

I rely on a different kind of material in chapters 6, 7, and 10. In these, I substantiate my claims about the social differentiation of the private sector and the emerging new private sector elite by analyzing three stratification surveys. These surveys, taken in 1981, 1986, and 1993, queried representative samples of the Hungarian adult, noninstitutionalized population. The first two were conducted by Tamás Kolosi, who generously made these data sets available to me for analysis. The 1993 Social Stratification Survey was supplemented by a probability sample of the Communist *nomenklatura* of 1988 and the economic elite of 1993. This supplemented survey, funded by the National Science Foundation, was directed by Iván Szelényi and Donald J. Treiman. I participated in its design and execution.

Between 1990 and 1994, I spent many hours interviewing private entrepreneurs in Hungary. These in-depth interviews, which provided a valuable additional perspective on the unfolding private economy, inform the book as a whole.

I also consulted a wealth of secondary sources. The Hungarian Statistical Office has gathered important data on Hungarian society and economy over many decades. Most of these data are now available, though they are not all in published form. The professionalism of the Hungarian Statistical Office historically has been very high, but data gathered since 1990 have been less reliable. The Statistical Office has had trouble adjusting to the difficulties of collecting information in times of rapid institutional change. Their data on the rapidly growing small private sector have been particularly deficient. The Hungarian State Property Agency, which has been in charge of privatization since 1990, has published a vast array of materials. Although an agency that documents its own activities is by no means a disinterested source and many details of its highly politicized first four years will probably always remain inaccessible, its currently available papers are useful nonetheless.

Last, but not least, I profited from the riches of Hungarian scholarship on economic history, economics, and sociology. I am deeply indebted to these scholars for the high quality of their research.

Plan of the Book

The second chapter of this book examines the ideological roots of the one-nation-one-factory model, tracing it back to the Industrial Revolution and the writings of Karl Marx. This chapter establishes the relationship between economic concentration, the state, and the private sector under socialism. Here I also give a brief outline of my preferred theory of social action contrasting it to conventional rational actor models. My principal claim is that strategic action requires stability, which is provided by institutions and ideology in mixes varying in history, whereby one can substitute for the other. The third chapter describes the "Great Transformation," the early years of Communism in Hungary. This was the period during which the socialist vision was put into practice by eliminating private ownership of capital and land, the chief obstacles to modern large-scale production, and by eradicating the labor market and replacing it with a new institution, universal state employment, specific to state socialism. The fourth chapter describes this institution and analyzes its central role in maintaining social order under state socialism. The fifth chapter identifies the contradictions and difficulties that were created by this new institution, investigates the ways the Hungarian leadership tried to cope with them in the 1960s and 1970s, and explains how a private sector survived and developed in spite of the leadership's efforts. The sixth chapter presents a snapshot of the social composition of the private sector at the end of the 1970s, showing that at that time private sector participants consisted mainly of those who were faring worst in the system of universal state employment. Chapter 7 explains why the Hungarian leadership reluctantly decided to embrace small private production after 1979 and what unintended consequences followed from this decision. The contrast between this chapter and the previous one highlights some of the reasons why the leadership could not return to its earlier policies. My claim here is that once the very social groups on which the leadership relied for support got involved in the private sector the gains of the private sector were securely locked-in against any serious retrenchment instigated by hard-liners in the leadership. Chapter 8 describes the course privatization of state property took in the last two years of Communist rule and examines how communism collapsed. This is the period when the very top of the Communist hierarchy defected into the private sector, securing the path to a negotiated farewell to communism. Chapter 9 discusses privatization in the post-Communist period, contrasting the post-Communist transformation with the Great Transformation of the early years of state socialism described in chapter 3. The final chapter examines the social processes behind the emergence of the new economic elite of the private sector.

CHAPTER 2

One Nation, One Factory: The Modernistic Vision of the Soviet-Type Economy

Ideology, Institutions, and Social Action

The most dramatic events signaling the end of state socialism were those associated with the collapse of a political order. Budapest's spectacular funeral for Imre Nagy, the prime minister during the ill-fated 1956 Hungarian revolution; the opening of the Berlin Wall; the mass demonstrations in Prague's Wenceslav Square; and the armed overthrow of Nicolae Ceauşescu provided vivid visual images of the last days of undivided Communist rule. Yet state socialism was more than an authoritarian political order, more than a particular mode of political government. It was a peculiar economic and social order as well, coordinated by a comprehensive vision of society and history. Never before had there been so great an effort to create a consistent system in which each element was expected to conform to an explicit general vision that, in turn, was meant to direct everything, from politics, paper and pork production, property and philosophy, to law, linguistics, literature, and leisure.[1] This all-embracing ideology provided the standard to which each communist country had to measure up. It cemented the uniformity of the Soviet bloc by forcing a surprising similarity onto such diverse countries as East Germany and Bulgaria. The common core of the socialist experience can be traced to Marxism-Leninism and its underlying vision of development as an unceasing march toward increasing concentration and a modern economy organized as a single factory.

Rooted in the great transformation of the nineteenth century, this modernistic vision was built on assumptions that were widely shared both in form and content by social theorists of the time, Marxist and non-Marxist alike. The belief that society in its entirety could be rendered transparent to scientific investigations modeled on those of the natural sciences and that history could be reduced to some simple, comprehensible driving force was an article of faith embraced by social thinkers since the Enlightenment. This idea had special appeal for nineteenth-century thinkers facing the chaos wrought by rapid economic, political, and social change at a time when—to quote the famous phrase of the *Communist Manifesto*—all that felt solid seemed to have "melted into air" (Marx and Engels [1848] 1986, 38). Much of the grand social theory that characterized the newly emerging social sciences was an attempt to find the driving force of history, the natural laws of social transformation, or the master narrative of large-scale change. Whether they chose to focus on the shift from the metaphysical to the positive scientific age, from militant to industrial society, or from Gemeinschaft to Gesellschaft, or on the imposing force of the increasing division of labor, the rationalization and bureaucratization of social life, or the accumulation of capital, theorists were grasping different aspects of the same, seemingly overwhelming, historical experience. They were grappling with different aspects of a great transformation: the imperious advance of science and technology, the rapid concentration of people in cities, the centralization of power in the hands of modern states, and the accumulation of capital in the form of vast industrial empires. Discovering the moving forces of history promised to lead to the mastery of the future; it suggested the possibility that the uncertainty of things yet to happen could be transformed into the confidence of scientific foresight. Their potential for harnessing chaos accounts for the emotional power with which these theories gripped the human imagination.

There was a curious harmony between the content of the sweeping historical changes of the nineteenth century that the theorists were examining and the form in which they were attempting to grasp these events. The most radical statement of the idea that reality and our understanding of it both follow the same path was elaborated by Hegel, who argued that the two are manifestations of the same Universal Reason. Hegelian thought profoundly influenced nineteenth-century social theory in general, and Marxian theory in particular (Hegel [1821] 1967; Hegel [1840] 1956; Marcuse 1960; Avineri 1972). Social theorists moving away from speculative philosophical systems discovered similar correspondences between the object and the method of their investigations: just as the variety of local customs and rules had been replaced by a single, unified, state administration and just as the diversity and idiosyncrasy of craft production had been supplanted by a few large factories built by rational design, it seemed possible to assemble the incongruous facts of social life and reduce their multiplicity to a unified, rational theory that would explain past, present, and future. The changes of the nineteenth century were momentous, touching on everyone's fate in a similar manner, rendering people's experiences more and more alike. Furthermore, improved means of communication compressed distances, making it easier for people to share their experiences. Thus, it seemed entirely plausible that the unity that Christianity, and later philosophy, asserted in the metaphysical realm, and that the natural sciences promised in the physical world, was there to be discovered in the social universe as well.

Although many of the theories developed in the nineteenth century have influenced history in complex and indirect ways, none has had the direct influence on the flow of history that Marxism attained in socialist societies. By turning social theory into an active ideology, Marxism became one of the primary moving forces of social change in socialism. Designing large-scale social change requires precisely the kind of modernistic vision so common among nineteenth-century thinkers. Those who wish to carry out such change must be guided by a theory that simplifies the immense complexity of society to an explicitly stated and consistent set of propositions and one that offers knowledge about something beyond the bounds of human experience: the future. Simple laws of history offer exactly this kind of theory. Theory of this type, which conforms to the needs of strategic action rather than abstract methods of inquiry, I will call ideology.[2]

This conception of ideology complements the more general theory of social action that underpins this book. Its point of departure is that social actors always face an intractably complex environment and an inherently unpredictable future (Schackle 1972; O'Driscoll and Rizzo 1985).[3] Thus, strategic or intentional action would be impossible if there were no way to simplify our environment (Simon 1957, 1981) and anticipate the future (Denzau and North 1994). Ideology creates the conditions of social action because it reduces the complexity of the world around us and provides us with clear expectations and thus a measure of certainty about what is yet to come. In erasing the ambiguities of past, present, and future, ideology installs stability and order in the place of chaos and uncertainty. Thus, ideology is not false consciousness. It is not a form of knowledge but the bridge between knowledge and action. Ideology depends directly on theories, but, in order to facilitate action, it is more simplistic and inflexible. Ideology should also be distinguished from the much wider concept of culture, as ideology is cognitive, explicit, and reflected upon.[4]

Ideology is, however, only one way of obtaining mastery over the complexity of the present and the uncertainty of the future. Social institutions—sanctioned rules of conduct—can achieve these same goals. Rules, just like ideologies, simplify reality and stabilize our social world (North 1990). They point to information from the present that is relevant for action, and they make the future a predictable extension of the past. Ideology takes on crucial importance when institutions themselves are in the process of being fashioned and thus cannot yet provide stable guidance.

When institutions are in flux, as they were in the nineteenth century or as they are during political revolutions or in periods when a new social order is being implemented, ideology rises to prominence.

As socialism developed in the twentieth century and its institutions were put into place, Marxist-Leninist ideology played a prominent role. Marxism of a peculiar kind supplied the blueprint for institutional change. The modernistic vision of Marxism-Leninism was one of the constitutive forces of socialism, and as such it brought about societies that would have been profoundly different without it but that also turned out to be profoundly different from the Marxist-Leninist vision itself. Thus, Marxist-Leninist ideology serves as a useful point of departure, but only as such, in understanding the nature, collapse, and aftermath of socialism. While the importance of ideology was paramount in the early years of state socialism, over time institutions fostered by ideology gained influence. During the postcommunist transition, another time of turbulence and rapid institutional change, ideology returned to the forefront. Thus, ideology waxes and wanes as institutions weaken and strengthen. Stability necessary for strategic action is maintained by the inverted movement of the two.

In this chapter, I present a short historical reconstruction of the type of Marxism that acted as the master scheme for socialist societies in Eastern Europe. This plan identified concentration as the primary force of social change. In this context, concentration refers to the uniting of dispersed resources in central locations with the goal of turning scattered pieces into organized and vastly more powerful assemblages.[5] The master plan depicted history as the unrelenting march toward ever-increasing economies of scale and centralization of ownership, which in turn would lead to the abolition of private ownership of labor and property and the substitution of universal state employment for the labor market. The task Marxist-Leninist ideology handed to the Communist Party states was twofold: to carry out proletarianization, that is, to turn everyone into an employee by taking away their property; and to do so in the absence of a labor market, that is, by absorbing everyone into the state sector as employees of the state.

Ideological Origins of State Socialism

It is far from obvious how Soviet-type society developed out of the chaotic historical experiences of the last century. As with any tradition that survives for a long time, Marxism is full of internal ambiguities, competing and contradictory interpretations and practices, which made it somewhat flexible under unforeseen historical circumstances and allowed it to amalgamate with other, local traditions. Claiming a one-to-one correspondence between Marx's writings and their most successful ideological translations, Marxism-Leninism, is naive for two reasons. First, Marx's vision of history as increasing concentration was widely shared among social theorists outside the Marxist tradition, such as Emile Durkheim[6] and Max Weber.[7] Thus, it is not my claim that only Marxian ideas could spawn an ideology of this kind. Second, Marx's often contradictory ideas are open to several interpretations. Therefore, I do not argue that the ideology underpinning state socialism was the only possible extension of Marx's theory and critique of nineteenth-century capitalism. This, however, does not mean that Marxism lacked an ideologically coherent dominant streak, an established orthodoxy, upheld by the Second Socialist International, the Comintern, and finally the Cominform.[8] Such an orthodoxy most certainly existed. It exercised a profound effect on the economic and political institutions of socialism and fought fiercely any competing variation of Marxist thought. The orthodox grand vision revolved around the idea of the national economy as one huge factory.

The origins of the ideology of "one nation, one factory" can be reconstructed from the writings of Marx (Selucky 1979). The factory system started its triumphant march in England in the textile industry between the 1780s and the 1830s. At that time it introduced a novel way of coordinating people separated by the division of labor, drawing them together into large units while at the same time allowing further division of tasks and greater specialization. Marx witnessed the triumphant rise of the factory system. In his time, factories gathered under a single roof individual machines run by one central power supply, usually a steam engine.[9] The factory system spread quickly all over the world, acting as the locomotive of economic progress. But coupled to this grand forward movement was urban misery of vast proportions. Marx's view of the nineteenth-century factory reflected this duality,[10] reconciled in his philosophy of history. Marx regarded the factory both as a degradation of human labor, and thus a violation of human freedom, and as a giant step toward conquering nature, and thus a dramatic contribution to human freedom (Marx [1844] 1967, 289). On the one hand, the factory replaced the dignity and skill of craft work with a mindless system that allowed for highly effective control of labor and the increased repression of workers. Laborers now faced long hours on the job and unhealthy working conditions in exchange for meager pay. They were highly regimented, as their relationships with others were defined in a strictly functional manner by analytically partitioning the labor process. They worked in an enclosed space where they were easy to supervise and where the architecture filtered out "unnecessary" communication among them (Foucault 1979, 142–46).

While Marx deplored the demeaning conditions of the factory, he also recognized two of its momentous achievements: economic efficiency and the creation of a labor process in which people worked collectively. The factory code, he wrote,

> is but the capitalist *caricature* of that social regulation of the labour process which becomes requisite in cooperation on a great scale . . . ([1867] 1974, 400, emphasis added)

For Marx, the factory was primarily a social organization accommodating the technological organization of machinery. Elaborating on arguments presented by Adam Smith, Charles Babbage, and Andrew Ure, Marx argued that the factory system achieved its spectacular increase in productivity by increasing the division of labor with the help of machinery. Marx admired the technological efficiency of the factory and its utilization of human labor. He was convinced that this mode of production would soon spread beyond the boundaries of industry, reshaping agriculture and every aspect of the economy (432–35, 474).

Marx was equally impressed by the organizational efficiency of the factory, the very same efficiency that subjected workers to a subhuman existence. He argued that the two could be separated; factories were not necessarily inhumane, and large-scale machinery could be the servant of man. Only under capitalism was this relationship between machine and worker insidious (394–96). Marx acknowledged that the factory regime, in one form or another, was inevitable in large-scale production, while at the same time leaving open the possibility that the factory could shed its odious features.[11]

When Marx entered the scene, the discussion within the socialist movement was dominated by small artisans and craftsmen whose guild system had been shattered by the market and the overpowering success of the factory system. They resented both developments and sought to erect a new social system based on the voluntary cooperation of small producers. Their leading theoretician, Pierre-Joseph Proudhon, attacked the concentration of property and wealth and called for a society of autonomous producers and their voluntary associations. These groups would exchange their products at a fair price based on the amount of human effort required to produce such goods (Proudhon [1840] 1970, [1846] 1972).

Unlike Proudhon, Marx realized that the concentration and centralization of capital and production were unavoidable in the foreseeable future.[12] It was from this insight that the novelty and formidable power of Marx's theoretical stance arose. Marx recognized that the labor movement had to be built around the industrial proletariat, which was multiplying with the advance of the factory system and had to leave behind disgruntled artisans, craftsmen, and journeymen, the primary constituency of the early labor movement.

Marx's vision was at once modernist, in its embrace of concentration as progress, and anticapitalist, in its criticism of the historical form of modernity. In a vicious polemic attack on Proudhon, Marx laid out the wider historical lessons of the factory system.

> Society as a whole has in common with the interior of a workshop that it too has a division of labour. If one took as a model the division of labour in a modern workshop, in order to apply it to a whole society, the best organized for the production of wealth would undoubtedly be that which had a single chief employer, distributing tasks to the different members of the community according to a previously fixed rule. ([1847] 1963, 135)

This "previously fixed rule," which one might call the central plan, has the advantage of creating rational and potentially humanized relations between producers, and it stood in stark contrast with the chaotic, irrational, and warlike competition of the market.

For Marx, the only alternative to the market as a system of distribution, under the constraints of scarcity and at a high level of division of labor, seemed to be the system found in the workshop, where both resources and tasks were pooled and rationally redistributed in an organized manner according to the necessities of production. Once the raw material or semifinished goods arrived at the carefully guarded premises of the factory, all factors influencing production within it could be arranged to minimize outside interference. Climate-controlled buildings made it possible for factories to operate continuously. Simplified and standardized tasks made it easy to replace individual workers, and coordinating and monitoring labor maximized time spent on production. Thus, the factory was able to maintain an extraordinarily stable environment where the flow of production could be carefully calculated and planned to ensure that the product traveled as fast as possible from start to finish but always at an even pace. In this sense, the internal organization of the factory was the historical prototype of centralized planning (Katsenelinboigen 1978).

The factory successfully solved the problem of the concentration of labor and equipment by creating an organizational plan of such superiority that it provided a good model for society as a whole. Because factories outstripped all other forms of production, they would soon dominate society. Concentration was expected to increase economies of scale in production, which in turn would further centralize capital in a self-reinforcing spiral. Large-scale production would be positioned to consistently outbid small producers, who would then inescapably disappear. In this process private property would accumulate in the hands of fewer and fewer individuals, dividing society sharply into two camps, workers and capitalists (Marx and Engels [1848] 1986, 41, 47). With the demise of small producers, private property—property based on private labor—would also vanish, and only capitalist property—property based on the labor of others—would remain. Capitalism was to destroy itself, as concentration would undermine both of its pillars: competition and private property. Monopoly would choke competition, and capitalist property would suffocate small private property. Capitalist property would not last long, however. It carried within it the contradiction that labor was now social, that people's work visibly depended upon that of others, while appropriation remained private. The capitalist alone pocketed the surplus produced by the worker. This was the injustice that caused so much pain for the working class, and this was the catalyst that would incite revolutionary action.

> Along with the constantly diminishing number of the magnates of capital, who usurp and monopolise all advantages of this process of transformation, grows the mass of misery, oppression, slavery, degradation, exploitation, but with this too grows the revolt of the working-class, a class always increasing in numbers and disciplined, united, organised by the very mechanism of the process of capitalist production itself. The monopoly of capital becomes a fetter upon the mode of production, which has sprung up and flourished along with, and under it. Centralization of the means of production and socialisation of labour at last reach a point, where they become incompatible with their capitalist integument. The knell of capitalist private property sounds. The expropriators are expropriated. (Marx [1867] 1974, 715)

Note that in Marx's view the importance of the factory went beyond its role as the locomotive of economic progress, beyond its embodiment in miniature of the future social order. With the participation of the proletariat, emerging from the lair of the factory, the power of centralization that created the factory as an economic force would also destroy the capitalist order.

Marx never elaborated the economic and social structure of the system that was to replace capitalism.[13] This task was left to his disciples. After his death, the two men who did most to consolidate Marxism into an orthodoxy were Frederick Engels and Karl Kautsky, the Second International's two most influential theorists. Engels turned Marx's ideas into a coherent ideology accessible to political activists. Kautsky, who was younger, adjusted Marxism to fit a new historical situation in which the collapse of capitalism seemed imminent. Whatever complexities and ambiguities remained in Marx's ideas were smoothed out by the two men's ministrations. Both Engels and Kautsky understood society as an entity that, with all its contradictions and internal struggles, operated on the basis of a few unifying principles. The discovery of these master principles was the purpose of theorizing, and Marx had already satisfactorily identified the key principles. Three years after Marx's death, Engels wrote the following summary of the Marxist theory of history:

> [W]hile in all earlier periods the investigation of these driving causes of history was almost impossible—on account of the complicated and concealed interconnections between them and their effects—our present period has so far simplified these interconnections that the riddle could be solved. Since the establishment of large-scale industry, that is, at least since the European peace of 1815, it has been no secret to any man in England that the whole political struggle there turned on the claims to supremacy of two classes: the landed aristocracy and the bourgeoisie (middle class). . . . But how did these classes come into existence? . . . The bourgeoisie and proletariat both arose in consequence of a transformation of the economic conditions, more precisely, of the mode of production. The transition, first from guild handicrafts to manufacture, and then from manufacture to large-scale industry, with steam and mechanical power, caused the development of these two classes. ([1886] 1986, 624–25)

The driving cause of history is class struggle, which in turn is propelled by a more profound force, the concentration of production. Because Engels and Kautsky conceived of society as driven by a few simple principles, tendencies that seemed to contradict or compete with these principles, or ones that pointed away from the mainstream of progress, could be conceived of only as historical residues, bound to disappear eventually.[14] The vision of society as an organic totality working according to a single logic was succinctly put by Kautsky in *The Agrarian Question.*

> Human society is an organism, not a plant or an animal organism, but of its own kind. Nonetheless it is an organism, not merely an aggregate of individuals, and *as an organism must be uniformly* [*einheitlich*] *organized.* It would be absurd to think that in a society one part could develop in one direction, and another, equally important, could develop in the opposite direction. It can develop only in one direction. ([1899] 1966, 294, emphasis added)[15]

Kautsky was even more fascinated than Marx was by the "triumphant march of capitalism," in general, and the factory system in particular. The future, a logical extension of the present, held little mystery.

> Under these conditions the factory rules, and the days of handicraft, of independent production, are numbered. What remains is carried on chiefly by unfortunates who cannot find places in the factory system. ([1891] 1910, 17)

People (such as small producers) who did not get integrated into this new organization of production were bound for misery and were fleeting historical residues. From this perspective, even factory work acquired an unexpected, if relative, desirability. Following Marx, Kautsky firmly believed that concentration would boost efficiency and productivity. He further reasoned that the concentration of production was a historical necessity. The result of this process was to be an ever-increasing force urging the socialization of the means of production.

> That which renders the socialist society necessary is large production. . . . In socialist society, as in society today, large industry will develop more and more and increasingly absorb small industry. ([1891] 1910, 131–33)

Kautsky keenly emphasized that small production and socialism were mutually exclusive. In socialism the concentration of the productive forces would continue and the means of production would not be redistributed among the population (136). Who would be put in charge of this huge economic organization? The state, which already had taken up a large part of this role (105).

When all property was handed over to the state, the only factor of production remaining in private possession would be labor. This concentration of production required careful planning and the cooperation of a large number of people. Kautsky was honest enough to admit that such an organization of production was incompatible not only with any form of private property but also with any form of the labor market (149–52). The partitioning of the labor process, now on a national scale, would assign each worker to a task.[16]

Kautsky's views about the transition to socialism were challenged even within the German labor movement itself. If concentration seemed to be the inevitable destiny of humankind for most of the 1800s, in the century's last decades small production still resisted its advances in many areas of the economy. In fact, even in the more developed parts of Europe, small producers continued to outnumber large ones. Eduard David (1903) pointed out that agricultural production was characterized by certain peculiarities not found in industry, and thus family farms were likely to defeat large-scale agribusiness (1903). In the celebrated revisionist controversy, Eduard Bernstein maintained that small production would survive in industry, as well, for at least three reasons. First, in many industries there was a division of labor between big and small, as in metalwork, where factories created semifinished goods and artisans completed the process. Second, wherever closeness to the customer was important, small outfits would prosper, a point proven clearly in services. And, finally, large-scale production itself gave new life to small producers. Mass-produced machinery and materials made small production less expensive, and as workers became superfluous in factories they were pushed back into small trades ([1909] 1961, 60–62).[17]

The revisionist challenge was intellectually profound. Not only did it question the inexorable law of concentration, but it also voiced skepticism about the existence of fundamental laws of history. By abstaining from offering a historical vision of their own, however, revisionists undercut their chances of shaking the orthodoxy of the movement, which received the strongest defense from Rudolf Hilferding.[18] Hilferding acknowledged that small shops could survive, at least for a while, but only as appendages of large firms. This made the petty bourgeoisie a lackey of big capital and an enemy of the working class ([1910] 1981, 344–47). Hilferding argued that property was concentrated not through competition and the elimination of the weak by the stronger but through banks, which linked enterprises through their common interests in large conglomerates (199). Finance capital, along with trusts and cartels, were important steps toward socializing capital.[19] This was significant because it meant that now associations of capitalists, and not competing individuals, controlled the means of production. As capitalists became more organized, capitalism became more resistant to economic crises. At the same time, it also became more vulnerable to political challenges. Now revolutionaries could command the entire economy simply by taking control of the few central switches of a hierarchically interdependent network of capital in which power was concentrated. Just as comprehending the central dynamics of society gave one intellectual command over the most important aspects of social knowledge, so would apprehending the "six large Berlin banks" give economic command over the most important spheres of German industry ([1910] 1981, 368).

The arrival of the World War I, which led to the fragmentation of the labor movement, invigorated the state's role in the German economy. For many, this increased state intervention looked like the next, and possibly the last, step on the road to German socialism.

The Soviet Example

Socialism, however, triumphed not in Germany but in Russia, a country with a small industrial sector and a correspondingly weak industrial work force, which was both unskilled and ill disciplined. The material conditions Marx had assumed capitalism would achieve fell to socialism to create. The leaders of the Revolution were strongly influenced by Hilferding and Kautsky's earlier works (Howard and King 1989; Kolakowski 1978, vol. 2). While still engaged in a civil war, the Bolshevik leadership set out to modernize Russia, trying to create the key ingredient of economic progress, namely, large-scale industry. Along with building factories, the Bolsheviks, now relying on the coercive apparatus of the state, were eager to create a social base to underpin Communist rule.

The first step was to eliminate large-scale private capital through nationalization. Because the size of the state sector in the economy had been considerable before 1917 and existing industry was highly concentrated (Tugan-Baranovsky [1907] 1970; Gerschenkron 1960), nationalization of the "commanding heights" of the economy did not prove difficult. The real task turned out to be accommodating labor within the emerging new economic system. In a speech in 1920, Trotsky argued in support of the recently introduced Compulsory Labor Service.

> The regulation of labor does not use the spontaneous means of buying or selling, but is based on an economic plan which encompasses the whole country and embraces all the working class. This is the program of labor service which has always been part of the socialist program. . . . And once we have recognized this, we thus recognize fundamentally, not formally but fundamentally, the right of the workers' state to send every workingman and workingwoman to that place in which he is needed to fulfill an economic task. In the same way, we recognize the right of the state, the workers' state, to punish the workingman and workingwoman who refuse to fulfill the orders of the state. (Quoted in Kaplan 1968, 351)

Where there is only one employer who can "buy" labor, the abolition of the labor market, together with other forms of the market, is quite logical (Bukharin [1920] 1971). In socialism, Lenin explained:

> *All* citizens are . . . transformed into hired employees of the state, which is made up of the armed workers. All citizens become employees and workers of *one* national state 'syndicate.' All that is required is that they should work equally, should regularly do their share of work, and should receive equal pay. The accounting and control necessary for this have been *simplified* by capitalism to the utmost, till they have become the extraordinarily simple operations of watching, recording and issuing receipts, within the reach of anybody who can read and write and knows the first four rules of arithmetic. . . . The whole of society will have become one office and one factory, with equal work and equal pay. ([1917] 1971, 83–84, emphasis in the original)

Thus, once "this factory discipline, which the proletariat will extend to the whole of society" takes hold, the rational simplicity of the social world can shine through, unencumbered by political entanglements. In socialism, society will be transparent and simple (Nove 1983, 32–39).

Lenin was much less critical than was Marx of the despotic features of the factory. In 1918, describing the immediate tasks of the Soviet government, he advocated the adaptation of Taylorism in revolutionary Russia ([1918] 1974a, 259).[20] The same year he wrote:

> When the working class has learned how to defend the state system against the anarchy of small ownership, when it has learned to organize *large scale production on a national scale,* along state capitalist lines, it will hold . . . the trump cards, and the consolidation of socialism will be assured . . . Socialism is inconceivable without large-scale capitalist engineering based on the discoveries of modern science. It is inconceivable without planned state organization, which keeps tens of millions of people to the strictest observance of a unified standard in production and distribution. (Lenin [1918] 1974b, 338–39; emphasis added)

Many elements of the Bolsheviks' program paralleled those of other contemporary, nonsocialist programs of modernization and industrialization, especially those in Germany. The crucial difference between the two countries' efforts, Lenin noted, was that the ultimate power in Soviet Russia rested with the workers, while in Germany the Junkers held the reins of power.[21]

The underlying modernistic vision of history, now the unquestioned foundation of the orthodox line, had been laid out in great detail a year earlier by Bukharin and Preobrazhensky in *The ABC of Communism.*

> THE LARGER THE UNDERTAKING, THE MORE PERFECT IS THE TECHNIQUE, THE MORE ECONOMICAL IS THE LABOUR, AND THE LOWER IS THE COST OF PRODUCTION. . . . Large-scale production effects economies in every direction: in buildings, machinery, raw materials, lighting and heating, cost of labour, utilisation of waste products etc. In fact, let us suppose that there are one thousand small workshops, and that there is one large factory which produces the same quantity of commodities as all the little workshops put together. It is much easier to build one large factory than a thousand small workshops; the raw materials for the workshops will be used far more wastefully; lighting and heating will be much easier in the case of a large factory; the factory will have the advantage in the matter of general supervision, cleaning up, repairs etc. In a word, there will unquestionably be in all respects an economy, a saving, in running the large factory. . . . All these advantages attaching to large-scale enterprise explain why small-scale production must invariably succumb in capitalist society. Large-scale capital crushes the small producer, takes away his customers, and ruins him, so that he drops into the ranks of the proletariat or becomes a tramp. ([1919] 1966, 48–50, capitalization in the original)

Capitalism was "like a badly constructed machine" (69) which turned out but was then unable to accommodate the mighty force of large-scale production. Concentration and centralization of capital were to lead to communism, which was superior, because it would clear class struggle and wasteful market competition from the path of further concentration (76).

When the era of the New Economic Policy began in 1921, Lenin altered his position somewhat. The NEP relaxed state control over the economy. While keeping tight rein over the commanding heights of industry, concessions were made to petty commodity production. Whether this adjustment was a temporary tactical retreat or a real change in the mind of the leader of the Bolshevik revolution has long been a matter of scholarly debate.[22] The model so closely imitated by the Eastern European socialist countries was that which emerged in the Soviet Union following 1929, after the NEP was abandoned. This model of Stalinist industrialization finally put the one-nation-one-factory idea into practice.

The Stalinist version of historical materialism promoted the development of large-scale mass production as the centerpiece of historical progress. The concentration of production, inevitably superior to any other form, was the justification for the collectivization drive (Jasny 1949, 26–30), and it gradually became the ultimate justification for socialism. As Stalin recounted the now well-rehearsed incantation, under capitalism:

> In place of the handicraft workshops and manufactories there appear huge mills and factories equipped with machinery. In place of the manorial estates tilled by the primitive implements of production of the peasant, there now appear large capitalist farms run on scientific lines and supplied with agricultural machinery. . . . But having developed productive forces to a tremendous extent, capitalism has become enmeshed in contradictions which it is unable to solve. By producing larger and larger quantities of commodities, and reducing their prices, capitalism intensifies competition, ruins the mass of small and medium private owners, converts them into proletarians and reduces their purchasing power, with the result that it becomes impossible to dispose of the commodities produced. On the other hand, by expanding production and concentrating millions of workers in huge mills and factories, capitalism lends the process of production a social character and thus undermines its foundation, inasmuch as the social character of the process of production demands the social ownership of the means of production; yet the means of production remain private capitalist property, which is incompatible with the social character of the process of production. . . . This means that the capitalist relations of production have ceased to correspond to the state of productive forces of society and have come into irreconcilable contradiction with them. This means that capitalism is pregnant with revolution, whose mission it is to replace the existing capitalist ownership of the means of production by socialist ownership. ([1938] 1972, 325–26)[23]

State socialism was a historical necessity because only state socialism, with its large-scale, bureaucratic, hierarchical, social, and political organization, was able to accommodate the large-scale, bureaucratic, and hierarchical nature of mass production.

The Stalinist model was built on the maximum mobilization and concentration of resources, including labor. The drive to industrialize took away from individual households all resources—both the means of production and consumption—and concentrated them in the hands of the state.[24] The relatively free labor market of the NEP era disappeared. Forced industrial expansion generated a virtually unlimited demand for workers, and the ensuing labor shortage, already apparent in 1929, created a sellers' market for workers (Filtzer 1986, 49–63). As workers took advantage of their market position, high turnover rates, lax discipline, and high absenteeism followed. The labor code of 1933 codified forced labor, but until 1938 Stalin continued to believe that moral exhortations and socialist labor competition could solve at least part of the problem. The famous Stakhanovite movement, first introduced in 1935, reflected that belief. Within a few years, however, persuasion and competition had to be fortified with draconian labor laws.

Soviet labor relations in the late 1940s and 1950s were shaped by a series of decrees dating back to the late 1930s. In 1938 the workbook was introduced, modeled after a system put in practice two years earlier in Nazi Germany (Schwarz 1951, 101). Workbooks, which workers took with them when they moved from one firm to another, contained their work histories, rewards, and punishments. These books were always deposited with the employer, who made all the entries.

Other decrees criminalized absenteeism, making it punishable with up to six months of forced (correctional) labor at the place of employment and up to a 25 percent wage cut. Being 20 minutes late had already qualified as absenteeism; now two such offenses could result in a prison sentence. Quitting was prohibited, except under special circumstances, for which special permission had to be secured. Specialists were assigned to jobs, and up to one million young people who had just completed their educations were required to enroll in "labor reserve schools" for training (Nove 1982, 261). These laws were so cruel that even the courts seemed loath to carry them out. A campaign had to be launched against liberal and slow prosecutors who engaged in "criminal inactivity and direct cover-up" (263).

It would be a mistake to explain these repressive measures as necessitated by the Soviet war effort. The laws were introduced before the war began and they were not changed until 1956, although they were somewhat relaxed before then. At a time when popular support was indispensable, this level of repression could have served little practical purpose. What is more, these measures were justified officially on ideological grounds rather than with reference to temporary, war-related emergencies (Nove 1982, 263). These policies represented the final step in eliminating the labor market, a goal deeply embedded in Soviet socialist ideology.

The Soviet model developed into an ideological orthodoxy and was quickly disseminated in the socialist countries that followed the Soviet example.[25] Scientific socialism, ossified into a "scientific" discipline, was taught in schools and in special courses, and it was invoked as the final arbiter of debates about social reality. All over Eastern Europe the textbooks in the early years were translations of the authorized Soviet manual. The textbook used in Hungary in the 1950s hammered away at its main point. Even the slowest student could not fail to learn what underlay the new socialist order:

> Large-scale industry—the material foundation of socialism. The essence of socialist industrialization. Socialism can be built only on the basis of large-scale mechanized production. In villages and in cities only large-scale production can guarantee the quick increase of labor productivity that is necessary for the victory of the new social order.
>
> In this context Lenin pointed out: "The material foundation of socialism can only be mechanized large-scale production, which is able to transform [not only industry, but] agriculture, as well." (Ostrovityanov et al. 1955, 369)

When the Communist governments of Eastern Europe took power after World War II, they were guided by this historical vision. The ideology that they inherited had been elaborated and modified by the Russian experience, but the fundamental idea that the iron law of history is concentration had stood unaltered since the 1840s. The power of size, the economies of large scale, was writ large on the socialist program of industrialization. Concentration was seen as the way of the future, the necessary precondition of rationality and efficiency, the key to economic development. The shift in the locus of production away from households and small workshops and toward the factory, the office, and other large and specialized spaces, a process already well under way in capitalism, was to be completed.

The Eastern European Communist governments thus set out to create an economy that was to be homogeneous (Preobrazhensky [1926] 1965, 231), having only one sector, and that controlled and directed by the state. The private sector was to be erased. Private property was to be eliminated by concentrating all property in the hands of the state. Workers were to be parted from their tools, some of which were to be collected for use in factories and some of which were to be discarded as obsolete. Workers themselves were to become employees of the state, dependent on their employer for their wages, their jobs, and their instruments. Wages were to be set by carefully planned, centralized wage policies in which the personnel needs of the economy, the macroeconomic balance of goods and purchasing power, and aspects of social justice would be considered. Labor would no longer be for sale. Laborers and tasks would be matched not haphazardly but by conscious design. The worker was to be assigned to one job, one position, by the plan. The economy was envisioned as a totality. It was a large machine, wherein each worker acted as an indispensable cog, lever, wheel, or whistle. Agrippa's tale[26] of the interdependence of the different body parts was retold with an industrial slant, substituting the imagery of machinery for that of the body.[27] All the units of production were to work together in happy unison toward the general interest of society.

In the aftermath of the tremendous disaster and dislocation created by World War II, and with memories of the Great Depression still lingering, this ideological vision had a strong appeal in all Eastern European countries for a small segment of society, which soon formed the avant-garde of the communist movement. It was up to them to carefully plant these ideas in the national soil of each country. Not surprisingly, the degree to which they succeeded depended in no small measure on how fully they were able to utilize the historical traditions of their respective countries and meet the most pressing tasks of postwar reconstruction. During the decade and a half following the end of the war, the vision of victorious concentration was translated into a series of institutions and, ultimately, into a new social order. The socialist Great Transformation already under way in the Soviet Union began in the other socialist countries after 1945.

This chapter gave a short overview of the ideological origins of state socialism and, ultimately, the origins of the institution of universal state employment. Marxism-Leninism organized the key conceptual elements of social design, such as property, economic organization, labor management, and social structure into the coherent and powerful cognitive framework of the one-nation-one-factory model.

In the next chapter I demonstrate that the elimination of private property and the establishment of universal state employment was driven by this ideological framework. The economic and political self-interests of the communist leadership were framed by this ideology and whenever those were in conflict with its most deeply held article of faith, the belief in the power of economic concentration, faith prevailed over interest, as it always happens when institutions are in too much turmoil to undergird strategic calculations.

CHAPTER 3

The Great Transformation: The Elimination of the Private Sector in Socialist Hungary

Guardians of the New Social Order

On March 25, 1948, at 4 P.M., 600 people gathered at the headquarters of the Metalworkers' Union in Budapest in response to an invitation to attend an unspecified event. Each had to pass the close scrutiny of security guards before being allowed to enter the large conference hall. The primarily working-class guests, many of whom had just arrived on the morning train from other parts of the country, had little inkling of what was to follow.

On the podium sat a selection of distinguished politicians. The first speaker, Árpád Szakasits, the president of Hungary, announced that the Council of Ministers had issued a decree that morning taking all industrial firms with more than 100 employees into the care of the state.[1] Then Ernő Gerő, the Hungarian Communist Party's economic policy czar, congratulated the astonished guests on their new posts as directors of these companies. The just-appointed managers, confused and overwhelmed, listened to the state secretary of industry read a long list of managerial duties, which ended in threats of meticulously specified prison terms for those delinquent in carrying out these tasks (Fábián 1986). When the people were called to the podium individually to receive the document appointing them to their new positions, some wavered. One man, assigned to run a meat factory, protested that he had never seen a meat factory from the inside. "Are you a comrade?" he was asked, and the matter was settled. Another, who had been a worker in the factory of which he was now in charge, returned to the plant that same evening. The night watchman, whom he knew well, greeted him and asked if he had left something in the shop. "No," he replied, and informed him that now he was the director of the company. "You are such a funny man," the watchman responded, laughing (Cserhalmi 1983).

While the new directors were stunned by the sudden and radical turn in their careers, the nationalization of factories that lifted them into directors' chairs was only one, relatively late, measure in a long-term strategy of the Hungarian Communist Party (HCP). As part of a larger design to create a modern economy as understood in the Marxist-Leninist ideology (i.e., one in which all obstacles impeding the concentration of production are cleared), private property was being eradicated in favor of state ownership. Aladár Mód, one of the chief ideologues of the HCP explained the Party's approach this way:

> Modern, large-scale industry came into being in the race for profit, but producing for profit now blocks its development by limiting the consumption of the working masses, by obstructing the industrialization of nondeveloped regions, by its economic crises, and by its imperialist clashes. Thus, industrial development in all countries today depends essentially on how much the people's needs and improvement of their welfare is put in the center of production against the profit interest of big capital. The socialist mode of production achieves this best by far, by taking the means of production into collective ownership. (1946, 439)

It was first and foremost this boundless faith in historical destiny and not economic or even political rationality that drove the Communist elite to carry out its plan with such merciless consistency. It took legal prosecution, moral haranguing, everyday harassment, coaxing, cajoling, threats, and physical violence to eliminate almost every form of private ownership and concentrate nearly all the means of production in the hands of the state. The process moved from the nationalization of big banks, large landholdings, and giant factories to the takeover of family stores, small plots, and artisan workshops. The Great Transformation, borrowing Karl Polanyi's phrase to highlight similarities between the advent of factory production in the nineteenth century and in early socialism, was completed in 1961 with the successful conclusion of the collectivization of agriculture. It reduced the overwhelming majority of the population to wage labor, including many previously self-employed individuals who were forced to take jobs as employees in the socialist sector. This proletarianization was unique not only because it managed to achieve a much higher degree of concentration of ownership than did the great transformation of the nineteenth century but also because it carried out this process without allowing a labor market to develop. The goal was to nationalize labor along with capital and land. Proletarianization without a labor market is historically unique to socialism, and it was the essential and distinctive feature of the socialist version of the Great Transformation.

This chapter chronicles the way in which the private sector was gradually eliminated and a new method of nationwide labor management developed to replace the labor market. During this initial period of "laying the foundations of socialism," which in Hungary lasted from 1945 to 1961, the institutions that were intended to serve as the cornerstones of the socialist order were constructed at great cost in money and suffering. The blueprint for this great transformation was Marxism-Leninism, and state power wielded by the Communist Party was its earth-moving equipment.

In 1945, at the outset of the Great Transformation, Hungary, having fought on the losing side in the World War II, was occupied by the Soviet army. Evidence of war devastation was everywhere: bridges and roads were impassable, rail lines and power stations were in ruins, streets were littered with the decaying bodies of humans and animals, land lay fallow, livestock was decimated, and industrial production was at a standstill. The state, which had played an active role in the war economy since 1938 but had fallen apart in the last months of the war, had to reconstitute itself in order to help pull the country out of its postwar malaise. Since December 1944, the bulk of state power had rested with the Communists, who had ridden into power with the occupying Soviet army and maintained a leading role until their electoral defeat in November 1945. Despite this defeat, and despite the fact that the right-of-center Independent Small Holders' Party received 57 percent of the vote, the HCP members were given important portfolios in the newly formed coalition government, including that of the Interior Ministry, which was responsible for law and order and state administration.

In the last month of 1945, the Economic Chief Council (Gazdasági Főtanács), or ECC was formed under Communist leadership. Since this body was accorded real power in economic matters, the center of economic decision making slipped out of the hands of the governing coalition. The Communist Party could not claim undivided power over the state apparatus until 1949. In the meantime, however, its command of the ECC, and of key ministries, along with the active support of the occupying Soviets, allowed the HCP to direct day-to-day affairs and set the stage for the socialist industrialization of Hungary. The Party's conspicuously absent social constituency was expected to emerge as a result of the Great Transformation. The Party had its mandate from a not-yet-existing working class, one that would toil in not-yet-existing factories. The justification for the HCP's program lay in the future, one mapped by the laws of history.

Nationalization and the Rise of the State Sector

The Appropriation of Large Companies and Commerce

The process by which the state eliminated private property was implemented from two directions. Acting through the ECC, the state used indirect measures to regulate and coordinate the economy, taking control out of the hands of property owners. At the same time, the government launched a vigorous campaign of directly appropriating private property. Non-Communist political forces grudgingly accepted increased regulation and state intervention as economic necessities. Nationalization met with considerable political and ideological resistance, however, especially from the leaders of the Small Holders' Party. Thus, nationalization proceeded in a gradual, piecemeal fashion.

Before 1945, the state held important monopolies in the economy. It owned the railways, the postal service, numerous mines, and several large landholdings. Before the war ended, 10 percent of all workers in industry were state employees. State involvement took two forms. Most state firms were joint stock companies wherein the majority of the shares belonged to the state. The state exercised its ownership rights through its representatives on boards of directors. The firms' budgets were completely separate from the state budget; they were simply a source of revenue to the Treasury. In the second type of involvement, the enterprise was directly owned and operated by the state. The state appointed its managers and regulated its day-to-day operations. Its budget was part of the state budget, though it was a separate item. Final responsibility for the enterprise's performance lay with the appropriate minister.

Postwar reconstruction provided the state with a new and dominant role in the economy. By the spring of 1945, the government already controlled the distribution of most vital materials such as steel and coal.[2] The five largest heavy industrial firms were completely occupied with delivering products to the Soviet Union as part of Hungary's war reparations. In late 1946, the state took formal control of the firms. As heavy industry was already highly concentrated, through this takeover the state acquired 100 percent control of metallurgy, 60 percent of the steel industry, and over 50 percent of machine building. Nationalization of much of the energy industry soon followed. By the end of 1946, roughly 43 percent of the workers employed in industry and mining were state employees (Pető and Szakács 1985, 79–81]. Many of these large private enterprises had been key players in the war effort, and thus they had been under strict state supervision since 1938. As strategic industries, they were appropriated by the advancing German army. They later became targets of military attacks and were wrecked by Soviet firepower. Many of the original owners had left the country and were reluctant to return to claim their badly damaged companies.

Under pressure from the Communists and the Soviet Union, in July 1947, the Hungarian government declined to participate in the Marshall Plan. Thus, Hungary had to carry out its ambitious designs for reconstruction and modernization relying solely on internal resources. The country was in an extremely difficult situation. A large portion of its already insufficient resources had to be shipped to the Soviet Union as war compensation. The only way to stabilize the economy was to get the Soviet Union to agree to a delivery schedule that was both flexible and considerate of the difficulties the Hungarian economy was facing. The power to negotiate with the Soviets to gain concessions on deliveries became one of the HCP's most important political assets.[3]

The importance of large banks, captured in great detail by Hilferding and Lenin, did not escape the HCP. In May 1947, large banks were placed under state supervision and half a year later they were nationalized. Since all the capital kept in these banks was also placed under state control, the capital market dissolved. Any private firm seeking credit was now at the mercy of the state. A week later, the Council of Ministers decided to appropriate the aluminum and bauxite industry, securing state control over Hungary's most abundant natural resource.

The decision to nationalize all industrial firms with more than 100 employees, revealed first at the conspiratorial meeting at the headquarters of the Metalworkers' Union in March 1948, affected nearly 600 firms and 160,000 workers.[4] All remaining large private enterprises were confiscated, and the state sector became dominant in all branches of industry. The enterprises became part of the state bureaucracy, as each was assigned to a specific ministry. Top managers, hastily selected in secret, became subordinates of state bureaucrats, just as chief engineers or department heads in each company were subordinates of the top manager, forming an unbroken chain of command from the ECC to the workers on the shop floor.[5] The final act of expropriating large capital occurred during the first days of April, when the National Federation of Industrial Employers was disbanded.

The state's grasp was weakest over industries composed of smaller firms. For instance, in paper and food processing the private sector retained a share of 46 and 45 percent, respectively. Most of these smaller firms fell during the second wave of nationalization, announced on December 20, 1949, when the state took possession of all companies that employed at least 10, and in certain cases as few as five, people. The preamble of the law supplied this explanation:

> The successful execution of the law 1949/XXV about the five-year economic plan makes it necessary that the Hungarian People's Republic concentrate in its hands those productive and transportation instruments in industry, mining, and metallurgy, as well as transportation, which either in their current form or after the appropriate

reorganization are *suited for large-scale, factory-like production.* (Balogh 1986, 191, emphasis added)

The large trading enterprises were nationalized along with large factories, but expropriating smaller companies proved to be more difficult. In the aftermath of the war, small-scale commerce assumed an important role. The complete breakdown of domestic trade forced city dwellers to barter with peasants in the countryside, exchanging clothing, jewelry, even furniture for food. A black market quickly developed, attracting marketeers of all kinds. The postwar government took immediate, strong measures to quash this free market, where gold watches were exchanged for a dozen eggs, but it fought a losing battle. The immensity of postwar shortages made it impossible to restrain prices without controlling the supply of goods. Authorities could easily crack down on unlicensed traders, but forcing entrepreneurs to charge less for their highly sought after wares was much more difficult. Consequently, while in 1940 there were 83,000 traders in the whole country, within months of the war's end, tens of thousands of new commercial licenses were issued (Berényi 1985, 16, 28). The world's highest inflation further fueled speculation. Fighting profiteers and speculators soon became one of the government's most popular causes. In the first half of 1946, the economic police, a unit assigned exclusively to economic crimes, investigated 14,000 cases of profiteering, criminal stockpiling, and illegal currency and gold trading. Profiteering carried a five-year prison term, but in special instances the death penalty could be meted out (Pető and Szakács 1985, 75).

Private traders soon became the scapegoats of postwar hardship, and with their blackened reputations the marketplace itself grew tarnished. Increasingly, they were identified with criminal opportunism. Yet the majority of private traders were not big-time speculators but legitimate small merchants, grocers, and shopkeepers. Since the interwar period they had played an increasing role in commerce. Ninety-five percent of these small businesses were individually owned, and 60 percent had no employees. The few large firms dealt mainly in agricultural produce. Some had been created by large industrial manufacturers as retail outlets for their products.

The state's approach to wholesale trade was somewhat different. Many of the large wholesale firms had relatively few employees and little fixed capital to appropriate. Their most important possessions were their accumulated experience, expertise, and national networks of personal contacts. These were much harder to confiscate. The government considered the control of domestic trade pivotal because a breakdown in this area could have brought the collapse of the newly stabilized economy. Instead of taking over commerce shop by shop, the government began to build its own system of wholesale trade, while at the same time drastically limiting the freedom of private trading companies by setting prices and regulating trade. The state also used its rapidly increasing control over production, its monopoly over banking, and its own distribution system, pieced together from the marketing departments of the newly nationalized manufacturing firms, to further undercut private companies.

By the middle of 1949, the state had its own system of commerce in place,[6] but there were still 1,820 private wholesale traders left in the country. In October the state appointed Party cadres as chief executive officers in all private wholesale companies. As of February 1, 1950, it prohibited all private wholesale activities. Private retail trade was not outlawed; it was suffocated. Now that the state monopolized wholesale trade, private retailers simply were not supplied with goods. By the end of 1952, the number of private retailers had dwindled from over 40,000 in 1950 to less than 3,000, and almost all of these ran small food or variety stores in rural areas where the state was unable to open shops of its own (KSH 1956, 146; Berényi 1985, 360).

Public sentiment was not favorable to either large capital or commerce. Opinion polls indicated that there was a general mistrust of big bankers as well as industrialists; the appropriation of banks and large businesses thus found some popular support (Blumstock 1977). Many in the small private sector applauded the nationalization of large capital. In contrast, the appropriation of small capital and modest landholdings, besides being economically counterproductive, was both highly unpopular and politically very dangerous. The appropriation of large-scale industry had been motivated by political and ideological considerations. The crusade against small industry, at least initially, was driven predominantly by the faith, buttressed by the Soviet example, that there was no room for small production in a developed and modern economy. That this faith was misplaced was a lesson the Communist Party was slow to learn. In the end, the Party would have served its own interests much better by not nationalizing small production.

The Abolition of Small Private Property

After the war, in both industry[7] and agriculture, the small enterprise was a vital part of Hungary's economy. Because their scale of operation provided greater flexibility, small producers were able to recover from the destruction caused by the war relatively quickly. It was easier and less expensive to restart a small workshop than a factory, a private farm than a large estate. Thus, the urgency of reconstruction increased small production's share in the economy.[8] This expansion was most pronounced in manufacturing, industrial repair, and construction. The consumer service industries declined, as the impoverished postwar environment provided little effective demand for consumer services. According to contemporary estimates, the share of small industry in industrial production jumped to 43 percent in 1946 compared with 28 to 30 percent during the 1930s (Nevelő 1973).

By 1948, as nationalization gained momentum, the proportion of large- to small-scale production returned to its lower, prewar level. Yet, in terms of employment, small industrial production continued to be very important: approximately 40 percent of industrial workers worked in small shops. Excluding family members, on average, shop staffs numbered less than two persons,[9] the holder of the license and either an employee or an apprentice. The majority (80.6 percent) of small units were in manufacturing; only 7.5 percent were in the service industries. In 1948, the most common professions were much as they had been before the war: shoemakers (14.4 percent of all license holders), tailors (12.7 percent), blacksmiths (6.8 percent), carpenters/cabinetmakers (6.7 percent), barbers/hairdressers (5.7 percent), and masons (4.8 percent) (KSH 1961). Most of these professions served the needs of the population directly and produced the kinds of goods that constituted the major investments of households at that time (shoes, clothing, housing, furniture, etc.).

These small workshops were not highly mechanized. In 1948, 35 percent had no electricity, and the average capacity of all motors per shop was only .68 kilowatt (Tellér 1973, 11). Most artisans who lived in the countryside were part of the peasant community. About a fourth of them had landholdings larger than a cadastral yoke (1.4 acres), and many engaged in seasonal agricultural labor, working for others. These artisans' customers were primarily local peasants, whom they supplied with tools, housing, and clothing.

The basis of small production was the household. Workshops were usually in the same building where the artisans lived. For those whose work was done elsewhere, as in construction, for example, the home was still important as a base for storing tools and negotiating business deals. Small artisans' households also supplied a ready pool of reserve labor. Family members frequently helped out. Overall, in 1948, there were 22,988 helping family members, about one-eighth of the number of licenses held in that year (KSH 1961, 69).

In addition to producing essential goods, artisans had another important function. They trained young apprentices in the skills and knowledge of their trades. Even after the war, when the number of apprentices decreased by a third, 81.7 percent of the industrial skilled labor force had learned their trade in small production (Nevelő 1973). Every fourth artisan had an apprentice. In certain highly skilled fields, such as printing and radio repair, the ratio was much higher, as young people anticipated growing demand for these professions. After finishing their apprenticeships, apprentices either opened their own shops or applied for skilled jobs in factories. Indeed, the apprentice system provided skilled workers for the steel and textile mills, the machine factories, and the chemical plants. Skilled factory workers regularly left the factory to set up their own shops, so there was constant flux between the artisan stratum and the industrial proletariat.[10]

Industrial small producers—especially in the cities—were better educated than the average citizen, and they tried to provide their children with an education that would allow them to enter careers as professionals or civil servants. They regarded themselves as part of the middle class or petty bourgeoisie, if not the "gentlemanly middle class" (*úri középosztály*), which was the focus of their social aspirations.

Between 1945 and 1949, the Communist Party took great pains to voice its support for small producers. This temporary leniency was more than merely a tactically prudent move. It found justification in the Party's ideological view of "productive labor" as an activity transforming nature. This definition, in its simplified, ideological version, put physical labor at the center of production, granting decreasing legitimacy to economic pursuits the further removed they were from manual labor. Consequently, entrepreneurship and work in commerce, banking, and even bureaucracy came to be seen as nonwork, unnecessary and suspect. This bias usefully coincided with existing traditions in popular culture. In the countryside, the peasantry had long held a notion of work very similar to the HCP's own (Lampland 1995). People who did not earn their living by the "sweat of their brow" and those who made a living by "taking advantage" of people rather than nature were objects of contempt and distrust.[11]

Thus, unlike big capitalists, small producers who worked with their hands for their livelihoods and property enjoyed limited ideological legitimacy in Communist politics for a short time, and farmers, artisans, and even small shopkeepers were included among the "working people" (*dolgozó nép*). Historically, the cleavage between small producers and big capitalists and the owners of the *latifundia* (large landholdings) had been deep and wide (Kövér 1982), while the cleavage between small producers and workers and peasants had been narrow and often superficial. Owning small farms or engaging in artisanry traditionally had not served as a stepping stone to large-scale land or factory ownership in Hungary. Large-scale production had been established by merchant capital and large landholdings had belonged to the aristocracy and the Catholic Church.

Moreover, in the years immediately following the war, the work and political support of small producers was indispensable. The Communist Party could not directly challenge them.[12] Thus, to gain political control over this group, the Party took a circuitous route: it started to promote cooperatives. Importantly, the Communist leadership distinguished between cooperatives and "pseudocooperatives" (*álszövetkezetek*). The latter were co-ops established before the war and newly created associations that did not toe the political line of the Communist Party. These pseudocooperatives hid black marketeers and acted as covers for "reactionaries" (Rákosi 1947, 286).

As late as April 1949, in the propaganda campaign that accompanied the launching of the first five-year plan, the leadership repeatedly stressed that "working small artisans and tradesmen" were to play an important role in fulfilling the goals of the plan.[13] These statements were harder and harder to take seriously, however. Even though artisans were urgently needed, especially in residential construction and agriculture, they were unable to procure materials and credit, their organizations were abolished, more and more small firms were "suspended," farmers were harassed, and a series of new laws made all small producers' lives increasingly difficult. To obtain the necessary permission to open a small business, one had to present proof of citizenship, an affidavit concerning one's political history (based on postwar denazification procedures), and a police document attesting to one's "good morals" (*erkölcsi bizonyítvány*) secured within the previous six months. This proof of "good morals" testified to a person's reliability not only in a moral (i.e., criminal) sense but also in political terms. Even those who could secure such proof might be subject to further scrutiny. If any question arose concerning their political reliability, small producers could be investigated by the local council of the Popular Front for Independence (Függetlenségi Népfront). Given the Communist-controlled police apparatus, a "backup procedure" of this nature was quite remarkable. Regulating the actions of local councils was much harder than securing the cooperation of the police. Yet the effort was deemed necessary in order to ensure the elimination of those who had managed to slip through the first net.

In March 1949, the Department of State Economy (Államgazdasági Osztály) of the CP had outlined its future policies on small business. Paraphrasing Lenin, who had declared that "small production engenders capitalism and the bourgeoisie daily, hourly, spontaneously and on a mass scale" (quoted in Nove 1983, 42), the secret document asserted:

> [Small artisans] are the stratum that re-creates capitalism every day, but they are the stratum with which (or the larger part of which) we

> have to work together for a long time. We must find the organizational form that allows us to reeducate this stratum, and enlist them in the building of socialism. The cooperative movement is the organizational form through which we can bring small artisans into the socialist sector of production. (PIA/276.94/121/1949, 162–63)

The cooperative was conceived as a temporary, transitional form halfway between independent small production and large-scale factory work. Members would work under the same roof, fulfilling the central plan, and they would be paid according to centrally set norms (PIA/276.94/121/1949, 164). Membership was open only to those who were either small producers or engaged in a few specified trades. Small producers could bring their employees into the cooperatives if those workers would otherwise be unemployed. Each member had to participate in the actual production process; a member could work in a nonproduction job (e.g., as a cashier) only if he or she had previously been self-employed. Only under exceptional circumstances could cooperatives hire employees.

How little autonomy the Party intended to accord to the already decimated private business sector is clear from the early drafts of a five-year plan drawn up in 1949 in the aftermath of the May elections (PIA/276.94/121/1949, 164–72).[14] The work of a special committee of the CP was devoted specifically to the five-year plan for the small private sector in industry, construction, and services. The committee's goal was to devise a schedule for the gradual elimination of private tradesmen, partially by absorbing them into state firms and partially by herding them into cooperatives. In preparation, a list of 16 ways to vanquish small private industry was compiled. Ideas included banning new licenses, cutting supplies from state factories to private artisans, eliminating credit, increasing taxes, banning purchases of machinery, and limiting the number of employees to three per private business (PIA/276.94/111/1949). The final plan called for reducing every trade by 75 percent over the next five years. In addition, entire professions were to be erased from the private sector, such as watchmakers, weavers, opticians, bicycle and other vehicle manufacturers, welders, lathe operators, furriers, paint makers, millers, cheese makers, distillers, glaziers, brick makers, and coppersmiths.

In December 1949, an executive decree announced that, with a few exceptions, all licenses would require approval from the appropriate minister. Thus, if one wanted to enter business as a locksmith, no one less than the minister of Industry had to approve the application. Local authorities could make the decision only when two conditions were met: that the applicant lived in a town with less than 3,000 inhabitants and at least one locksmith in the area had recently given up his business. A series of measures restricting small production followed. The number of employees was frozen, artisans had to buy their materials at retail prices and could not keep more than a month's worth of supplies in stock, and many expenses could not be included in the product's final price. Other decrees were aimed at particular occupations. For instance, tailors in urban areas were banned from selling the clothes they made and builders could not employ skilled construction workers of any kind (Gervai 1960, 302–3).

The plan for eliminating the private sector was quite successful, though by 1953 it had only succeeded in entirely abolishing four professions: chimney sweeps, canners, distillers, and printers. The first trade was absorbed by the local councils, the second was appropriated, and the last two fell victim to state monopolies on liquor and printing. The largest drop occurred in food processing. Private bakers and butchers disappeared almost completely as the state took control of virtually all foodstuffs not produced for self-consumption and used health inspections to withdraw the licenses of small producers (PIA/276.94/111/1949, 77–80; PIA/276.94/142/1950, 29–30).[15] The chemical, rubber, and leather industries also saw a large decline because of the state's firm grip on materials. Another big loser in absolute numbers was small-scale construction; industrial construction absorbed most of these artisans (PIA/276.94/121/1949, 182–83). The smallest loss occurred in textile manufacturing, where rope and fishnet makers proved resilient. Their traditional trade was not amenable to factory-type mechanization (table 3.1).

TABLE 3.1. Planned and Actual Decrease in the Number of Self-Employed Persons by Economic Category, 1949–53

Economic Category	Actual Decrease (%)	Planned	Number in 1953
Food processing	98.6	87.0	343
Paper and printing	85.6	35.7	212
Chemicals	81.4	96.4	163
Rubber and leather products	81.1	40.2	523
Construction	80.5	67.9	5,196
Lumber (carpenters, etc.)	73.6	46.7	6,597
Metal processing	73.3	55.6	6,941
Leather wear (shoemakers)	73.2	55.0	8,233
Building materials	72.8	65.9	428
Service industry	72.6	74.1	4,515
Textile wear (tailors)	69.0	76.5	9,125
Textile manufacturing	59.1	54.2	756
Overall	77.1	66.0	43,032

Sources: PIA/276.94/142/1949, 188–90, 222–25; KSH 1961, 30–35.
Note: Domestic, miscellaneous, and itinerant trades are omitted.

The eradication of small production met few immediate obstacles; turning artisanry into factory work was far more difficult. In the trades in which factory production was most practical, such as the shoe industry, the artisans preferred cooperatives to factories. Although cooperatives were organized like factories, they did not carry the stigma of proletarianization, because cooperative workers were called members and not employees. Cobblers and shoemakers resisted the state's efforts to recruit them into factories. Thus, shoe factories in the state sector had to make do with whatever labor they could manage to attract. In other trades, large-scale production made little sense. Whetters, bakers, electricians, barbers, and others who could not benefit from the modern organization of production either set up cooperatives, in which they continued to do what they had always done but now under bureaucratic control imposed by the state through the cooperative, or were absorbed into factories where they worked doing something different from—though sometimes related to—their original trades.

With a few exceptions, large-scale production could not fill the void created by the destruction of small private industry.[16] Consumers were not the only ones to suffer. State firms could not subcontract artisans for small jobs in the rush to meet their plan targets. As the combination of restrictions on the private sector and an accumulating demand created an ever-improving market for an ever-decreasing number of tradesmen, the need for tighter regulations and more vehement ideological exhortations grew. Some artisans indeed contrived to circumvent restrictions by using the cooperative as a legal front, but these pseudocooperatives were harshly prosecuted.

By 1953, the small private sector had been absorbed into the state sector. The number of licenses held in 1953 was less than a third of the 1948 figure (KSH 1961, 45), and the number of employees had dropped from 120,958 in 1948 to 2,747 by early 1953. Apprentices had almost vanished. This precipitous decline was the result of a new system of industrial training introduced in 1949, which had moved the locus of industrial education to factories and newly created trade schools in order to tailor the work force to the needs of the socialist plan (Darvas 1984). By 1953, there were only 59 apprentices working with artisans.

Collectivization: The Nationalization of Land

By 1949, all but two of the major factors of production had been nationalized and appropriated by the state: these were land—now given to the peasants—and labor. The private ownership of land and labor were the two remaining obstacles to the establishment of a homogeneous, one-sector economy based on large-scale factory production and centralized planning.

The prewar land system had been dominated by large estates or *latifundia.*[17] In 1935, a meager 0.8 percent of estates with holdings greater than 60 hectares accounted for 44.2 percent of arable land, and 35.7 percent of all those working in agriculture owned no land whatsoever. Between the upper crust of the rich landlords and the bottom stratum of the agrarian proletariat and semiproletariat lay a continuum of small and middle peasants. At the upper end were the rich peasants who needed and could afford to employ others. This group made up little more than one-fourth of those who drew their incomes primarily from agricultural production (Donáth 1977, 22).

The unequal distribution of land had been a key political and economic concern for decades. After the war all political parties agreed that "the land should belong to those who cultivate it" (*a föld azé, aki megműveli*), but divisions occurred over how best to carry out land reform. The Small Holders' Party, representing the interests of the small and middle peasantry, wanted to create a new land structure with viable smallholdings—an agriculture based on small, independent farmers. The Communist Party, in alliance with the National Peasant Party supported by the poor peasantry, wanted to satisfy the land hunger of as many poor peasants as possible. This position generated some support for the Communists within the ranks of a politically inexperienced, yet sizable, social stratum: the agrarian proletariat. The two radical leftist parties set at a much lower level the minimum size of plots to be appropriated and distributed than that advocated by the Small Holders' Party plan. It seems likely that the CP, believing that the future of agriculture lay in large-scale agricultural factories, regarded land reform as politically inevitable and that they evaluated the viability of these smallholdings with the future of collectivization in mind. In the 1945 land reform the Communist plan triumphed. When the Small Holders' won the first postwar parliamentary elections in the fall of 1945, the land reform was already in full swing, and it was too late for the government to make any major changes (Donáth 1977, 38–45). Moreover, the reform enlarged state property by placing forests, lakes, and certain agricultural lands under state ownership.

Interestingly, the idea of redistributing land without compensation was never considered.[18] Peasants had to pay for the expenses associated with administering the land reform (e.g., the cost of surveying), and they also had to pay for the land itself. The state assumed responsibility for compensating the owners of large estates and for collecting payment from the new landowners; the peasants thus became indebted to the state and not to the previous landowners. These debts later provided the government with crucial leverage to force peasants into joining the cooperatives. The state performed its middleman role less than evenhandedly. It assiduously enforced and collected payments from the peasants, especially in the late 1940s and early 1950s, but was considerably less conscientious about compensating the previous owners. Most received nothing for the land they had surrendered. This was hardly surprising, as the state was facing a severe postwar economic crisis involving inflation as well as debt. Even if it had intended to honor its commitment, doing so would have been very difficult. Furthermore, the state, then already controlled by the CP, did not conceal its ideological hostility toward the landed upper class, so the promise to repay reactionary class enemies was not given in good faith.

No matter how flawed and precarious the existence of the newly created agrarian petty bourgeoisie was, their share in the Hungarian economy increased dramatically. They comprised only 30.4 percent of the economically active population in 1930 and 28.7 percent in 1941. Their numbers jumped following the land reforms, however, and their share stood at 43.8 percent by 1949 when the brutal policies of collectivization began (Pető and Szakács 1985, 144).

Unquestioned faith in the superiority of large-scale agricultural production over small-scale private farming coincided with the need to wring more produce and labor out of the countryside to serve as a basis for socialist industrialization. But collectivization was not yet politically feasible in 1945. The CP remembered the fiasco in 1919, when during its short-lived tenure in power it tried to force collectivization on a hostile, land-hungry peasantry.

Constituting over half of the entire work force, the peasant population was an important economic and political factor by virtue of its numerical weight alone. The land reform of 1945 was intended to dispel lingering suspicions among the peasantry about Communist intentions. These suspicions, strongly ingrained by the post-1919 counterrevolutionary regime's propaganda between the two world wars, and reinforced by news of ruthless collectivization in the Soviet Union, were difficult to put to rest. After 1945, they became one of the Communists' greatest political liabilities.[19]

These circumstances necessitated the use of other instruments of control. The first measure was a 1944 law mandating delivery obligations for all agricultural producers. The amount of produce farmers had to deliver for free or at below-market prices was prescribed according to the value of the farmer's land. These quotas originally were devised as emergency measures to feed the country at war, but they continued to determine agricultural policies until 1956 (Závada 1986, 17).[20] In the late 1940s and early 1950s, the 1944 law was consciously wielded as a political weapon. Beginning in 1945, delivery quotas were established in ways that discriminated against farmers with larger landholdings, specifically those with more than 25 cadastral yokes (35.3 acres) or with land valued at more than 350 gold crowns.[21] In 1945, a peasant with three cadastral yokes (4.2 acres) had to deliver 50 kilograms of wheat, 60 kilograms of barley, millet or rye, or 150 kilograms of maize per cadastral yoke. A peasant with 40 cadastral yokes (56.5 acres), on the other hand, was liable for four, three, and two times more of these grain products, respectively, per cadastral yoke (Závada 1986,. 310). The political thrust of these measures was clear to everyone. They were designed to break the *kulaks*—the most successful small producers in agriculture.

Between 1945 and 1948, delivery quotas decreased for peasants with less than 14 acres and increased for the rest. From 1949 on, and especially after 1950, there was an across-the-board increase, as the hardship these deliveries inflicted on the peasantry was successfully used to coerce them into joining the cooperative farms.

The second weapon at the state's disposal was the credit system it had controlled *de facto* since 1945 and *de jure* since 1947. Interest rates were high, and peasants with newly acquired land in need of start-up capital had to take on a serious debt burden (Halász 1975, 106–7, nn. 39, 40).

The third way the state began to take greater control of agricultural production was by increasing administrative interference. With the declared purpose of decreasing unemployment, state bodies regulated the use of horses, oxen, and cows, limited the rental fees for draft animals, and prohibited the use of harvesting machinery (Simon 1979, 19). Machine stations played an important role in the fight against agricultural small production, as they gave the state a monopoly over farm machinery. Neither cooperatives nor private farmers were allowed to buy large farm equipment like tractors, threshing machines, and combines; their only access to this kind of machinery was through the machine stations. Private peasants' requests to use the machines were routinely denied, so those with larger properties had to employ nonhousehold labor during harvest time. This immediately made them "exploiters," even though they often would have been able to work by themselves had the stations provided them with the machines they requested.

The work process itself was also brought under state control. From the spring of 1949 on, state agencies issued a series of time schedules, which were inflexible and oblivious to local variations and needs as well as to the unpredictability of the weather. Regardless of circumstance, everyone was expected to adhere to schedules that mimicked the way industrial tasks were allocated in factories (Pető and Szakács 1985, 185–87; Balogh 1986, 213, 406–16). Different committees were responsible for overseeing peasant obedience. If peasants didn't comply, they were soon denounced as saboteurs, risking serious consequences ranging from harassment, discrimination, and fines to lengthy jail sentences.[22]

Not all forms of state coercion were this onerous. Some relied more on exhortation than punishment. For instance, peasants were called up to participate in work competitions. Farmers challenged each other, and villages challenged neighboring villages. Few took these challenges seriously, but it was unwise to refuse to participate. These competitions were an agricultural parallel to the Stakhanovite movement in industry. Indeed, there were peasants who succeeded in overfulfilling their delivery quota by several hundred percent. Moral pressure and more stringent forms of coercion were necessary partly because agricultural prices were kept low and provided little incentive for high levels of production, partly because urgent industrial needs for a large influx of labor constantly siphoned workers from agriculture, and partly because traditional peasant culture, which emphasized individual ownership and independence, clashed head on with Communist ideological goals.

The push for collectivization gathered force in 1949. Agitators (*népnevelők,* literally "educators of the people"), mostly zealous young people from the cities or poor local peasants enlisted in the Hungarian Workers' Party (HWP),[23] went to the countryside to harass, convince, pressure, coax, and threaten peasants into joining the cooperative farms. This is how one agitator recounted her experience.

> During the kolkhoz organization . . . we of course went out to agitate. Those people hid wherever they could! In the attic, in the outhouse, in the beet pit, or the ice pit, even though it was so cold that one could freeze in there. We knocked all over in the house, but no answer. Then, suddenly, we heard a baby crying. From the ice pit!
>
> "God bless you, come on up! We are humans, we just came to talk." No, they did not want to talk. . . .
>
> "But you will freeze to death down there, my God, with that little baby, and, I see, your wife is blue and green already!"
>
> "No, we will not come out, we are just fine down here." And it was impossible to beg them out of that place. They would not come out. This is how it went, with painful agony. (Quoted in Magyar 1986, 338)

Initially, the political semantics of the campaign were purposefully confusing. As in industrial small production, the slogan "cooperativization" (*szövetkezetesítés*) was very ambiguous. Cooperatives could be anything from consumer co-ops or loose cooperation for using machinery or selling produce wholesale to the Soviet-type *kolkhoz* in which, having lost their independence, farmers worked like employees.

The idea of cooperatives in agriculture was not a Communist invention. There had been cooperatives in the countryside before 1945. These had been based on loose and voluntary cooperation of independent small producers, and they had operated only in specialized areas, marketing dairy products and procuring credit. The largest of these older cooperatives were the Hangya (Ant), which was mainly a consumer co-op, and Futura, which was a wheat-marketing association. After 1945, marketing cooperatives such as Futura were instrumental in enforcing delivery quotas. Nonetheless, the Communists were distrustful of these cooperatives and introduced their own designs. They classified cooperatives into three categories. The first, cooperative groups (*termelőszövetkezeti csoport*), had a very loose organizational structure. Peasants kept all their property but consented to coordinate and cooperate in certain tasks. The second, specialized cooperatives (*szakszövetkezet*), were formed by people engaged in cultivating the same crop, usually labor-intensive produce like vegetables or fruit. Each kept his or her own land and equipment, but there was a common fund for buying more, which then became the collective's. Finally, there was the classic cooperative (*termelőszövetkezet*), modeled after the Soviet *kolkhoz,* in which land, equipment, and livestock were formally owned by the collective. Members had no independence; they were simply employees. This last form was considered the "most advanced" or "most collective." According to the political ideology, the first two forms would eventually develop into the third (Donáth 1977, 125–27).

The first *kolkhoz*-type cooperatives were founded mainly by poor peasants, those who had the least to lose by joining. In June 1949, there were 584 cooperatives sharing 55,000 hectares of land. Four years later, 5,224 *kolkhoz*-type and other cooperatives were in operation, farming 1,620,000 hectares (Pető and Szakács 1985, 181). Another 489 state farms cultivated 963,300 hectares (Donáth 1977, 128). In 1953, the average *kolkhoz* worked 310 hectares.[24]

The number of agricultural co-op members peaked in 1953 and then dropped as a result of the New Course, a temporary relaxation of political pressure after Stalin's death (see table 3.2). But as the New Course faltered, co-op membership figures climbed. Following the uprising of 1956, co-op membership again decreased dramatically.

Agricultural co-ops stood between the state and the private sector. The state did not regulate wages and the labor process in these organizations, as it did in state farms. Instead, it retained control through strict and detailed plans prescribing what agricultural cooperatives had to produce and how much they had to deliver. Cooperative members were subject to a central control as effective and ruthless as that applied to workers in state-owned large-scale industry, while at the same time they were denied the benefits of state employment. Co-op members were not paid a salary or wage, nor did they receive social security benefits. Unlike workers in state enterprises, where the bosses were appointed by the state, co-op members did have the right to elect their chairmen, but, since these elections were staged by the local Party apparatus, they were little more than a charade (Pünkösti 1988).

From the beginning, the *kolkhoz* provided members with a household plot (*háztáji*), just as the Soviets had done in the Soviet Union after 1935. Household plot size was limited to .57 hectares. The household plot and necessary inputs such as fodder, straw, and fertilizer were payments in kind for work done at the *kolkhoz.* Household plots relieved the authorities from their obligation to provide for the food needs of the *kolkhoz* members, and, in the early years of socialism, they saved peasants from starvation (table 3.3).

The symbiosis of small family plots and large estates was not a historic novelty introduced by collectivization. In prewar Hungary, the owners of large landholdings typically gave small family plots to the peasants employed at low pay on their estates (Juhász and Magyar 1984). The plots made possible subsistence farming and ensured that the peasant and his family survived—at the cost of expending additional labor. Because of these plots, labor could be kept constantly cheap, as agricultural workers did not have to spend money on food and could even sell some produce

TABLE 3.2. Number of Agricultural Cooperative Members and State Farm Employees, 1949–58

Time	Cooperatives	State Farms[a]
1949	37,000	79,000
1950	120,000	160,000
1951	256,000	213,000
1952	339,000	260,000
1953	360,000	316,000
1954	245,000	331,000
1955	257,000	320,000
1956	309,000	319,000
1957	154,000	85,000
1958	166,000	276,000

Source: KSH 1959b, 62.

[a]State farms include tractor stations and state firms engaged in forestry and agriculture.

from their plots. Before the war, certain state employees outside agriculture, such as those who worked for the National Railways, had received small plots of land as a fringe benefit. After the 1949 collectivization began, many workers and state employees who lived in the countryside kept small plots despite strong pressure from the state to surrender this land.[25] These so-called auxiliary plots provided them with a little produce to improve their diet.

The proportion of privately owned and cultivated land decreased from 96.6 percent in 1949 to 56.2 percent by 1953 (Pető and Szakács 1985, 181; KSH 1959, 138). Still, even as late as 1959, private peasants produced a greater overall volume of agricultural products than did the "socialized sector" (KSH 1959b, 49).[26] It took the second collectivization drive, between 1959 and 1961, to finally draw nearly everyone (94 percent) into the socialist sector (Donáth 1977, 171).[27]

The Abolition of the Labor Market: The Nationalization of Labor

An economy without a private sector needs a way to manage its workers. As the overwhelming majority of Hungarian working people became employees of the state, a new system of employment had to be constructed. The contours of this new arrangement could be seen as early as June 1945, when obligatory "public work" four days per month was introduced to help complete major postwar reconstruction projects. A month later, a new bill established "public work" (*közmunka*) as a permanent institution. This meant that any able-bodied adult could be assigned to any job if the state, acting in the "public interest," deemed it necessary. Accordingly, all women between 18 and 42 and all men between 18 and 60 were instructed to register with the state. Peasant males had to register after their sixteenth

TABLE 3.3. Proportion of Agricultural Cooperative Members' Income from Private Plots

Year	Percentage
1951	36
1952	47
1953	35
1954	49
1955	42

Source: Pető and Szakács 1985, 215.

birthday (Baksay 1983, 37). The registration of 3.5 million people was a formidable bureaucratic task, requiring 20 wagonloads of paper and a competent administrative apparatus (Baksay 1983, 44). The old state apparatus, which before the war had been both strong and sizable, suffered few changes in its lower ranks in the aftermath of the Communist takeover. Since these workers' bureaucratic experience was indispensable, the state had to see to it that they did not exploit their strong position.

One important instrument for controlling the state administration itself was the "B-list" promoted by the Communists occupying the Interior Ministry. The list's purpose was to single out for possible dismissal employees of the state apparatus who had been "politically compromised" earlier. At the same time, the B-list was designed to trim the bulky state administration, which had swollen during the war (Balogh 1975, 206–16). It was supposed to contain about 100,000 names,[28] but the need for a well-functioning bureaucracy and resistance from other political parties in the coalition government saved about half of those targeted. Beyond "weeding out" those who resisted the direction of the social and economic transformation, however, the B-list served the additional function of creating an atmosphere of uncertainty within the bureaucracy.[29]

The new labor regulations that followed the registration of the work force were very strict. Once individuals were assigned a job, they could not leave on their own initiative unless they received special and individual permission from the appropriate minister or they developed some health problem serious enough to warrant their departure. This strict regime was not kept up for long, however. By 1946, demobilized soldiers and prisoners of war poured into the labor force looking for some kind of employment, and households sent all their members job hunting as they saw their incomes devoured by staggering inflation. The B-list also created a new type of unemployed worker, the educated, middle-class bureaucrat looking for a manual job in industry.

As unemployment soared, the coalition government shifted its attention and efforts from regimenting the labor force to creating new jobs. It initiated many large projects to create employment, and in 1947 it sent 4,000 guest workers to Tito's Yugoslavia.[30] In 1948, 5 percent of the total population—roughly 9 percent of the work force—was unemployed, despite the fact that the 1945 land reform had given land and work to a large number of peasants. Under these conditions it was completely unnecessary as an economic measure to keep the system of compulsory "public work." Yet, the system was not abolished and lived on as a political weapon. Even at its inception, the political thrust of this program was not disguised. There was a special annual six-month compulsory labor provision for people who were members of the Arrow Cross Party (the

Hungarian Nazi party) or other rightist organizations, together with anyone of any age who had changed his or her family name to a more Germanic one, presumed to be an expression of support for Nazi Germany. After January 1, 1945, people committing such economic crimes as tax evasion, unfair price setting, black marketing, and shirking were subject to similar treatment under the law.[31]

Work was traditionally believed to have therapeutic value. The popular proverb "Work ennobles you (*A munka nemesít*)" received a narrower interpretation in Communist ideology: "supervised, industrial, manual work ennobles you." This kind of labor developed into an important part of the criminal justice system. Prisoners were put to work and people convicted for lesser crimes were sentenced to "educational-correctional labor." Members of the clergy—monks and nuns—were to avail themselves of the beneficial ideological effects of supervised, industrial, manual labor. Many Communists seem to have believed that this course of action would quickly eradicate the clergy's superstitious, religious worldview. Inmates of asylums were expected to recover from their mental illness as a result of undertaking "productive labor."[32] The factory as an institution had come full circle. Factory labor, modeled in large part on the organization of correctional institutions (Foucault 1979), became valuable on its own, and found its way back to prisons and asylums.[33]

The generally acknowledged importance and value of work only compounded the concern over the lack of jobs. By late 1948, unemployment was especially severe in construction, a reflection of the difficult economic times. In the metal and machine industry, on the other hand, as well as in the leather, fur, rubber, textiles, and clothing industries, unemployment was a result of the short supply of raw materials. Very much concerned about unemployment, the CP decided to change its strategy in November. Until then, productivity growth in industry and construction had been considered to be the locomotive of economic growth. Now the utilization of new resources, primarily labor, was to take over this function, ushering in the "era of extensive industrialization." The first five-year plan had called for a 50 percent increase in the number of people employed in industry. This figure was constantly revised upward, and by the the time of Party's Second Congress in 1951 it stood at over 100 percent. The creation of a large industrial proletariat became the regime's top priority. Four different strategies were used to expand the size of the industrial work force: (1) members of the old propertied classes, from aristocrats who had formerly owned large landholdings to artisans who had managed their own small workshops, were put to work; (2) the unemployed were given jobs; (3) women were drawn into the work force; and (4) the distribution of the labor force was changed by funneling people from agriculture into industry.

New factories needed not only new workers but also new managers unquestioningly loyal to the political leadership. The removal of capitalists and their "lackeys" meant that new cadres had to be promoted quickly to take charge of state companies. Most of these new managers were selected from among trustworthy workers, mainly from the skilled ranks, with some also drawn from among the engineers, lower managers, supervisors, and foremen. Much as with the worker-directors who had been appointed to head the newly nationalized factories in 1948, the new cadres found themselves transformed into managers overnight. Having had little preparation for their new jobs, they were often bewildered and overwhelmed by the immensity of the tasks placed on their shoulders. According to one survey, over half of the new managers had had no more than six years of formal education (Fábián 1986). They were completely dependent on—and indeed very closely supervised by—the Communist Party. Those who were not already Communist Party members were soon drafted. Inevitably, many of the new directors disappointed the Communist leadership; in certain branches, a third to a fifth of the company directors were replaced annually (Lengyel, n.d.).

To ease the acute shortage of politically reliable and properly skilled executives, planners ordered the education of 100,000 middle-level and 40,000 upper-level new officials by 1954 (Kovács and Örkény 1991, 13). Forty thousand of these cadres were to be promoted from the ranks of skilled factory workers. Meeting that goal would have required promoting one in every four skilled workers into some management position.

In early 1949, as new investment projects were begun, unemployment receded rapidly. The first signs of a labor shortage appeared in the spring of the same year in high-priority industries. In the cement industry, for instance, a labor shortfall spurred the Central Planning Office into action as early as July: trucks and loading machines were hurriedly dispatched to make up for the lack of workers. Mechanization was not the dominant method of dealing with labor shortages, however. Shortages were to be eliminated by increasing the size of the industrial work force.

As soon as the labor market became a sellers' market, workers began to take advantage of their new position, just as had occurred in the Soviet Union in 1929 at the onset of Stalinist industrialization. By the end of the summer the severity of the situation forced the CP to put this problem at the top of its agenda. On August 31, Party leader Rákosi gave a speech. In earlier addresses the wasteful utilization of materials had been identified as the chief concern.[34] This time Rákosi focused almost exclusively on labor problems.

> Discipline [in production] has slackened recently. Some [of the workers recently promoted to directorships] commit the mistake of not enforcing discipline sufficiently among their colleagues. They have no

> heart or courage to enforce with iron hands the discipline that is absolutely necessary for the building of socialism. (*Magyar Nemzet,* September 2, 1994.)

The freshly promoted worker-directors had not forgotten their roots. They faced terrible psychological pressures when they had to discipline people who had so recently been their coworkers. Abuse of sick leave, absenteeism, and tardiness were rampant; the quality of products also suffered enormously.

In certain areas of industry, factories vied with one another in a constant competition for labor.

> Recently there have been hundreds of cases of one state factory enticing workers away from other state factories. *It is even more common that workers leave to work with small artisans, in their workshops* [*kócerój*]. Many times they are able to get their four-weekly pay on Saturday, and by Monday they continue to work in another factory or with an artisan. They just laugh at those who do not understand these manipulations. This problem, too, should be treated more strictly. (*Magyar Nemzet,* September 2, 1949, emphasis added)

The high turnover rate hampered the execution of important plan objectives. As labor was cheap, and labor-saving machinery was in short supply, in order to execute very ambitious plan targets industrial enterprises had to rely upon a steady work force. Thus, the constant movement of workers was a major concern for enterprise management as well as for the government.

The National Council of Trade Unions, whose leadership was carefully selected by the Communist Party, joined in exhorting laborers to work harder. In September 1949, at the Trade Union Congress, the different union branches competed, each outbidding the other in their enthusiastic support of the five-year plan. Promises to work even harder abounded. The Congress as a whole resolved to "solidify labor discipline," vowing to enforce the principle of individual responsibility (*egyéni felelősség elve*) at the workplace. This was an unusual declaration from an organization supposedly built on solidarity and mutual help among its members.

In May 1950, implicitly acknowledging that lower-level trade union cadres often were not complying with central directives, the Presidium of the National Council of Trade Unions issued a decree that called upon trade union functionaries to tighten control over workers. No tolerance was to be shown for tardiness, absenteeism, "strolling around during the work day," underutilizing work time, leaving work early, handling materials, tools, machinery, or public property irresponsibly or carelessly, or producing goods of low quality. Finally, union functionaries were reminded of their duty to fight any liberalism on the part of management that might jeopardize discipline or undermine work quotas.

> Our unions, and shop-level functionaries should give more help to management with regard to any measures taken to restore and solidify work discipline. They should assure that enterprise disciplinary boards take strict measures against those committing quota tinkering (*normalazítás*) and wage cheating. (quoted in Balogh 1986, 239)

The trade unions' effort failed to fully satisfy the HWP, and in July 1950 it chastised the National Council for not fighting wholeheartedly. The council accepted the criticism and promised to push even more vigorously for "the development of production," extension of the Stakhanovite movement, and "realization of the socialist wage system" (Balogh 1986, 266–70).

Turning trade unions and all other workers' organizations into a cruel mockery of their original purpose deprived workers of a "voice" for protest (Hirschman 1970), that is, for organized struggle within the firms. This left them with few options. Through sporadic, individual actions of resisting industrial discipline they could acquire a very limited "voice" within the factory. The other option—which many took—was "exit," the individual strategy of going elsewhere to improve one's lot. This option was quickly eliminated. Reviving strict measures introduced in 1945, "arbitrary quitting" (i.e., leaving a job without the consent of the employer) became a civil offense in 1950 and soon was deemed a criminal violation.[35] The penalty usually did not exceed a fine and "corrective labor" at the workplace, but in certain cases a prison sentence could be levied.

Political leaders linked the poor behavior of the work force to its lack of socialist consciousness. It is difficult to dispute that most of the newly recruited workers were ill suited for factory work. With their peasant background, these workers found it difficult to adapt to the organization of work and time that factory life demanded. Since residential construction in urban areas had to yield to industrial construction, it lagged far behind the pace of industrialization (Szelényi 1983). Thus, workers seeking employment in cities could not bring their families with them. Consequently, most new workers either stayed in the villages and commuted long hours to their workplace or moved into urban workers' hostels, living quarters with the domestic comforts of a military garrison. Either way, since these workers kept their primary residence in the countryside, it was natural for them to participate in agricultural work whenever necessary. As a result, absenteeism in factories soared in the summer months when workers returned home to help their kin with agricultural work (Gyekiczky 1984).

The state made every effort to keep the movement of labor under tight control. All hiring had to be done through employment offices under the auspices of the Office of Labor Reserves, which replaced the National Office of Labor Policy in 1950. These employment offices were responsible for channeling labor into high-priority areas like construction and heavy industry. Their efforts were aided by comprehensive wage policies designed to induce as many people into the labor force as possible (table 3.4). Wages were set very low, so no family could afford to keep an able-bodied member at home. The official explanation for the low wage policy was that most day-to-day needs would be satisfied free of charge by the state. Housing, medical care, recreational facilities, and transportation were supposed to be provided to all workers through their workplace. While the actual delivery of such services was only intermittent at best, they nevertheless effectively tied workers to their jobs because only state employees in good standing were eligible for the benefits.

Direct industrial recruitment began in 1950, with people in the countryside being drafted for industrial work. Those who signed the employment contract were given a sum of 200 to 400 forints (fts), totaling roughly half of their future monthly wage. Besides acting as an incentive to the prospective members of the industrial proletariat, this small sum also

TABLE 3.4. Employment and Real Wages between 1949 and 1955

	Industrial Employment		Real Wages in the State Sector (1949 = 100)	
Year	All Employees	Workers in State Sector	All Employees	Industrial Workers
1949	782,000	407,000	100.0	100.0
1950	812,000	464,000	101.3	107.4
1951	871,000	544,000	89.7	94.1
1952	957,000	620,000	82.3	84.5
1953	1,054,000	685,000	87.0	87.9
1954	1,123,000	706,000	102.3	103.9
1955	1,139,000	712,000	106.0	107.1

Source: Belényi 1993, 25; Pető and Szakács 1985, 221.

served the useful purpose of fortifying the legal case against those who later arbitrarily quit their jobs. Failure to pay back recruitment money upon leaving a company was considered either a special case of embezzling state property or simply theft. In 1952, some 7,000 cases of "refusing to continue employment" were brought to trial, but many more cases were brought on charges of theft, embezzlement, "crime against the plan" (*tervbűntett*), and "endangering the public by shirking" (*közveszélyes munkakerülés*). As factories facing taut production targets were reluctant to lose workers, offenders were rarely jailed. Most were punished with wage cuts and correctional labor at the workplace. Still, the egotistic and undisciplined behavior of workers persisted.

Low wages, harsh discipline, and poor working conditions made factory work unappealing, so it took enormous pressure to make peasants give up farming, turn over their land to the state, and leave for industrial jobs in the cities (Závada 1986; Magyar 1986). Between 1949 and 1953, 300,000 people (roughly every seventh worker) left agriculture. The effects of this drain on agricultural labor were soon felt on agricultural production. By 1951, the state could not accept any more land from peasants because there were not enough hands to cultivate it. Very soon, local authorities responsible for the delivery of agricultural produce prohibited families still working on the land from leaving and even began to try to summon peasants—especially the *kulaks*—back from the factories (Belényi 1993, 32–42). Not surprisingly, the industrial firms vigorously resisted this solution and let only a very few workers go.

If recruiting factory workers was difficult, enlisting future cadres also encountered unexpected obstacles. The most talented skilled workers were supposed to be sent for a special crash course (*szakérettségi*) to prepare them for entering college. Factory directors could not afford to give up their best workers, but neither could they directly refuse to do so. Therefore, they sent the people whom they needed least. As a result, many of these future cadres were physically infirm, suffering from tuberculosis, kidney ailments, heart trouble, or nervous problems (Kovács and Örkény 1981, 105).[36]

The New Course

By March 1953, when Stalin died, the Hungarian economy was spinning out of control. Real wages were 20 percent lower than they had been in 1949, although in many places workers were forced to work seven days a week. The drought of 1952 brought the threat of famine (Rév 1987), and some collectives, formed in the face of bitter peasant resistance, began to disband (Barla Szabó 1981, 1). The state machinery was overburdened;

courts and jails overflowed. Between 1951 and May of 1953, the police prosecuted 850,000 people for minor offenses; since 1950, the courts had charged 650,000 individuals and convicted 387,000 of them (Balogh 1986, 500). Villages were bitterly divided, friends were pitted against each other, and families were broken (Závada 1986; Magyar 1986).

Nudged by Moscow, where the new leadership was determined to curb the worst excesses of Stalinism, the Hungarian leadership announced a New Course in June 1953. The document outlining this New Course, which was not published for decades, presented a long list of past mistakes and outlined the new policies. It acknowledged that industrialization and collectivization of agriculture had been rushed, that consumption had fallen, and that "administrative measures" had been used indiscriminately.

Private artisans and tradesmen, the document admitted, had been eliminated too hastily, and as a result the population did not have sufficient access to certain goods and services. Their absence was felt most acutely in home maintenance and repair, but small villages also lacked barbers, tailors, and cobblers. Therefore, new licenses were to be issued "if necessary" (Balogh 1986, 507). Private peasants had also been neglected, to the detriment of agricultural production. They were to be given more fertilizer and free veterinary help; *kulaks* were to be contained and isolated but not harassed (Balogh 1986, 506). Neither here nor in subsequent documents was the idea ever entertained that the private sector was, or should be, a permanent part of the economy, though it was now recognized that it would fade away more slowly than originally predicted (Barla Szabó 1981, 46).

The New Course brought temporary relief. Prices of many necessities were reduced, new resources were committed to residential construction (especially in Budapest and other, large, industrial cities), and real wages were raised. The pace of forced collectivization was slowed. A subsequent law reinstated small private enterprise as a civil right. Now, anyone with the necessary credentials and without a criminal record could get a license. Exceptions designed to protect state firms from losing too many workers to the private sector included those who quit their jobs arbitrarily or were dismissed through disciplinary action. These individuals had to wait a year before applying for a license. The new rules prompted a jump in the number of new operating licenses granted in the private sector. In addition, for the first time, certain part-time private activities could be undertaken without a license. Since most families in the countryside participated in building their own homes, a 1954 law gave permission to relatives and friends of the family to assist in the construction without a license. The same law also authorized concierges to do minor repairs in the houses left to their care. Licenses for part-time private activities were still unavailable, however (Gervai 1960, 295–98).

In the socialist sector, the Nagy government modified the labor code to protect workers' "right to recreation" by curbing the powers of firms to force them to work overtime. Some of the draconian penalties meted out for violating labor discipline were also eased, and measures were enacted to increase work safety and protect pregnant women and young workers (Habuda 1980, 45). Moreover, the Party promised to return to the norms of "socialist legality" and vowed to end arbitrariness in the criminal justice system.

Still, resistance to these central directives remained considerable at the local level. Local Party bureaucrats were slow to act, uncertain how long this change of course might last.[37] Their foot-dragging paid off. The New Course was reversed in February 1955, after having spawned frictions and tensions that hard-liners were eager to emphasize. One of the most politically sensitive charges against the new policies was that their liberalism encouraged many peasants to leave the collectives and return to the private sector. In the first year of the New Course, 130,000 people, over a third of the members, left the collectives (Donáth 1977, 145). At the same time, the number of artisans almost doubled. In certain branches, such as construction, the number of workers employed by the state dropped dramatically as state workers left to pursue self-employment (Belényi 1993, 111). Those who stayed in the socialist sector grew increasingly restless and ill disciplined. Turnover rates increased; in the first five months of 1954, one-fourth of the industrial work force changed jobs (Barla Szabó 1981, 21–22).

The Finale of the Great Transformation

The return to the classical model of socialism was interrupted by the 1956 revolution. During the revolution, in just a few months, 40 percent of the agricultural cooperatives formally disbanded. Overall, about 50 percent of the members left their cooperatives; many others fell apart without legal declaration (Pető and Szakács 1985, 301). Most of the people who stayed were peasants who had not brought much land into the collectives. In 1957, the number of private peasants was back to what it had been in 1949, almost wholly erasing the effects of eight years of collectivization.

Although Russian troops had put down armed resistance by the end of 1956, the new government, led by János Kádár, needed time to consolidate its power. During its first year, one of the main tasks facing the new leadership was to fill stores with consumer goods depleted during the fights and strikes of the revolution. The government was keenly aware that its shaky legitimacy hinged on its ability to project a clear promise of prosperity.

Small Private Industry and Trade

Just as in 1945, the small private sector was the first to rise from the devastation caused by the armed struggle. The Kádár government recognized the political advantages of supporting the small private sector.

> The party supports private small industry in its pursuits to satisfy the needs of the population. We also appreciate the useful activities of private retailers. However, if certain commercial activities are harmful, [and] increase speculation, we must take measures . . . (Kádár 1987, 234)

In 1957, several measures were introduced to again encourage the private sector. New credit was made available to artisans; income and social security taxes were cut to draw them into the "work of country building" (Kádár 1987, 118–19); state firms were allowed to subcontract craftsmen; and there were even vague promises of restitution of property for small artisans (Tellér 1973, 223).[38] Small retailers were also encouraged, especially in the countryside, and a new law was introduced to clarify their limited rights (Berend 1983, 89). The newly emerging private sector contributed significantly to economic normalization. Very soon, though, it began to exhibit objectionable characteristics.

The number of private entrepreneurs grew much faster in cities than in villages, where "they were needed most." They often strayed from their primary mission of providing consumer services and turned more and more toward state companies for contracts. While helping some state companies, they encroached on the territories of others and found devious ways of securing materials, easily besting their state competitors. As these entrepreneurs competed successfully for materials, so did they attract the best skilled workers from the socialist sector, offering better pay. High incomes in the private sector were a constant irritant to the leadership as well as to many workers in the socialist sector.

From early 1958 on, official rhetoric became increasingly hostile toward private entrepreneurs, dwelling longer and longer on their alleged tax evasion, profiteering, and price hiking (Kádár 1987, 394). New laws imposed higher taxes and more restrictions on private business.[39] By October 1958, the role Kádár envisioned for the private sector had narrowed considerably.

> Small [private] industry, small tradesmen, and other petty bourgeois elements do have their particular tasks, and they can attend to them surely for many, many years. We believe the time will come when they

> will have to step from the small capitalist platform down to where tradesmen in cooperatives stand, where the rest of the people stand, where only work is the foundation of life. (Kádár 1987, 486–87)

The number of artisans peaked in 1958 and declined steadily after that. Between 1948 and 1960, the composition of small producers changed. The drop was largest among artisans engaged in different forms of metalworking and food processing, such as smiths, butchers, bakers, and millers, while the number of radio mechanics and artisans producing rubber and plastic goods in 1960 was the same as it had been 12 years earlier. There were fewer artisans engaged in construction-related work and in the service sector, but their proportion among artisans increased from 12 to 15 percent and from 7 to 9 percent, respectively, due to the faster decline of other occupations. A comparison of the decline in metal processing and the increase in construction is instructive. Both construction and metal processing were at the heart of socialist industrialization. Recruitment into both sectors was aggressive from the late 1940s on. Yet, there were two important differences. While metal processing could be concentrated in factories, construction could not, despite attempts to shift to prefabricated structures. The success of concentration in metal processing brought economies of scale. This made simpler metalwares that could have been manufactured by small producers, such as pots, pans, nails, and wire, inexpensive and available. Private manufacturing of metal household items, therefore, was not very lucrative. The second difference was that, while many of the products in metal processing were intermediate (i.e., not directly usable by consumers), construction catered directly to private customers. It was much more difficult to control consumer purchases than to bar companies from buying semifinished goods from the private sector.

Small producers were not just losing ground in many branches of the economy; they were also aging. In 1948, 40 percent of small producers were over 50; 12 years later, 48 percent were in that age group, and 21 percent were over 60. The vanishing occupations contributed most to this aging, but so did professions like watch- and shoemaking, which did not disappear but had to be content with a more limited demand. The youngest professions were the most dynamic ones: on the one hand, radio repairman, electrician, and precision toolmaker—highly skilled industrial occupations servicing the latest technology; on the other, photographer, hairdresser, and beautician—personalized service providers.

As the majority of artisans grew older, their exclusion from the social security system became more and more troubling. Since they were not eligible for any form of pension, they were forced to keep working until the end of their lives. In 1962, a new law incorporated the small-scale private sector into the social security system.[40] The inclusion of artisans into the social security system was partly a by-product of the extension of the system to the peasantry, a move intended to sweeten the second and final collectivization drive. In addition, however, the state realized that in the foreseeable future it would have to rely on artisans to attend to the consumer needs of the population.

> As our society develops the interest of the population will require *for quite a while* that we provide opportunities within the limits of the law for the private small-scale industry engaging in honest work. Private artisans and tradesmen will survive as long as the state and cooperative industry and trade will not satisfy the growing material aspirations of the population better in all respects than the private sector. The work of private artisans and tradesmen also helps the development of our society. However, their capitalist tendencies must be restricted. The party wants the private artisans and tradesmen to participate actively in the common socialist effort of the working people, and to gradually—and voluntarily—find their way to socialism. (decree of the Eighth Congress of the Hungarian Socialist Workers' Party, November 1962, MSZMP, 586, emphasis added)

As more and more artisans "found their way to socialism," giving up their trades and joining workers in factories, their numbers declined steadily. In 1964, the government, concerned about the poor quality and limited availability of services, began to grant part-time operating licenses to retirees and people employed in the socialist sector. Credential requirements in certain areas were lifted, and the state drew the boundaries of admissible activities in the countryside less rigidly. A cabinetmaker, for instance, now could do any kind of woodwork, including construction carpentry, and was not limited to making furniture.

In the same year, the economy slid into a recession and the state had to cut back on expenses and raise new revenues. It decided, among other things, to increase the taxes of the "affluent urban private artisans." In official statements a dual image of the private sector began to emerge. On the one hand there were the good, honest, hardworking artisans living modestly in villages and performing useful services such as home appliance repair, house painting, or well digging. On the other hand, there were the reactionary, capitalist artisans who grew rich from profiteering and speculation. This group tended to reside in the cities. They increased prices unfairly and usually engaged in manufacturing overpriced and useless objects, like plastic bags and T-shirts, or they sold overpriced semifinished products, like screws, to state firms hard pressed by shortages. The ideological bias of Marxism toward manual work as the only truly productive form of human labor is impossible to miss in this distinction. The good private sector sweated its money through manual work; the bad private sector barely lifted a finger, merely taking advantage of the urgent needs of others. The entrepreneur who made money through recognizing opportunities was depicted as a shady character linked to the capitalist past.

Making money in commerce did not have the saving grace of manual labor. Thus, small private traders were in an even more precarious situation than were artisans. By 1967, there were only 9,000 retailers left in the country; 62 percent of them were over retirement, age and another 8 percent were handicapped. Most sold fruits and vegetables or ran tobacco shops, second-hand goods stores, or haberdasheries. Some, too old to tend the store themselves, rented their licenses to others. This was illegal, but it was condoned by the authorities for charitable reasons (PIA/288.5/137/1967, 20).

The Collectivization of 1959–61

The large drop in the number of private artisans at the end of the 1950s was related to another, as yet unmentioned factor. As soon as the Kádár regime tightened its control, it set out to complete the unfinished business of collectivization. This final drive, which was put on the agenda of the leadership in the spring of 1958, gave a clear signal to artisans that the new regime was not committed to a prosperous private sector. Collectivization, in driving most of the private peasants back into the collectives, simultaneously undercut the livelihood of many rural artisans who worked primarily for that market. Coopers, cartwrights, and blacksmiths either went out of business or joined the cooperatives. As many of them had some land of their own to bring to it, they often chose the second option and took a job in their profession in a collective.[41]

The final collectivization drive was completed by the end of 1961. Several factors lay behind this unexpectedly quick success (PIA/288.5/223/1961, 65). On the one hand, peasants recognized that the Kádár regime had consolidated its power and had the coercive means to break any resistance. On the other, the leadership also realized that it had to offer peasants some incentives. New laws incorporated members of the collectives into the social security system, thereby providing health care and pensions, and ensured rent for the land and compensation for the livestock and equipment they brought to the *kolkhoz.* And this time members could elect their own leaders in the collectives with less state interference than in the past.

The central authorities also pumped resources into the newly forming cooperatives, providing aid to buy fertilizer and machinery and assistance in building new facilities. It was an expensive victory. Between 1957 and 1960, the government had to invest two-thirds more than it had planned in agriculture, draining resources from industry. Even that much was not enough. One of the biggest difficulties was how to house the farm animals peasants brought into the collectives. Providing well-equipped stables for cows and pigs proved so expensive that it was soon decided that a large number of the animals should be kept where they had originated—in the peasants' barns (PIA/288.5/223/1961). With this decision, household farming became something different. It ceased to be simply an activity that the peasant carried out on his own behalf. Now it was elevated to an activity on behalf of the collective, and thus it was granted a measure of political support. However, this support began to fade as soon as collective leaders found out that members often paid much less attention to their work in the collective than they did to their household plots. By providing members with a measure of independence, household farming impaired the collective leaders' ability to keep a well-disciplined work force. Household farming became a constant source of tension.

Collectivization also increased peasants' purchasing power. Compensation, rent, pensions, the savings that free health care provided, and the fact that investment ceased to be their concern left relatively large amounts of money in peasants' hands. With the meager supply of consumer goods, this quickly led to shortages and spurred the leadership, which staked its political legitimacy on rising living standards after 1956, to speed up the production of such expensive consumer durables as refrigerators and television sets (PIA/288.5/200/1960). These made their first appearances in urban shop windows in the late 1950s.

By 1962, only 150,000 peasants, or about one in nine, remained in the private sector. The rest either had joined the collectives or—and this group numbered about half a million—had given up agriculture altogether and gone to work in industry. With collectivization, the private sector in agriculture dwindled to a small group of intransigent peasants. Private farmers worked on small plots of land using traditional cultivation methods and sold their goods in their villages or in the marketplaces of nearby towns. To supplement their small incomes, these farmers took advantage of the horses and carriages they owned and offered hauling services (PIA/288.5/384/1966, 121).

Final Consolidation

The successful conclusion of collectivization in agriculture appeared to have removed the last impediment from the path of concentration and progress. The private sector was all but eliminated, and state employment became the institution through which the economic activities of over 90 percent of the population were coordinated. The average size of state companies increased dramatically. The average industrial company had 96 workers in 1948 (Pozsonyi 1987, 16), 483 in 1955, and 641 in 1960 (KSH 1967). The first step in concentration came in 1948–49, when companies were reorganized after nationalization. If they manufactured more than one type of product, the companies were broken up and the parts reassembled so that each new company had a homogeneous line of products. A group of companies were brought together to form an industry center (*ipari központ*), and industry centers were gathered in industry directorates (*ipari igazgatóság*). The latter were under the jurisdiction of one of the ministries, usually the Ministry of Industry (Pető and Szakács 1985, 104–20; Pozsonyi 1987, 18). After the initial reorganization, the number of industrial companies stabilized and stood at around 1,400 until 1963. From 1950 on, the increase in size was the result of the quick expansion of the industrial labor force, which doubled by the early 1960s. In 1963–64, as yet another step in the process of concentration, state companies in industry were merged and consolidated into even larger conglomerates.[42] In certain industries, such as silk, glass, wine, sugar, and paper, only a single company was left. This feat was achieved by reducing the number of industrial companies to 839.

With this level of concentration, Hungary surpassed Western developed countries substantially, and among socialist countries it was equalled only by Czechoslovakia and Russia (though others soon followed suit). Concentration of production was hailed as another sign of the historical superiority of socialism because, many argued, modern technology required large companies.[43] The experience of Western countries cast some doubt upon this belief, but more importantly there were signs within Hungary itself indicating that it was not technology but ideology and political control that made these mergers necessary.

The new giants were often composed of several plants scattered around the country, connected only by poor roads and overloaded railway lines. Documenting and coordinating the daily life of plants in faraway places overwhelmed the existing administrative staff, requiring an increase in the proportion of white-collar workers (KSH 1967). The value of machinery per worker declined overall with size once a company reached 1,000 workers, despite efforts to concentrate investment in large companies. Although in some industries (e.g., machine manufacturing; construction materials; leather, fur, and shoe manufacturing; textiles; and food processing) the largest firms were the best equipped, in others (e.g., mining, metallurgy, electricity, and handicrafts) the relationship was either reversed or nonexistent.

In terms of economic performance, the conglomerates proved to be a disappointment. Productivity was highest in companies with less than 1,000 workers and began declining as one moved toward the giants with 10,000 workers or more. The diminishing return to scale was especially spectacular in mining, metallurgy, electricity production, and the textile and food processing industries. Overall, then, the largest companies had greater overhead, were worse equipped, and were less productive than the others (tables 3.5–7). Nevertheless, it was assumed that the proper implementation of science and technology would eventually prove the power of size.

The Capitalist and Socialist Versions of the Great Transformation

The Great Transformation in the Communist world was a self-conscious historical project, guided by an ideology rooted in the historical experiences of the nineteenth century. The great transformation of the nineteenth century wrought social devastation, starvation, sickness, dislocation, and poverty on the masses of the working class. It also shattered communities and severed human ties. Its twentieth century socialist version carried similar consequences. If the Great Transformation in Hungary, despite its considerable horrors, was less destructive and shorter than its nineteenth-century counterpart, it was largely because much of the country's industrialization had already taken place before 1945. Hungary had made a down payment of suffering on its industrial future before the Communist takeover.[44]

One of the most influential twentieth-century critics of nineteenth-century capitalism, Karl Polanyi, attributed the social catastrophe in Eng-

TABLE 3.5. Change in the Number of White-Collar Workers per 100 Manual Workers between 1960 and 1965 in the State Sector (cooperatives excluded; 1960 = 100 percent)

	Size			
Industry	1,001–5,000	5,001–10,000	10,001–	Industry Average[a]
Heavy	113.7	136.8	120.0	114.3
Light	140.0	109.1	NA	100.0
Food	148.3	NA	NA	135.9
Total	122.2	136.8	120.0	113.7

Source: KSH 1967, 20.
[a]Includes companies with fewer than 1,000 workers.

land in the wake of the Industrial Revolution to laissez-faire liberalism. The self-regulating market was allowed to impose itself on every realm of social life, threatening society with complete disintegration. Polanyi argued forcefully that by developing an unrestricted market in labor as well as in land and money, the market vastly overstepped its legitimate boundaries and began to encroach on social institutions. He pointed out that the market did not develop spontaneously but was an ideological project propped up first by the mercantile and then by the liberal state ([1944] 1957, 111–62).[45]

The Communist version of the Great Transformation was similarly a state-sponsored ideological project, even if its objectives seemed diametrically opposed to laissez-faire capitalism. The plan, by completely suppressing the market in labor, land, and money, demolished social institutions and loosed great suffering and humiliation on large segments of the population. The Party was keenly aware that any form of preexisting social organization, be it formal or informal, from chess clubs, professional associations, and church groups to friendship and kinship net-

TABLE 3.6. The Value of Machinery per Worker by Company Size in the State Sector (cooperatives excluded, 1,000 forints)

	Size				
Industry Group	101–500	501–1,000	1,001–5,000	5,001–10,000	10,001–
Mining	63	58	361	78	64
Electricity	1,232	1,126	1,084	—	—
Metallurgy	118	273	194	309	243
Machine manufacturing	51	56	71	68	93
Construction material	30	91	69	136	—
Chemical and rubber	235	212	285	182	—
Timber	22	59	30	—	—
Paper	—	—	—	218	—
Printing	80	62	95	—	—
Textiles	76	51	71	91	111
Leather, fur, and shoes	17	16	24	103	—
Clothing	15	—	11	—	—
Other manufacturing (handicraft and homecraft)	24	9	18	—	—
Food processing	86	97	81	200	—
Total	101	178	135	120	110

Source: KSH 1967, 21.

works, created competing loyalties and provided autonomous resources to individuals. Formal associations were simply abolished or taken over by the regime (Hankiss 1990, 32–35). Informal networks were harder to crack. Forced occupational and geographic mobility tore people away from friends and acquaintances. The workers-turned-company-directors described at the beginning of the chapter were easy to manipulate, for they had left their support networks behind and depended solely on the whims of the Party. Others saw their communities shattered by fear or the purposefully divisive politicking of the authorities.

Polanyi attributed the destruction of social institutions to the market, which knew no human motivation but greed and released the economy from the grip of social norms. With historical hindsight, it seems that the market was only one, and possibly not the most important, of the factors responsible for the erosion of social life. The economy was equally inconsiderate of and detrimental to existing social norms in the first period of socialism, even though the market was suppressed as much as possible.

The common element between laissez-faire capitalism and early

TABLE 3.7. The Value Produced per Worker by Company Size in the State Sector (cooperatives excluded, 1,000 forints)

	Size				
Industry Group	101–500	501–1,000	1,001–5,000	5,001–10,000	10,001–
Mining	262	79	400	112	94
Electricity	671	579	300	—	—
Metallurgy	491	555	468	380	337
Machine manufacturing	156	192	188	215	186
Construction material	90	166	103	175	—
Chemical and rubber	410	475	379	268	—
Timber	129	180	166	—	—
Paper	—	—	—	252	—
Printing	143	114	149	—	—
Textiles	199	247	156	151	140
Leather, fur, and shoe	95	119	140	255	—
Clothing	194	—	183	—	—
Other manufacturing (handicraft and homecraft)	115	87	126	—	—
Food processing	650	667	402	412	—
Total	303	327	234	203	168

Source: KSH 1967, 22.

socialism was that both were social forms designed to accommodate large-scale mechanized production. The factory required a clear spatial and temporal demarcation between the norms of work and other activities in life, laying the groundwork for the separation of the economy and other aspects of social life. Factory production made an economy embedded in the complexities of social relations as feasible as allowing workers to attend to family matters while working on the assembly line.

It was the scale of large industry and agriculture that introduced new and separate rules of conduct, ones that clashed with previous institutions. These rules were formal, written, and explicit. Large-scale and direct cooperation, restricted to the military before the advent of factory production (Weber [1922] 1978, 1156), required such rules of conduct among the parties, making identities, norms, and processes unambiguous and laying out clearly in space and time who was to do what and how. They created the predictability and stability that were necessary for strategic action on a large scale.

It was the rapid rise of factory production that created the social shock, which then was exacerbated by strong states intent on carrying out aggressive ideological agendas, be they of the laissez-faire or the Marxist-Leninist type fixated on factory production. Thus, proletarianization, the reduction of small producers to wage labor to create the social preconditions required for factory production, proved to be disastrous both with a completely free labor market and with the complete suppression of a labor market of any sort.

The historical details of the socialist Great Transformation reveal another, more general lesson of theoretical importance. My contention is that state socialism emerged from the ideology of Marxism-Leninism with its infinite faith in the power of concentration and the central notion of the national economy as one single factory. Economic theories of institutions depict institutions as least cost solutions to transaction cost problems, which emerge in a series of iterated games (Alchian and Demsetz 1973; North 1977; Schotter 1981; Tsebelis 1990). This may explain how cooperation comes about in certain, peculiar situations characterized by great stability, by a handful of parties with approximately equal power and with a shared understanding of what is to be accomplished. In these situations the only problem to be solved is how to reconcile well-defined but diverging interests. The kind of large-scale institutional design that gave birth to communism, however, was far more complex, and it was constructed under circumstances where none of the preconditions mentioned were present. Moreover, being a revolutionary design, state socialism did not have the benefit of the gradualist, iterative, learning process, even though once it was put in place the model did go through modifications and reforms.

Ideology can play an important role even if it points in the same direction as economic or political rationality. These instances, however, hardly persuade those skeptical about the importance of ideology. Therefore, in this chapter I have pointed out decisions where ideological prescriptions were followed by the leadership at the expense of economic or political expediency. Most importantly, the eradication of small private production was both economically and politically unnecessary and harmful. Its sole justification escapes anyone unfamiliar with the one-nation-one-factory vision.

Still, the overtly ideological origins of state socialism did not fail to produce solid institutions. Once ideology was institutionalized and shared understandings started to develop about practical tasks, these societies began to experience a measure of stability. From then on, institutions, not ideology, furnished primarily the stability necessary for strategic action.

CHAPTER 4

Social Order: The System of Universal State Employment

In light of the recent upheavals in Eastern Europe, it is difficult to comprehend that in the 1960s and 1970s socialism in Hungary was a stable system that looked stolid and stale compared not just with its own first decade and a half of social turmoil but with Western capitalist countries, which were swept by political protest in the 1960s. This social order, which had been erected by 1961, survived until 1990. Its bedrock was the institution of universal state employment, which was to harmonize society with the vision of one nation, one factory. After World War II, state socialism began as an ideological project, with the Party-state intervening repeatedly to correct the unanticipated consequences of its earlier decisions. The leadership was in constant turmoil, rushing to put out fires only to cause new ones. Though initially it had only a small group of reliable cadres, the Party-state had to be present everywhere to prevent the collapse of its design. The creation of large enterprises, these models of the future, raised a series of problems. There were not enough managers who were reliable and competent, and there was a shortage of skilled labor that was willing to tolerate factory discipline. Building the facilities and machinery involved great expense, diverting resources from consumption. Over time, however, self-reinforcing mechanisms developed that locked in the economic dynamics of concentration.

This chapter describes and assesses the institutional structure that emerged all over Eastern Europe by the early 1960s, after the marginalization of the private sector. Here the focus is on the mutually reinforcing logic of the pieces that formed the skeleton of social order. Chapter 5 examines the internal tensions and contradictions that came to characterize that order.

The Institution of the System of State Employment

The stability state socialism achieved by the 1960s in Eastern Europe was the result of the success of the Great Transformation in establishing a set of institutions that people followed primarily, not as a matter of political conviction, Party loyalty, or even fear, but as a practical necessity to promote their own interests. Managers and planners no longer regarded concentration as an ideological goal. Now it was a rational strategy that happened to be in harmony with ideological objectives. From the perspective of the enterprise managers, increasing size and disregarding diseconomies of scale made sense for several reasons. Low wages created no incentive for economizing on labor. Companies had no reason to invest in labor-saving machinery; what they wanted was machinery for which human labor could not substitute. It was not merely that labor was cheap. More importantly, it was a cost paid ultimately by the central budget and not the firm. The only constraint on hiring more and more workers was the availability of labor.

There were also positive incentives for companies to grow. Hiring more workers than were actually needed provided companies with an insurance policy against future labor shortages. The more difficult it was to find workers, the more companies would hire unnecessary labor, making the labor shortage even more severe. Largeness also made firms internally more flexible. Because production flowed unevenly among companies, they had to mobilize extra resources internally to make up for materials, spare parts, or semifinished products that failed to arrive from the company preceding them in the production chain. For example, if a clothing factory did not receive the necessary textiles in time to keep production from coming to a halt, it could dip into its own reserve supplies, provided it had some. If, however, the supplier dumped a large amount of textiles on the clothing factory just before the end of the plan period, the clothing factory, in order to meet its own targets, could mobilize extra hands to finish the job before the deadline—provided it had workers who under normal circumstances were unnecessary but now could be put to work at full speed (Frey 1979). Larger companies could hide more extra resources, and extra resources made companies larger.

The method by which plan targets were set also forced companies to grow. Companies were required to increase their output compared with their performance the year before. It was unthinkable for a company to scale back its operation because planners saw increased production as a desirable end in itself. The easiest way to meet bigger targets was to make the company bigger. Large size also gave managers more leverage as they bargained with central planners (Bauer 1981). Even though the enterprise managers recently promoted from the shop floor were in a very precarious position, and thus rarely made open demands, the leadership could not allow large companies to fail and would help these firms, even at the expense of smaller ones. Finally, large size had a benefit that managers never overlooked: their bonuses were directly related to firm size (Soós 1986).

If managers had many reasons to expand their companies, the leadership had no reason to stop them. Their initial ideological commitment was soon complemented by other considerations. First, in the absence of competition there was no point in having different companies doing the same thing. It made much more sense to create a single large company providing for all needs in a given area. Second, planners soon realized that it was much easier to command a few giants than many dwarfs. Planners faced a complex task; adding more companies would have made their job intractable. Third, once the plan was written, monitoring a few competently run companies was easier than overseeing many poorly managed ones. Since competent and politically reliable managers and experts were in short supply, concentration was a natural choice. Fourth, if a company was failing, the simplest solution was to merge it with another, more successful company. Thus, big enterprises constantly grew, swallowing smaller ones. Companies were captives of their own pasts. Those starting out large were destined to grow larger still simply because they had begun big; small firms were bound to shrink and disappear simply because they had begun small.

Finally, the leadership initially believed that a third world war was imminent. In preparation, it committed a large amount of resources to war industries, where large size had real advantages. The fact that Hungary, a country with no comparative advantage in steel production, had an oversized steel industry even in the late 1980s, was the result of decisions made during the war psychosis of the late 1940s.[1]

For the one-nation-one-factory model to succeed, more was needed than managers and planners interested in the concentration of production. There also had to be a set of social institutions that made society compatible with this new model of concentration and ensured a stable social order in which people could be managed according to the requirements of socialist industrialization.

The unique feature of socialist industrialization was that it successfully divorced proletarianization from the commodification of labor. By disappropriating all productive property, it reduced the working population to wage labor, but at the same time it did not allow a labor market to develop. If the state was to be the only employer, why develop a labor market?

What began as an ideological project soon turned into an economic necessity. With the first labor shortages, it was clear that the infinite appetite of companies for workers and a regime of low wages would have been incompatible with any form of a labor market. Wages had to be kept low so that more could be spent on new factories and new machines. But it was the successful coupling of low wages and high investment that fueled the urgent need for more workers, which in turn put upward pressure on wages. To make things worse, peasants, who constituted the largest pool of potential industrial labor and had just recently had their dreams fulfilled by the land reform, were not interested in leaving their newly acquired plots for factory work.

To replace the labor market, the Party-state organized a quasi civil service, a universal system of state employment. In the early stages of creating this new institution the state resorted to political coercion. But once alternative ways of making a living were suppressed the system began to administer itself through centralized wage and labor policies. Party hardliners initially resisted this shift. Nevertheless, as we will see in the next chapter, by 1962 state employment had become the principal way in which the Party-state exercised its power. As a result, it could afford to dispense with political mobilization and coercion as the paramount means of keeping social order. Ideological zealotry became unnecessary. It was enough to be willing to work "honestly," strictly within the parameters set by the state. The system required cooperation, and the higher up one was in its hierarchy the more important it was to follow directives from the top. A large part of the population became both boss and subordinate. Workers were enticed to exploit the weight of their positions as they enforced cooperation from those below them, while at the same time they were pressured to cooperate obediently with those above. To make the system fail-safe, the Party stood vigilantly on each rung of the hierarchy, ever ready to intervene.

In addition to replacing the labor market as a means of integrating labor with production, universal state employment offered the state a means of nationalizing the last factor of production still in private hands: labor. Labor was the last resort of the private sphere because it could not be divorced from the body of the individual. Nationalizing labor, therefore, was an altogether different and much more difficult task than was nationalizing land or capital. The system of universal state employment gave the state strong control over the labor process. It was the key to its ability to plan and to organize the economy as a whole. Equally important, this system also provided the state with power over people's lives outside as well as inside the workplace. Manipulating wage and employment policies influenced social stratification by narrowing or widening material differences among the various social groups. The state could maintain control over the life chances of individuals without being overtly coercive or directly interfering in people's private lives. The state also had the power to move individuals and groups up and down in the social hierarchy and divide groups by introducing elaborate internal hierarchies where none had existed before, as happened in agriculture in the 1960s (Juhász 1979; Lampland 1987). It even had a limited ability to change the overall structure of the social hierarchy by changing the proportions of different occupations, as occurred when it radically increased the number of industrial workers and depleted the agrarian work force. The management of social structure through state employment enabled the state to reserve its political might for extraordinary cases only.

By 1961, over 95 percent of the Hungarian work force was employed in the socialist sector. The working lives of the overwhelming majority thus were directed and administered through the institutions of the system of state employment. Although it was a system of organized dependence, universal state employment had many features attractive to workers. It provided security, and it made people's lives predictable and calculable. By taking a job, people could be certain that as long as they showed up on time and performed their assigned tasks they were entitled to a modest but stable income. People could make long-range plans about how to move up in the hierarchy at their workplace, knowing that in 10 or 20 years they would be working for the same company. They also knew that seniority alone would improve their circumstances. State employment erased the anxieties of unemployment; not finding a job became a thing of the past. The new institution made a range of social services accessible to a large section of the population for the first time in history. From the late 1950s until the late 1970s, state employment gave people a sense that their lives were improving surely, if slowly.

Historical Precedents

State employment was not a communist invention, but extending it to the entire population was unique to socialism. "To organize the whole economy on the lines of the postal service" was the way Lenin outlined the immediate task of the Russian Revolution (quoted in Nove 1983, 32). In many important respects, the prewar Hungarian Postal Service and the Hungarian National Railways, the largest company in Hungary, had provided previews of the kind of labor relations that would characterize Communist rule. From their inceptions, both services had been run by the state and neither had labor relations shaped by collective bargaining. In each, trade unions and all forms of political organization had been discouraged or forbidden (Szpirulisz 1972).[2] Their unusual organizational structure was loosely modeled after the military: employees had ranks as well as salutations and uniforms indicating them. The emphasis on discipline and morale, as well as the language of the service, imitated the army. The military importance of these services was frequently reiterated as a justification for their strict disciplinary norms.[3] Employees were not simply laborers discharging their duties. Their employer required that these workers behave "properly" off the job, too. As civil servants they were expected to emulate the ethos of their employment. Thus, even their private, nonwork lives were subject to scrutiny.[4]

State employees had fringe benefits about which other workers could only dream. They received special supplies of coal and timber, travel passes, housing in company settlements, medical care in company hospitals, and a decent postretirement pension. They were often provided with small garden plots for growing vegetables, herbs, or fruit for their own consumption. These benefits, together with a decent salary and relative job security, made state employment very much coveted by members of the lower and lower-middle classes. It is not surprising that when the Communists offered their own version of state employment after the World War II, they gained some initial popular support.

Before 1945, many large private enterprises sought to preempt autonomous workers' organizations (like militant labor unions, which were not tolerated) by emulating the paternalistic and military type of labor organization found in state firms. They had their own welfare system, and some built and virtually ran their own towns, where the company provided housing, electricity, health care, and a library.[5] Discipline within and even beyond the factory was strictly enforced.

In many respects, these large enterprises resembled the pre-1945 manorial estates in agriculture, where landless peasants lived and worked on premises owned by the landlord and where a similar system of organized dependence had developed much earlier (Lampland 1995). The landless peasant (*cseléd*) was not a worker who contracted with the landlord but a "member of the landlord's household" (Lörincz 1974, 380–39). Living in huts provided by the landlord, the *cseléds* were completely dependent on their employer for every aspect of their lives. The law prohibited any form of organization among these peasants. It was the landlords' responsibility to see to the welfare of their workers. Opportunities to improve one's life were limited. The *cseléds'* mobility was restricted by the *cselédkönyv,* a little booklet these peasants had to carry and turn over to their new employers each time they changed jobs.

Thus, most of the industrial workers coming from agriculture were used to a paternalistic work organization, and, even though industrial labor was quite different from agricultural work, many aspects of factory life would have seemed familiar to them.

The Communist System of Universal State Employment

The important difference between the prewar system of state employment and the Communist version that replaced it was that the latter was meant to be all-inclusive. Everyone was, eventually, to become an employee of the state.[6] This created a historically unprecedented social formation in which welfare and citizenship rights became tied to one's job, and thus employee status replaced citizenship.

In its classic form, as it existed until the 1980s, this system was built from a series of overlapping formal components designed to control and manage state employees. The scale of this system required explicit, written rules, which in turn depended on clearly defined employee groups and unambiguously classified employees. At the highest level there were wage and employment policy agencies, which controlled wages and the movement of workers among state firms. The Ministry of Labor and the National Planning Office made careful calculations about the number of welders, pilots, and music teachers the economy needed to fulfill current and future plans, and the number of students in each profession was regulated accordingly.

Workers' wages were determined by a centrally administered wage-tariff system. A classification scheme was formulated for the entire work force, which grew ever more baroque with time. This wage-tariff system was meant to express "the value-producing capacities and social judgment of certain jobs" (ÁBMH 1983, 97). What it actually embodied was an ideological commitment to workers in large-scale production, especially in heavy industry, and the "social judgment" that skill and authority should be rewarded.

From the beginning the tariff system was two-tiered, with different levels for manual and nonmanual workers. The first version of the system classified manual workers into 22 categories based on their experience, skill level, and degree of autonomy. These three criteria were supplemented by an assessment of the physical demands and the general working conditions of the job. Apart from this classification, wages were also based on the regional ranking of the firm (there were two ranks) and on whether the job was paid hourly or by a piece rate. White-collar workers were divided among 56 categories that differentiated them according to their authority level and skill type. The first wage-tariff system classified the worker rather than the job. So, as their experience grew, manual workers could move from one class to the next. The classification of nonmanual workers allowed for two or three salary classes per job; white-collar workers could climb upward through this range if their bosses deemed them deserving.

In 1952 and 1953, the state changed the tariff system and shifted the basis of classification from the worker to the job. The manuals distributed to the ever-growing clerical personnel administering the system contained a painstakingly detailed description, exemplars, and sometimes even pictures of each job in a given category. Now, in order for a worker to be moved from one category to another, he or she had to be moved from one job to another. Since all jobs were centrally allocated, this change increased the central authorities' control and decreased management's. The new system reduced the 22 manual categories to eight and introduced large pay differences across the various branches of the economy, reflecting the priorities of the Great Transformation. Workers in heavy industry received the highest wages; those who worked in light industry or agriculture made much less. As a result of the collectivization drive, unskilled labor was plentiful in industry, but skilled labor was already scarce. The new system stressed skill and paid little attention to the job's physical demands. In 1956, the number of categories dropped again, to three: skilled, semiskilled, and unskilled. For white-collar workers, the number of categories had decreased four years earlier, and separate schemes were put in place for industrial engineers, clerical workers, and other nonmanual laborers. Just as for manual workers, the ranges of salaries within categories became much wider. There were special tables for calculating wages in different sectors of the economy. Again, this was to promote the objectives of large-scale industrialization: the special tables gave preferential treatment to heavy industry.

In 1971, to reflect the increased autonomy granted to enterprises by the 1968 reforms (discussed in the next chapter), a third classification scheme was introduced. The new system dropped the practice of calculating wages separately by branches. It also gave managers more freedom, providing guidelines for classifying jobs rather than imposing a ready-made classification. Blue-collar jobs were classified on the basis of skill and a composite of various physical and psychological criteria. Skill was classified into seven categories: one category for unskilled, two for semiskilled, and four for skilled labor. Work conditions were determined by kinetic and static exertion, monotony, required attention, physical danger, temperature, noise and vibration, dirtiness, exposure to harmful chemicals, and levels of dust and light. All of these conditions were summarized in a single score. For white-collar jobs, the new system distinguished among authority levels, sorting white-collar workers into 10 groups. The first group was reserved for enterprise directors and their deputies and the second and third for department heads and their deputies. Within each of the three groups, managers were distinguished by the type of enterprise they managed, specifically, by the size and importance of their company.

The next two categories included managers of subdivisions and foremen. These were followed by three categories that encompassed staff who worked autonomously, grading the jobs by the educational credentials of their incumbents. In the last two groups were clerical workers, also separated by educational credentials.

Beginning in the 1970s, the complexities of the wage system grew to staggering levels as an increasing number of special measures were appended to the general framework. The appearance of new jobs and the disappearance of old ones kept the system in constant need of updating. In 1975, the Central Statistical Office introduced the Unified Classification System of Occupations (*Foglalkozások Egységes Osztályozási Rendszere* or FEOR). FEOR assigned an eight-digit code to each of the several thousand existing occupational titles. The first six digits described the occupation and the last two gave the position of the occupation within the wage-tariff system.[7]

Wage regulations sought to achieve three conflicting goals: one microeconomic, one macroeconomic, and one political. At the microlevel, they were designed to give proper incentives for both companies and workers to work harder and more efficiently. Here the state was interested in spending. At the level of the national economy, the regulations were to keep overall purchasing power within certain limits, maintaining a high rate of investment. Here the state was interested in saving. Finally, the state wanted the resulting income distribution to conform to its political objectives. This goal, by introducing a wholly different principle, posed an insoluble problem. How could wages be kept equal if at the same time the state pursued its microeconomic goal by paying more for good work and less for bad?

Between 1950 and 1956, the overall size of the wage bill of each company was determined together with the maximum number of people it could employ. If a company overfulfilled its plan target, it was allowed to increase its wage bill proportionately. After 1956, the plan imposed an average wage on each company, but the number of workers was also fixed by planners. Since the average wage was calculated by dividing the overall wage bill by the number of workers, prescribing any two of these three quantities was sufficient. Thus, shifting from total to average wages seems to have mattered little. Nonetheless, it was always easier to justify the need for hiring more workers than originally planned than it was to increase either wages or the wage bill. Managers could always argue that they needed more workers in order to fulfill their plan targets, but they could not argue that they had to pay their workers more. Now that the system had cast the average wage into stone, rather than fixing the total wage bill, companies that argued successfully for additional hires could grab new financial resources from the center more easily. Beginning in 1959, companies were gradually given more latitude in determining individual wages within given ranges. This increased the enterprises' incentives for hiring extra workers at below-average pay. Now they could increase wages for workers they wished to reward, while keeping the same wage average.

The 1968 economic reforms gave companies greater autonomy. The size of a company's work force was no longer determined by central planning. Companies were free to hire. The average wage was still centrally decided, but firms could make adjustments according to a constantly changing formula calculated against their profits. More profitable firms could raise their wage levels while less profitable ones could not. This increased inequalities, which turned out to be politically unacceptable.

In addition, new hiring practices exacerbated the already serious labor shortage. Hiring poorly paid "fillers," workers whose most important contribution to the company was their willingness to accept low wages, which allowed management to reward others more generously, became an everyday practice (Tímár 1981, 267). In 1976, in response to the worsening labor situation, the state tried the other option—fixing the overall wage bill. This approach was problematic, however, since it penalized economically strong companies that wanted to expand.

While policy agencies were battling to find the right classification systems and the correct formulas to set the general parameters of the system, other agencies were charting the individual careers of state employees. Workers carried workbooks, which made their entire previous work history accessible to each new boss and the central authorities. At each firm, the Personnel Department, representing the Party-state, was responsible for implementing "cadre policies," supervising promotions and job category changes, and keeping dossiers on employees. Personnel Departments had strong links to the Interior Ministry, which was in charge of the internal coercive apparatus of the state. The heads of these departments were the most feared figures at the workplace because of their far-reaching influence over employees' careers. They were usually Party members and were given continuous ideological training (Baranyai et al. 1981). The role of personnel management was summarized this way in an official personnel handbook:

> For the working class and the party *the cadre problem is related, first of all, to the central question of the socialist revolution; the exercise of power.* The Hungarian Socialist Workers' Party is a governing party. The working class exercises its power with the leadership of the party. The proper realization of this power and the correct representation of the fundamental interests of all working classes and strata depend to

> a large extent on the cadres. In our days, when the power of the working class is solid, the classes and strata of society, party members and nonparty members work in national unity for socialist goals, and the questions of cadre management are posed differently than they were during the consolidation of power. The decisive questions of socialist power under our present-day circumstances are economic construction and socialist education. (Juhász 1982, 7, emphasis in the original)[8]

Cadres were the standard-bearers of the system of state employment and thus represented the power of the Party-state.

In most companies, the Personnel Department worked in tandem with the Labor Department, which was in charge of the more mundane and technical details of labor management. In factories the Labor Department designed the labor correlates of the production process, determined workers' production quotas, carried out time and motion studies to optimize the efficiency of labor, and adapted wage policies to local circumstances.

The bosses were themselves supervised by the appropriate Party organizations. As managers moved up the hierarchy they came under the care of higher and higher Party committees. The Party had the right to propose or rescind appointments and vigilantly tracked the managers' actions and achievements. Personnel department heads were closely supervised by the Party organization of their companies and so were company managers. Top managers of important enterprises—mostly Party members themselves[9]—were the responsibility of the town or county Party organizations, which could consult Party leaders in the factory. Until 1973, local Party organizations could not veto appointments at their own levels. They informed higher Party organizations of their dissenting opinions, and the higher bodies made the final decision. Beginning in 1973, local Party organizations could tender their veto directly.

Positions of national significance came under the supervision of the Central Committee, or even higher units, such as the Secretariat or the Politburo. The list of these nationally important positions was called the *nomenklatura.*[10] The *nomenklatura* was introduced in 1950 after a careful study of the Soviet *nomenklatura* system. Originally it contained around 3,800 positions. This number later decreased, but in 1988 there were still more than 1,200 positions on the list. The number of people in those positions in 1988 was around 3,500. The list ranged from the top administrators of the state apparatus down to the department head level; it included the highest positions in the judicial system, all members of Parliament, and all diplomats; leaders of mass organizations, including trade union leaders and heads of the army; and the police and border guards. In addition, the *nomenklatura* covered heads of the largest state enterprises and state farms and powerful positions in the arts, education, and culture. The Central Committee approved the directors of science institutes, theaters, museums, presidents of the electronic media, and editors of newspapers and literary journals. The Central Committee's control was so pervasive that no full professor could be appointed at any university without its approval (T. Varga and Szakadát 1992).

The system of universal state employment was a system of organized dependence and supervision. The manipulation of economic opportunities became the substitute for overt coercion. People were dependent on their bosses, who acted as representatives of the state. Many actions, from travels abroad to adult education classes, could not be undertaken without written recommendation from workplace supervisors. Yet this system also provided security and real benefits that before 1945 had been available only to a small minority. In keeping with the slogan "socialism is the society of labor where goods are distributed according to work," most benefits were tied to employment.[11] Benefits that did not require active employment in the socialist sector were tied to previous performance as a worker and were given only to people who were either too old or too sick to work. Pensions, for example, were never considered a general right accruing to all citizens. Only a few social provisions, such as health care and education, applied to everyone regardless of participation in the economy.[12] Many benefits were dispensed directly by firms to their employees. For state employees, these included sick pay, housing loans, the use of vacation homes, meal and travel subsidies, paid maternity leave, child subsidies, child care, and emergency financial aid in case of a birth or death in the family.

These welfare provisions constituted a form of state control. They made it nearly impossible to pursue self-employment full time because, until 1975, full-time members of the private sector had to pay high social security taxes to be eligible for any pension. The welfare provisions also gave the state a more personalized leverage, allowing it to reward particular individuals rather than groups. In handing out certain provisions, especially those in short supply, firms had considerable discretion. Housing was an especially coveted benefit. The shortage of homes was severe even relative to the number of eligible applicants; it was up to the enterprise to select the lucky few who would get company housing. Those who were left out had no way to contest the decision.[13]

Some benefits were automatically assigned to state employees in need. Sick pay and subsidized meals were rights that bosses could not withdraw from workers. There was also full employment, touted as the great achievement of socialism. As there were plenty of jobs, unemployment vanished, and workers did not have to live in fear of losing their livelihoods.

The system of universal state employment relied primarily on a mixture of careful supervision and economic rewards to manage people in the economy. This required not only a nationwide organizational structure but also consumer goods to motivate people to participate diligently in the socialist economy. The Kádár government went further in the direction of consumerism than did most other socialist governments because its political legitimacy was very weak in the aftermath of the suppression of the 1956 revolution. The need for depoliticization was urgent. Originally, socialist propaganda emphasized the importance of collective consumption: public transportation, factory cafeterias, and communal resort homes. Even early on, however, the leadership was aware that most consumption cannot be collectivized and that collective goods were blunt instruments with which to motivate workers (table 4.1). But acknowledging the importance of private consumption implied an acknowledgment of a private sphere. Within the severe limits set by the state, people were free to spend their money as they wished. That, in turn, meant allowing private individuals or households to own property of some sort. The state took great pains to separate this property for consumption from property that played an active part in the economy. A sewing machine bought by a worker to use at home was personal property. The same machine used by an artisan was private property (Szabó 1967). The former was endorsed; the latter was censored. The ability to distinguish between personal and private property hinged upon a clear separation between consumption and production, household and enterprise, the private world of leisure and the public realm of work. People went to work as employees of the state, got paid, and then went home to spend the money they had earned to "recreate their labor power."

Conceding the existence of a private domain of consumption did not mean that the state gave up on influencing people's private behavior. Guidelines for proper deportment outside the workplace were offered by the most popular board game of this period, Manage the Smart Way! (Gazdálkodj Okosan!). The game, which has sold around one million copies since its introduction in 1959, was modeled after Monopoly, but with the proper socialist message.[14] The object of play was not to become rich by buying and selling real estate but to save enough money to buy an apartment home and outfit it properly with furniture, kitchen cabinets, a radio, a sewing machine, a washing machine, and a vacuum cleaner. Later versions of the game added televisions, refrigerators, even ping-pong tables, and dropped sewing machines, reflecting the shift in consumption patterns. (The automobile somehow never made it into the game.) Unlike

Monopoly, in which participants are constantly engaged in commerce, Manage the Smart Way! allowed no interaction among players. All goods were sold by the bank, which represented the state. Everything had a set price, there was no haggling, and each item was to be obtained from the proper state store. There was no credit, but homes—the only item with this option—could be paid for in installments. There was no rent of any kind, except for interest on savings, which was meant to inculcate frugality. The importance of prudence was emphasized by encouraging players to buy insurance.

The money one earned was won in lotteries of various kinds, or it was handed out as a reward for frugality or for completing a circuit around the game board. To remind players that the ultimate source of money must always be labor, prizes were awarded for good work and workplace innovation. Like Monopoly, Manage the Smart Way! was highly moralistic. Players were warned against drunkenness, smoking, traveling without a ticket on public transportation, jaywalking, and lengthy calls on public phones. They were also lectured on the pleasures and benefits of reading and sports (without any apparent consequences for the game). Players were also expected to go to museums, movies, and the opera. In the context of the game, this meant spending funds on diversions that depleted the players' savings and impeded their progress toward middle-class comfort and, ultimately, winning the game. The winner was the first to own a furnished home and acquire a savings account of a certain amount.

Much as in the game, in real life the public sphere of state employment, where one worked for the greater glory of the country, was supplemented by a carefully guarded private sphere of consumption, where one sought a modest, middle-class lifestyle.

TABLE 4.1. Patterns of Consumption, 1960–80 (number per 1,000 people)

Year	Refrigerators	Washing Machines	Cars	Motorcycles	Radios	TV Sets
1960	3.8	45.2	3.1	23.6	222	10.4
1965	25.1	114.3	9.8	38.6	245	81.8
1968	61.5	151.5	16.0	50.0	245	136.2
1970	102.7	178.7	23.1	59.0	245	171.2
1975	220.0	228.0	53.7	66.2	240	226.0
1978	264.0	283.0	76.6	65.0	242	246.0
1980	287.0	297.0	94.5	63.2	NA	258.0

Source: Berényi 1985, 359.

Was Hungary Unique?

To what extent was Hungary's development unique during this period, and to what extent did it move along the same path other socialist countries traveled? If the process of nationalization was primarily driven by ideological rather than economic considerations, one would expect similar developments in other Eastern European countries that had embarked on the same ideological project. The prewar economic conditions in these countries were very different. At one end was Czechoslovakia, a developed industrial country with only one-fourth of its work force employed in agriculture in the prewar period. At the other end was Bulgaria, a backward, largely agrarian country with more than three-quarters of its workers toiling on the land in the 1930s (Spulber 1957; Gerschenkron 1962). World War II leveled some of these differences but created others. Poland, Hungary, and the eastern part of Germany were devastated by the war, while Bulgaria and Czechoslovakia survived relatively unscathed (Teichová 1988, 115; McIntyre 1988, 88). Hungary, Germany, Romania, and Bulgaria fought on the losing side of the war and had to pay war reparations, while Poland and Czechoslovakia received compensation for their losses.

In spite of these differences, all Eastern European countries set out to implement almost identical economic policies and even tried to follow the same timetable. This was no coincidence, since by 1948 each country was dominated by a Communist Party pursuing the same Marxist-Leninist vision of economic development. Guarding their unity was the Soviet Union. Committed to the same vision, the Soviet Union held itself up as an example and coordinated the building of socialism in each country.

The importance of the direct involvement of the Soviet Union in this early period must be emphasized. Soviet advisers were present in the key offices of each Eastern European country to give guidance to the local Communist functionaries. The power interest of the Soviet Union and the force of ideology are difficult to separate because the second gave form to the first. The security and military interests of the Soviet Union were clearly paramount, but that does not explain why artisans had to be squeezed out of their workshops or why collectivization was necessary. One could argue that collectivization was much more dangerous and destabilizing than leaving peasants on their own would have been. Similarly, the Soviet Union could have attended to its political interests in Eastern Europe without becoming involved in the complete transformation of these societies and their economies. What impelled the Soviet Union was not practical necessity but historical mission. It needed to fulfill its self-declared mandate to bring about a future society.

By the mid-1960s, the one-nation-one-factory model and its companion institution, universal state employment, complete with the *nomenklatura* system, were firmly in place in the Soviet bloc countries (see table 4.2). One partial exception was East Germany, where the private sector was eliminated more slowly and nationalization was completed a decade later.[15] The other partial exception was Poland, where the task of collectivization was left unfinished. By 1965, 3.5 million small private farms still

TABLE 4.2. Elimination of the Private Sector in Eastern Europe

Country	Year Collectivization Completed	Number of Private Artisans in 1965
Poland	Incomplete	161,000
Czechoslovakia	1960	12,000[a]
East Germany	1960	98,600
Romania	1962	42,900
Bulgaria	1958	18,300
Hungary	1961	61,200

Source: Pozsonyi 1987, 42.
[a]In 1961. Figure is calculated from Pozsonyi 1987; and Teichova 1988, 105.

TABLE 4.3. Industrial Enterprises by Size, Socialist vs. Capitalist Countries (percentages)

Country	1–500	Number of workers 501–1,000	1,000+
Socialist countries in 1965			
Poland	80.5	9.6	9.9
Czechoslovakia	41.5	16.5	42.0
East Germany	94.5	3.2	2.3
Socialist sector[a]	88.9	5.3	5.8
Romania	47.8	25.7	26.5
Bulgaria	76.2	13.7	10.1
Yugoslavia[a]	72.1	14.2	13.7
Soviet Union	78.0	11.6	10.4
Hungary	56.5	13.2	30.3
Capitalist countries			
Netherlands (1968)	97.1	1.7	1.2
Finland (1963)	96.8		3.2
West Germany (1965)	94.9	2.8	2.3

Source: KSH 1971, 27.
[a]Calculated from Pozsonyi 1987, 54, 56.

remained in Poland, accounting for 85 percent of the country's arable land (Magyar 1982–83). Overall, by the 1960s the state sector dominated the economy of all Eastern European countries. Wherever the private sector survived, it was strictly regulated and supervised by the state. Private enterprises were constrained to remain few in number, small in size, and traditional in operation. Though these firms posed no political threat, the state shared Lenin's suspicion that small production would encourage capitalism and the bourgeoisie daily, hourly, and on a mass scale.

The result of the socialist Great Transformation was an unprecedented concentration of production. If the process was unique to socialism, to what extent was its result—an economy based on bloated megafactories—specific to these economies? During the two decades after World War II, production in many areas became more concentrated in Western developed countries as well, so is it possible that socialism was heading toward the same destination, though on a different path? The concentration of production in socialism was both much more pronounced and much more pervasive (see table 4.3). In Western countries there was a comparatively modest increase in certain branches of industry (e.g., in transportation and electricity), but in others there was a decrease (e.g., textiles, construction) (Ehrlich 1985; Hannah and Kay 1977).[16] The revisionist Eduard Bernstein was proven right. In the final analysis, Western capitalist countries preserved diversity in company size, and in some areas small production not only survived but remained a leading economic force. Only in socialism did concentration completely marginalize small production.

Among socialist countries, Hungary was not unique in the way it carried out its Great Transformation. Driven by the same ideology, the "laying of the foundations" of socialism created similar social and economic structures across Eastern Europe. However, this uniformity was not simply the consequence of a common ideology. It was a goal in itself. Eastern European Party-states were intent on following the same model and constantly worried about deviations. Ironically, many of the differences that eventually emerged were tied to the common problems created by the success of this first period. Hungary's solutions to these problems, specifically the ways in which it tackled the consequences of eliminating its private sector, are discussed in the next chapter.

CHAPTER 5

Consolidation, Reform, and Retrenchment

Prelude to Reforms

An Ideological Shift

The consolidation of universal state employment shifted the principal form of domination from moral and physical coercion to economic management. This made political demobilization and normalization possible. Now politics could be downplayed in everyday life. The socialist economic model, however, was unable to fully deliver the goods that acted as economic incentives, lubricating the system. Thus, as soon as the old private sector was vanquished, a new private sector began to emerge, filling the gaps left by large-scale mass production. By the end of the 1970s, the private sector had become an indispensable part of the consumer economy.

After the 1956 revolution, depoliticization was one of the priorities of the Kádár leadership, which could claim even less political legitimacy than could the first Communist regime in 1949. While the earlier regime resorted to manipulating elections, Kádár had established his power with the brutal assistance of the Soviet army. Kádár learned the lesson of the revolution: confrontational politics was dangerous. He also understood that hard-line Communists were a serious threat to stability. These men and women had been among the first to flock to the newly constituted Communist Party, renamed as the Hungarian Socialist Workers' Party (HSWP) on November 1, 1956. They saw no reason for the Party to change its course. The Party as a whole, however, was highly demoralized after absorbing Khrushchev's revelations about the horrors of Stalinism, delivered at the Soviet Communist Party's Twentieth Congress, and then having to absorb similar disclosures about the abuses of the Rákosi regime. By the end of 1958, Party membership stood at 416,646, still less than half of what it had been in August 1956, two months before the revolution began (Kovrig 1979, 448). Kádár needed to extend his base of support beyond his Party faithful. To reach out to the population, the new leadership had to shift its ideology. The basic modernistic vision was not altered, but class struggle was carefully deemphasized. The private sector, now greatly shrunken, was no longer depicted as a serious threat to socialism. Accordingly, participants were no longer suspected of collectively undermining the newly born system; they were treated with the condescension accorded to the losers of history.

Opposition to the New Direction

The new emphasis on economic domination was not universally endorsed. Hard-liners fought the system depicted in Manage the Smart Way! by rejecting the elevation of material incentives over political and moral ones. In 1961, a debate unfolded about the devastating effects of the new order established by the resurgence of materialism and consumerism, derisively labeled "refrigerator socialism." Its detractors railed against the egotistic, petty bourgeois (*kispolgári*) mentality that was corrupting the population.

> The desire to own personal goods is on the rise. . . . [D]on't the years of toiling for the television set, the refrigerator, the weekend house, the automobile develop the character of the petty bourgeois? Doesn't the struggle for personal property amplify the traits of selfishness, materialism, social indifference? And, if this person achieves his desires, doesn't the fact that he locks himself up in his apartment with his television, that he is isolated from pedestrians when sitting in his car and from the human occasions of social events in his weekend house, blunt him into a petty bourgeois and a Philistine? Isn't the mentality of the petty bourgeois being reproduced in this television-automobile-weekend-house-motorcycle lifestyle? . . . Some would put it sharply; on one side there is television, automobile, foreign trips, hoop skirts, and, on the other, declining interest in politics, languishing attention to the products of socialist culture, the revival of bourgeois morality, individuation. (*Új Írás* 1961/8, 737)

The petty bourgeois was guilty of worshipping consumer durables and seeking only his or her own economic advancement while disregarding the common good. The chief complaint against the petty bourgeoisie was that it used its newly acquired merchandise to barricade itself inside a cocoon of privacy. This posed a mortal threat to socialism.

> To make it clear: if opportunities of material civilization, which in and of themselves are welcome, just, and necessary, meet in the mind capitalistic seeds, even if these seeds are embryonic, they develop these seeds to an unheard of degree, and the car, the television set, clothing, and the instruments of a more carefree life serve purely

> harmful and malicious tendencies. . . . [These opportunities] turn against the social order and ideas that brought them into being. (*Új Írás* 1961/9, 839)

This criticism harkens back to Lenin's warning that in socialism small production reproduces capitalism every day. The alarm of the enemies of the petty bourgeois mentality was far from misplaced. Just when the private sector in production seemed to have been defeated, the new turn to socialist consumerism expanded a private, and thus unsupervised, domain—that of household consumption.

By 1962, the hard-liners had lost the battle. Kádár successfully recruited supporters for his moderate line from within the Party. In August, he prevailed in condemning Rákosi and Gerő, the two leaders most closely associated with the repression of the pre-1956 period, and at the Eighth Congress he filled top Party positions with his own loyalists. Still, the attack on petty bourgeois mentality had lasting effects. The petty bourgeois was now less identified with a specific class and more with a set of character flaws. The most important of these imperfections were materialist selfishness and a small-minded disinterest in the lofty ideals of socialism. An individual thus could be petty bourgeois to a lesser or a greater degree depending on how pervasively these shortcomings penetrated his or her personality. The critical distinction was no longer class membership but individual mentality. Thus, anyone and everyone could take this unsavory turn.

The hard-line crusaders of the early 1960s anticipated quite correctly that incipient consumerism would eventually lead to the revival of capitalist tendencies and ultimately to the resurgence of the private sector. Consumer items soon provided the tools, tasks, and motivation for private entrepreneurs. Some consumer durables were easily transformed into instruments of private enterprise. Large freezers allowed people to keep meat fresh at home, ready to sell at any time, thus enabling them to raise more chickens or pigs than they could consume or immediately sell. Automobiles could be used as taxis or—with small alterations—as minitrucks. The leadership was not blind to this specific danger. While no law explicitly barred individuals from buying buses, vans, trucks, or any special purpose vehicle, internal regulations prevented such purchases. Several years later, in 1970, the Ministry of Transportation and Postal Service suggested lifting the restrictions on vehicles for practical reasons. The internal memorandum acknowledged, though, that the problem was

> not so much a transportation but more a political question. Ownership of transportation equipment makes it easier to run a small pri-

> vate business in manufacturing or trade, and as a result the needs of the population can be better served. On the other hand, this would increase incomes [in the private sector]. (PIA/288.15/183/1970, 24)

This suggestion was turned down flatly by the top Party committee on economic policy (122).

Household appliances contributed to the private sector in another way as well. The production of low-quality consumer items in the socialist sector quickly generated a secondary market for repair and maintenance. Manufacturers, interested only in fulfilling their plan targets, had little interest in the afterlife of their products. State companies responsible for repair work were overwhelmed, and appliance, car, and home repair soon became a lucrative private business. While broken appliances created demand, working ones freed up time. Household chores could be executed faster. Although the state expected people to fill their newly gained free time with political and social activities, sports, studies, and other forms of self-improvement, many used it to make extra money in the private sector.

The most important way consumerism fueled the private sector was that it awakened material aspirations that many people could not satisfy using only the wages they earned in the socialist sector. Buying a car or a vacation home would have been no more than a dream for many had they not had extra income from the private sector. All of these factors emerged and grew over the decades following the 1956 revolution. In the early 1960s, however, when there were only four electric refrigerators and three automobiles per 1,000 people, the zealous admonitions blasting rampant consumerism seemed hardly justified.

The Need for Reform

As early as 1960, economic tensions began to emerge in the now dominant socialist sector. In December 1963, the plenum of the Central Committee decided to open discussions on economic reform.[1] One curious aspect of the debates that followed was that the private sector was seen as neither the problem nor the solution. The private sector was a relic, an outmoded thing of the past. The problem of "property relations had been solved"; the difficulties that arose did so at the level of the "relations of production" (PIA/288.5/375/1965, 33–34).

Scholars and policymakers have articulated the need for reform in terms of problems internal to the socialist sector, now comprising the overwhelming majority of the national economy. To be sure, the private sector did give rise to complaints of all kinds, but none was viewed as directly responsible for the problems the reforms set out to remedy. Most of the criticism of the private sector was focused on unearned prosperity. In a 1965 Politburo meeting, Kádár summed up the leadership's opinion in the course of a discussion about living standards.

> There is a popular perception that certain strata live very well. This is true, and we must take it into account. I don't know in what form this can be done, but we should draw the line at the petty bourgeoisie and self-employed professionals. We must confront this question. One man thinks about how to get something to eat, [while] another changes cars every year. (PIA/288.5/377/1965, 51; see also PIA/288.5/381/1965, 39)

It is telling that all Party documents since the 1950s have discussed the private sector not in conjunction with other economic problems but separately, under the heading of "social relations" or the "tasks of building a socialist society."

It was not the workings of the private sector that brought about the macroeconomic problems but its virtual elimination and the parallel construction of universal state employment. It was not the enemy that created difficulties but victory over the enemy. The first sign of trouble was that the foreign trade deficit increased as a result of an upsurge in wages and demands for consumer and investment goods. A jump in the hard currency debt was especially worrisome. Wages and aggregate purchasing power grew partly because peasants and, in lesser numbers, artisans, relieved of the burden of investing in their now nationalized businesses, had more money to spend. The supply of goods to match these claims was insufficient. Since investments also had been increased to keep afloat the new cooperatives, with new buildings, machinery, and fertilizer, the state had to expand imports. Foreign debt rose accordingly (PIA/288.5/200/1960, 45–53; Bauer 1981, 107–22). The state had taken possession of the private sector, and now it had to foot its bills. Meeting that responsibility at the expense of those in the socialist sector, mostly industrial workers, would have been politically unwise. In fact, after the revolution wages had been raised and benefits extended in industry, too, in order to improve the workers' mood. Moreover, to speed up economic growth, factories were given permission to start new projects. Indebtedness in 1960 was triple what had been planned, and a third of the debt was owed to capitalist countries (PIA/288.5/200/1960, 53).

Another impetus for reform was the sense that concentrating more and more decisions at the top overwhelmed the leadership and decreased its capacity to direct and control. In the 1950s, the leadership had focused on a few gigantic projects to which all others had been subordinated. Now they had to distribute their attention more evenly. The planners had to set and constantly update almost a million prices (PIA/288.5/375/1965, 53). Politburo meetings were spent on haggling over minutiae—deciding whether to raise the price of firewood by this or that amount, whether to allow a certain company to make a particular purchase abroad, and so on. In the first extended debate on larger changes in the economy at a Politburo meeting in November 1964, Kádár vented his frustration:

> to tell you the truth I am angry, when we, in the Politburo and the State Economy Committee have to think about where to send 5 kilograms of gravel. (PIA/286.5/352/1964, 62)

The realization that in taking on all these decisions, the state also took on responsibility for any failure in the economy, only heightened the leadership's despair. Speaking at another Politburo meeting, a year later, Kádár explained:

> There is something that is related to the economic reform, that responsibility will be better distributed among the government, the local authorities, and the workers than it is now, and I think that will be correct and good. Now, if things are available [people say]: long live the government; if things are not [people say]: down with it! (PIA/288.5/377/1965, 53; see also PIA/288.5/375/1965, 40, 56)

Concerned over macroeconomic disequilibria, diminishing control, and growing culpability, the leadership decided to pursue reforms, though it was ambivalent about making profound changes. The reformers argued that at this stage of socialism the economy could not be managed "as if it were one single large company in which divisions with little autonomy operate" (PIA/288.5/394/1966, 129). Companies were to be given more autonomy, especially regarding production, while keeping important investment decisions centralized. The view that prevailed continued to regard concentration as the ultimate engine and fate of the economy. As Kádár argued:

> The concentration of capital is necessary also in socialism. [One of the Politburo members interjected: "We have abolished the word capital, and use assets instead."] We know about the concentration of capital under capitalism. We know about the realities of the socialist system, and, in my opinion, we need some similar process at work there, as well, because otherwise production cannot be economical. . . . I don't know what to call it, but we need capital concentration in a socialist

> society, because otherwise production will not be economical. (PIA/288.5/375/1965, 39)

While it was admitted that in certain branches medium and small size could be more advantageous, there were explicit assurances that large companies, which often formed national monopolies, would not be broken up (PIA/288.5/426/1967, 112; PIA/288.5/394/1966, 131).

The Reforms of 1968

Large Firms and the Reforms (Managers)

The New Economic Mechanism, introduced on January 1, 1968, unfolded under the banner of enterprise autonomy. It eliminated quantitative planning and instructed enterprises to maximize profit according to a very complex set of indicators. A third of the prices were set by the central authorities; most of the remainder were determined partially or fully by the firms, as prices could move within established ranges or according to certain rules. For a few goods, prices were completely deregulated.[2] A large portion of the decision making was ceded to enterprise managers, who could decide what to produce and where to buy what they needed. They could also make decisions about smaller investments, technology, and credit. The reforms allowed them an increased flexibility in hiring, firing, and rewarding workers. Top managers were still selected by the central authorities, but they were removed less often.

The Private Sector and the Reforms

The economic reforms introduced a new, more relaxed atmosphere, and in this context the role of the private sector could be addressed more pragmatically. The Party memorandum discussing the private sector noted that the Party still endeavored to make the remaining "private artisans and traders gradually find the socialist way" (PIA/288.15/137/1967, 10). The final decree, issued by the highest organ of the HSWP, stated that in the previous 10 years the political profile of the private sector had moved in a "positive direction." Nevertheless, "especially in Budapest and in the larger cities, there are still many negative, corrupt tendencies." The decree called for more effective administrative measures against "parasitism" and "exploitative entrepreneurship" (MSZMP 1974, 123). These measures, together with tighter social control, were necessary if private activities were to be prevented from growing into larger enterprises. They would also help curb the rise of private artisans' access to orders from the socialist sector, an anticipated side effect of the new autonomy of state companies. New tax laws would guard against the accumulation of personal wealth (MSZMP 1974, 130–31). The part of the private sector that was deemed "socially useful," that met "society's needs" (i.e., consumer services as opposed to manufacturing) was promised better access to tools and materials, and the possibility of some new forms of private business partnerships was considered. With the exception of new partnership options, all the directives were enacted into law.[3]

The reforms also consolidated the position of household farming. As an acknowledgment of the importance of household farming in Hungarian agriculture, documents preparing the ground for the 1968 reforms classified cooperative members' household plots as part of the cooperative rather than the private sector (PIA/288.5/394/1966, 127). Since it was neither directed nor supervised by the central authorities, household farming was indeed part of the private sector, though it was highly dependent on the cooperatives. The latter supplied fodder, straw, fertilizers and pesticides, veterinary assistance, and transportation. In the 1960s, most of the produce raised on household plots was consumed by the family (Tóth 1970, 46), and the rest was sold, usually through annual contracts with the collective. Beginning in 1968, household plots were allowed to enter into agreements with state purchasing agencies. In 1970, the limit on the number of livestock per plot was abolished. Other supportive measures continued to be enacted until 1974 (Swain 1992, 67).

The Semiprivate Forms

If the reforms were circumspect in dealing with the traditional private sector, they also unwittingly contributed to the rise of a new gray zone between the private and the socialist sector. The increased autonomy of the agricultural cooperatives allowed them to solve one of their perennial problems: the cyclical nature and uneven rhythm of agricultural labor. During the spring, summer, and fall agriculture required varying amounts of work. Labor peaked during harvest time, when relatives and family members who had left agriculture for industry would return to help out, taking leaves of absence from their regular jobs. In the winter, however, people and machines often sat idle. The dream of the agricultural factory, with its controlled, smooth flow of production, was incompatible with the nature of plant growing and animal breeding.[4] Those required much more flexibility than is compatible with supervised factory production.

It was not just labor that fluctuated from day to day in the cooperatives. Their annual incomes also varied greatly depending on the harvest. Agricultural cooperatives thus were eager to find ways to keep their workers busy in the off-season to supplement their incomes and have some insurance against bad harvests and livestock disasters. A nonagricultural business venture, run as part of the cooperative, seemed an ideal solution. Such a side business also provided employment for the wives of collective members. Many jobs in the collective were considered unsuitable for women, but as social welfare support was tied to employment women could not receive maternity benefits or pensions unless they were employed (Juhász 1988, 206).

The reforms made it possible for agricultural cooperatives to start small, nonagricultural side businesses to complement their operations. What the leadership had in mind was explained in a 1966 Politburo resolution. Cooperatives were given the option of a side business to provide continuous, local employment for cooperative members and their families; to take better advantage of local resources; to increase the income of the cooperative, especially in areas where land and weather were unfavorable to agriculture; and to bring new revenue to the state. These side businesses were to be linked to the agricultural production of the cooperative, if possible, processing agricultural produce. Cooperatives were also encouraged to provide services such as transportation and machine repair in underserved rural areas. The document hastened to point out, however, that these small businesses would not be allowed to result in the "unwarranted deconcentration of industry" (PIA/288.5/406/1966). That these businesses could easily become semiprivate enterprises run by private entrepreneurs with the legal front of the agricultural cooperative was a fear that was raised in a Politburo discussion earlier that year.

> We cannot allow agricultural cooperatives to give only their office stamp to certain enterprises . . . , [allow] people who are not their members to work there, and recruit employees and workers into these nonagricultural side businesses who produce a certain amount of income that goes to the cooperative members not involved with that work. . . . I think the cooperatives cannot be allowed to earn money in this form, without working for it, regardless of whether the chairman or the members [benefit]. I don't want to exaggerate this, but it is possible, if we set no limits, that they would even build people's foundries.[5] These speculative undertakings should not be allowed. (PIA/288.5/384/1966a, 55)

Many of these fears proved to be well-founded. Cooperatives seized upon this new opportunity. Their nonagricultural side businesses turned out not only canned fruits and vegetables, dry noodles, goose down pillows, and comforters but also badly needed industrial products such as rubber gasket rings for espresso machines and pressure cookers, plastic bags, buttons, and wallpaper. Many subcontracted with large state companies to manufacture simple parts, and quite a few began businesses in construction. Most of the enterprises were extremely successful, as they were providing goods much needed but nowhere to be found. They were flexible, they could engage in short batch production unprofitable in large companies, and they were quick to respond to newly emerging needs.

Some of these enterprises were run by private entrepreneurs under the legal cover of the cooperative. The typical agreement involved a percentage deal, which specified how the entrepreneur and the cooperative were to split the value added by the enterprise (Rupp 1983). Apart from imposing this "tax," the cooperative gave the entrepreneur complete freedom. In many cases, entrepreneurs set up their enterprises at a physical distance from the parent cooperative. For instance, three cooperatives from villages around the capital formed a consortium to provide legal cover for businesses in Budapest engaged in moviemaking and the organization of exhibitions as well as for a printing shop in Gyál (the site of one of the three cooperatives). The Gyál cooperative ran 15 other businesses in the village, including a shop making lamps, one manufacturing springs, one turning out boxes, and another producing metalware. As if to fulfill the leadership's nervous anticipation to the letter, the cooperative also operated a foundry (PIA/288.24/1970/57/1970, 67–71). To preserve appearances, the workers in such enterprises joined the parent cooperative, as if they were peasants who just happened to switch to one of the cooperative's side businesses. Free of the regulations that constrained state companies, these side businesses paid good wages and thus found it easy to recruit workers from the state sector (Rupp 1983, 124). Side businesses multiplied rapidly. In 1965, nonagricultural goods and services accounted for only 9 percent of the total output of agricultural cooperatives. By 1970, this figure had risen to 23.2 percent (Rupp 1983, 44).[6]

State Employment

The New Economic Mechanism brought changes in the state employment system as well. The size of the labor force could not be further increased, labor shortages were severe, and state firms now competed with one another for labor. Population forecasts warned that the shortage of labor would worsen starting in the late 1970s. With the passing of the postwar baby boom, the overall size of the work force would shrink. In the 1950s, the creation of a unified system of state employment went hand in hand with the obliteration of the private sector. Labor from the private sector swelled the ranks of state employees as workers flocked to socialist firms.

Tapping the reserves of postwar unemployment and mobilizing women increased the number of people employed by the state. The suppression of the labor market made it possible to pay low wages. Initially this was a double bonus for socialist firms. Labor became cheap, while at the same time there was more of it. Low wages increased the supply of labor because families had no choice other than to send every one of their working-age members into employment. This increased female participation considerably.

After the success of the second collectivization effort, the socialist labor force arrived at its absolute limit. Labor shortages, previously confined to specific areas, became a universal problem. Every person who could had already joined the socialist sector. At this point one firm could hire new workers only at the expense of another firm. In this zero-sum game, the firms' options were limited. They could not lure workers from other firms with the promise of higher wages because wages were centrally regulated. In 1964, the state installed new penalties for quitting and gave firms more power to reward loyal employees and dismiss problem workers (Radnay 1985, 21). The latter option was rarely used because the labor shortage forced firms to hang on to every worker they could. The penalties for quitting were also softened since punishment was the responsibility of the new firm, which was so eager to recruit an additional worker that it was willing to be lenient. Serious problems of labor discipline ensued, and it soon became obvious that structural changes were needed (PIA/288.15/76/1964; PIA/288.5/327/1964).

The new labor code that accompanied the reforms gave more discretion to companies in regulating their labor relations and made it easier for workers to quit and look for other jobs (PIA/288.5/426/1967, 103–4). The workers' new freedom was not granted out of concern for their rights, however. Reformers believed that increased enterprise autonomy and limited market measures would increase productivity, dampen the demand for labor, and perhaps even lead to some unemployment. These measures were designed to make it easier to shuffle laid-off workers among enterprises (PIA/288.5/327/1964, 61).[7] To soften the expected blow of rising unemployment, the work week was reduced from 48 to 44 hours. This measure was also a political move, calculated to increase support among the population.[8]

Neo-Stalinist Retrenchment

The reform measures were controversial from the beginning. The armed intervention in Czechoslovakia that put an end to that country's reformist communism encouraged Hungarian hard-liners to believe that they could expect support from Moscow and other Eastern European communist parties (Berend 1990, 205). It was internal dynamics, however, that played the key role in retrenchment. The 1968 reforms were meant to correct problems emerging in the socialist sector by allowing more room for the play of market forces. The goal was neither to yield ground to the private sector, thus turning back the achievements of nationalization, nor to replace the system of state employment with a labor market of any sort. Yet both emerged as unintended consequences of the reforms and led to a neo-Stalinist reversal.

Loosening the state's grip on labor was originally supported by large companies because they expected to entice workers away from weaker firms. However, the unexpected winners of the increased mobility of labor were not the large state firms but the private sector and the small co-op side businesses. They siphoned off the best workers, those whose skills were in high demand. To make matters worse, the reform did little to diminish the firms' unlimited appetite for labor. The expected unemployment never developed (Nyitrai 1969; Fazekas and Köllő 1985). Companies continued to seek more employees; in addition, they now had to compete with the successful private and semiprivate sectors for the relatively small pool of workers with important skills. Hard-liners opposing the reforms soon found support among the managers of large state companies, who, in turn, could point to the indignation of their own workers, whose loyalty was now being repaid with wages lower than those of individuals who had switched, full- or part-time, to the private sector. Engineers, bookkeepers, and technicians unable to use their skills directly in the private sector were resentful and quick to complain. Skilled blue-collar factory workers, the vanguard of the working class the Communists claimed to represent, also felt left out. Their anger carried special weight. As early as the end of 1969, the regularly filed reports from local Party and trade union officials regarding the climate of political opinion were filled with complaints about the low pay of "honest workers" and the high incomes of "speculators." The Party organization of the Csepel Steel and Metal Works, one of the symbols of modern large-scale industry, stated dispassionately:

> In the Steel Works there were comments that real wages and real income of those who live from wages and salaries increase less than the national average. They say [that the national average] includes the incomes of people in the private sector and the self-employed, which, in their opinion, developed more favorably than the average. (PIA/288.22/1970/35a, 70)

A report from Videoton, the largest television factory, raised pointed questions:

> The press, various broadcasting agencies, and the legislature, too, have discussed the problem that some people with various "schemes can earn millions for themselves." (E.g., goldfish dealers, private designers, patent agents, etc.) In our quarters the question is posed: how long can this go on in this manner? "Wherever these things happen, is the Party present there?" "If it is, why doesn't it take measures?" "How long can those leaders who condone these things enjoy the trust of the Party?" (PIA/288.22/1970/35b, 46)

The National Council of Trade Unions, surveying a large number of companies, concluded that:

> In large factories—even where the profit is satisfactory—there were objections that industrial cooperatives and small firms pay better than the factories of national economic importance do. In the Enamel Factory in Salgótarján [a city north of the capital] the mood prevails that "it is not worth working in large-scale industry in the state sector." (PIA/288.22/1970/17, 159)

Reports also indicated that workers were upset about unstable prices. As one from a large lighting fixture company summarized the popular wisdom: "Everyone knows the political effects of price changes; they exercise the strongest influence on the [people's] mood of a period." As far as the workers were concerned, prices were set by "experts appointed by state authorities," and those producers who set high prices on their own were in violation of official policies (PIA/288.22/1970/34, 39–43). Those whose hikes were motivated by economic gain were considered particularly despicable. The term *nyereségvágy* (greed), associated with murder-robberies, was often used in this regard. Many pointed out that rising food prices benefited the peasantry (PIA/288.22/1970/18, 50–56), which already enjoyed the advantage of extra income earned from household plots.

> The workers and employees, while they regard the support of household farming important from the perspective of production, are worried that the increase in peasant incomes will continue. (PIA/288.22/1970/2, 35)

This advantage was further enhanced by the side businesses, which in earning money for the agricultural cooperatives also benefited the peasants.

While local secretaries transmitted these sentiments from the shop floor, Party school instructors diligently gathered the opinions of the Party cadres, who were required to enroll periodically in special courses. These covered current political issues as well as issues of less immediate concern, such as how Marx was able to overcome the influence of Feuerbach and how one could effectively refute the theory of an expanding universe. It is not surprising that these cadres had more general grievances, many of which echoed earlier complaints about the petty bourgeoisie.

> The opinion was often heard that the reform amplifies capitalist and petty bourgeois tendencies. As an example they brought up the disproportionate distribution of income and the "unwarranted" support of small commodity production. (PIA/288.22/1970/19a, 126)

They complained that the private sector fostered economic inequalities and supported a petty bourgeois, egotistic perspective and lifestyle. The preoccupation with economic self-interest was the main objection to side businesses because "their pursuit of profit diverts them from their main activities" (PIA/288.22/1970/19b, 13–14).

Egotism drove workers away from large state companies, but the increased mobility had an effect on those who stayed as well. Labor discipline was undermined because workers now had a choice. If management decided to enforce a stricter code of discipline, workers could leave. This development was noticed by the cadres. Students in one Party school objected to the loosening of labor discipline, debated the causes of labor mobility, and came to the conclusion that the two were related (PIA/288.22/1970/18, 139–42).

In September 1971, the Politburo cracked down on side businesses. Only those enterprises whose business was closely related to the main agricultural activities of the parent cooperative or those that responded to local consumer needs, and thus competed with the private sector, could remain in operation. Subcontracting with large firms was permitted only under carefully circumscribed conditions. For example, subcontracts had to include wages and side businesses could not pay more than 10 percent in excess of what a state company paid for comparable work. Around the capital, where side businesses had grown the fastest and state managers were complaining loudest about them luring workers away, all forms of subcontracting were suspended in certain industries. The Politburo's decree also called for frequent internal and external audits (PIA/288.5/563/1971, 31–32). These requirements effectively prodded side business back into the socialist sector.

In November 1972, the Central Committee decided to reverse the reforms. János Kádár, in his closing speech, offered this overall assessment:

> The way I would characterize the current situation is that the foundation is healthy, but on it there are quite a number of deposits, which

> have emerged again. The *forced*—but otherwise correct—turn and change that we had to carry out in the beginning of 1957 also opened the way to certain undesirable petty bourgeois and right-wing phenomena. . . . the worry and alarm that have appeared recently in our public opinion [as a result] indicate, in the final analysis, that the vast majority of *honest people—Communists and their allies*—are troubled by the main direction the party is taking. (*Társadalmi Szemle* 1972/12, 22, emphasis added)

To ease the worries of "honest" people, the Party had to combat these undesirable phenomena. Though Kádár never publicly declared the economic reforms a mistake, he observed that "we wouldn't have perished without them." The remedy he suggested was to strengthen state intervention and planning. To shore up support, the Central Committee decided to raise wages in large-scale industry. As an internal document pointed out a year later:

> Under our current conditions the labor of workers in large-scale, small-scale, cooperative, and private jobs is equally necessary; however, Lenin's pronouncements, that the solid core of the working class is the workers of large-scale industry concentrated in large plants, are still valid. The Party believes that the regular and gradual improvement of their condition requires coordinated, comprehensive, and special care from the central authorities. (PIA/288.5/621/1973, 40)

Perceiving the shift in the political climate and receiving direct orders from the leadership, the major newspapers and journals began to chime in.[9] Editorials sermonized against the petty bourgeois mentality, and scholarly articles built complex arguments to explain how the pursuit of private economic interest can surface in a country where the private sector has been all but eliminated. A typical explanation was belabored in the Party's ideological monthly. With remarkable insight the author explained that private production should not be equated only with private property, but rather it should include the private use of state property as well.[10] The socialist division of labor—that is, the system of state employment—gives everyone a task. Engaging in private economic activities outside this system

> can create damage at any point or position of the socialist economic organization by elevating secondary jobs to the rank of the primary job as a result of its peculiar private style of labor, and it demotes the

> primary job to secondary importance: it is the agent of the privatization of machinery, raw material, and especially of the human productive capacities, expertise, and ideas. (Bizám 1974, 47)

A series of measures clamping down on private producers followed. Small artisans and entrepreneurs who had pocketed undeserved income were ferreted out. In a string of well-publicized trials, small producers were sentenced to several years in prison for "profiteering" and disregarding regulations. A media campaign was launched against violations of regulations and the imposition of unjustifiably high prices. But the most fury was directed against individuals who had tried to cross over into areas reserved exclusively for the socialist sector. Usually this involved a private artisan or entrepreneur who had used a state firm as a legal cover for private business, in this way gaining access to materials and customers otherwise off limits to private enterprise. One such case concerned an artisan who had manufactured screws under the auspices of four cooperatives. Over the years, 27 million forints' worth of screws had been produced and sold by the cooperatives as their own products. Cooperative managers had received a share of the profits. When the scheme was uncovered, the artisan was fined and sentenced to a jail term of three and one half years (Hegedűs and Márkus 1979, 280). In another case, exposed by the Party daily, "overpriced" animal feed concentrate had been produced and sold by a private individual, again under the cover of a firm in the socialist sector. The article carried the ominous headline "Unlawful Profit—Inevitable Bankruptcy" (*Népszabadság,* January 7, 1973).

In August 1974, the City Council of Budapest formed a special supervisory body to investigate the prices and business practices of the 16,537 private artisans working in the city. According to newspaper reports filed during the first month of its operation, this body initiated criminal proceedings against 20 of the 30 artisans it investigated. Their offenses ranged from employing workers off the books and operating a second shop to irregularities in bookkeeping and working in unlicensed areas (*Népszabadság,* September 8, 1974; October 6, 1974). The fervor of the officials was not boundless, however. Difficulties in the service sector put the leadership in a bind. They had to preserve enough of the private sector to meet at least some of the demand for repair of faulty television and radio sets, dripping kitchen faucets, and broken down automobiles.

Those engaged in household farming fared no better than did the artisans. Household farmers suddenly found their net taxable income assessed higher than in previous years, even though they were not producing more. Many landed in the highest tax bracket, starting at 50,000 fts, above which taxes were steeply progressive (*Népszabadság,* July 13, 1975). This reassessment occurred when government wholesalers lowered their prices in response to central directives (Zsuffa 1975).

The Eleventh Party Congress, held in March 1975, emphasized that the "socialist ownership of the means of production must be strengthened," indicating the general direction the Party had adopted. The private sector was mentioned briefly. The document acknowledged that "there is still a need—primarily in the area of services—for small production based mainly on one's own labor and the activities of family members" (*Népszabadság,* March 23, 1975).

In a later decree, the Politburo added the assurance that "the private property of small producers primarily serving the public will survive in the future" (MSZMP 1983, 24). A year after the Party Congress, a document issued by the Secretariat of the Central Committee reiterated the position the HSWP had taken in 1968, suggesting that the economic problems that justified tolerance toward the private sector then had not yet disappeared. The similarity between the two documents is quite remarkable, despite the more matter of fact tone of the 1976 document. The Party took the position that as long as the private sector was completely isolated from the socialist sector and limited to consumer services, as long as it had no links to socialist firms and did not employ labor except family members, it should be tolerated. Indeed, it should even be supported, with the understanding that self-employed individuals constituted a "constantly shrinking and historically dying stratum of our society" (MSZMP 1983, 284). This document, like its predecessor in 1968, vaguely suggested the need for creating "loose partnership forms," advice that again went unheeded until 1981. In its final point, the document asserted revealingly that there was no reason why the strictly enforced compulsory membership in the National Association of Artisans (Kisiparosok Országos Szövetsége or KIOSZ) should be changed in any way. The leadership remained disinclined to loosen its grip over artisans.

Growing Concentration

The 1970s saw a further increase in the concentration of production. Ministries responsible for particular branches of the economy relied on large state firms for their success. The Ministry of Metallurgy and Machine Industry, for instance, could not afford the failure of the largest steelworks and machine factories, and the other ministries were similarly dependent on large companies. Soon ministries became advocates for their largest clients, lobbying together with the managers of these enterprises for special treatment.

In 1972, a list of the largest strategically important state companies was compiled. These 49 giants, the flagships of Hungarian industry, were elevated to special status, which made them eligible for tax breaks, subsidies, and extra investment funds. Most importantly, they were invited by the National Planning Office to participate in the formulation of the central plan. These select companies employed over two-fifths of the entire industrial work force, or about 700,000 people, and they claimed over three-fifths of all fixed capital in industry (Szalai 1989, 18; Berend 1990, 210). Between 1970 and 1978, the number of state companies in industry dropped from 812 to 700, and the average size of their labor force grew from 1,342 to 1,644 (Kopátsy 1983, 82).

The Central Committee spelled out its justification for this special treatment in a document written in October 1973. Discussing the general principles underlying efforts to improve the lot of the working class, the committee observed that:

> The advantages of the socialist mode of production appear primarily within the framework of large factories representing the highest level of social organization. Today the *theoretically well-established* advantages of large-scale production [*nagyüzemek*] are realized in the practice of large Hungarian industrial companies only to a relatively small degree. This is not only an economic problem, as it puts extra burden on the state budget, but it is also a political problem because it hinders the best organized segment of the working class laboring within the most concentrated setting in satisfying better its material and cultural needs and developing its consciousness of socialist ownership. (PIA/288.5/621/1973, 51–52, emphasis added)

At the Eleventh Party Congress in the spring of 1975, one of the leading hard-liners of the Politburo, Béla Biszku, publicly explained the leadership's position.

> The decisive condition of building socialism and the success of our people is the development of large-scale firms, the consistent implementation of the policies of socialist industrial development, in the manner most appropriate to our situation. In our circumstances, large-scale state firms give birth to and reproduce the working class. Therefore, the development of large-scale state firms is not only an economic question, but it is also an important political priority. When we saw that, for various reasons, the position of large-scale firms was inadequate and the development of the workers in large factories was faltering, we had to consider it as a political problem of the first order. . . . The Central Committee and the government put on the

> agenda the development of several large companies. . . . This also serves [to enhance] the strengthening of the class base of the society building socialism. (*Népszabadság,* March 19, 1975)

Similar plans were announced in agriculture, where mechanization and increasing size were supposed to turn cooperative and state farms into agricultural factories (*Társadalmi Szemle* 1975/04, 33; Németh 1975, 24–25). Between 1970 and 1975, the average size of the agricultural cooperative grew from 2,290 to 3,800 hectares; for state farms, the same figures increased from 5,550 to 7,200 (PIA/288.5/687/1976, 33). Although some of the leadership were eager to see this trend continue, by 1976 an alternative approach to industrializing agriculture prevailed. Agricultural cooperatives were encouraged to form agrarian-industrial associations with state firms mainly in food processing and distribution. These vertical organizations were aimed at bringing cooperatives and industrial firms into closer alignment and turning co-op peasants into socialist workers (PIA/288.5/687/1976, 30; PIA/288.5/694/1976, 37).

There were, however, two important points where the retrenchment was unable to turn back the course of the reforms. The reform effort may have been dead, but it was not buried. It had never even been pronounced dead officially, as hard-liners never amassed enough support to explicitly declare that the New Economic Mechanism had been a mistake. This was of more than symbolic importance. Bureaucrats involved in the design of the reforms were assigned to less important tasks or positions, but they were not even reprimanded much less purged. Most of them stayed in place and kept a low profile.

The second, even more important outcome of the reforms was the increase in the political power of the top managers of the largest firms. The hard-liners in the Politburo needed their support, and these managers did not want to return to the regimented ways of central planning. They preferred keeping their newly won autonomy combined with vigorous state intervention on their behalf. Top managers, who initially had been simple marionettes of the central authorities, came to life and, turning the tables, began to direct the actions of their puppeteers.[11]

Structural Difficulties

As it attempted to roll back the earlier reform measures, the regime encountered three immediate obstacles. The first problem was created by the newly implemented hard-line policies; the second and third were long-standing difficulties that the hard-line shift aggravated.

The crisis that the leadership had brought upon itself was a meat and fruit shortage, which followed in the wake of the aggressively repressive measures taken against household farms. The countryside responded to these measures quickly and creatively. Villages were filled with the customary festivities of pig slaughter, except that this time it was the mother hogs that villagers turned into sausages, hams, cracklings, bacon, and meat and stockpiled in refrigerators. As a result, the number of pigs from household plots, which had produced a fourth of all pork in 1975, dropped by more than 50 percent by 1977, creating meat shortages in urban areas. The drop in beef production was similarly dramatic (KSH 1981b IV, 81–82; Berend 1988, 13). Fruits also began to disappear from urban shops (KSH 1981b IV, 80). Faced with the choice between higher prices and empty stores, the leadership, amid much rhetoric about improving the lot of industrial workers, chose to retreat and embrace household plots once again (Zsuffa 1975; Hare et al. 1981, 245–47). This time the Politburo grasped that it would not be enough to simply support household farms. It also had to convey a long-term commitment to household farmers (PIA/288.5/684/1976).

The second worrisome sign was the decline in the number of newly built homes after the peak year of 1975 (KSH 1979). Originally, the state had promised to provide free housing for every citizen. Over time housing became one of Hungary's worst social problems. It had been hoped that the socialist sector would solve the housing problem by building large apartment complexes from prefabricated concrete panels. But in addition to their poor quality and dreary appearance these complexes proved to be very expensive. Transporting the large concrete pieces was extremely costly. Moreover, special sewer and water systems were necessary to accommodate the high density of residents. These apartment buildings assumed many of the characteristics of the factories where they had been fabricated. They were large and utilitarian, and they were subdivided into standardized units. Their rigid design discouraged community life, just as factory floor plans try to curtail unnecessary socializing among workers. Individuals were sorted into their identical apartments by assembly lines of elevators or, since these were frequently out of order, by narrow staircases. Often these units had no common spaces other than a small storage room on the ground floor, and they featured windows from which one could never see one's own building. People got to know their neighbors only through the noise that traveled unimpeded through the concrete walls. The architecture was as inflexible as the assemblage of heavy machinery that created it. Just as the machinery was unable to adjust to new designs, these prefabricated walls were unable to accommodate the changing needs of families. Walls could neither be removed nor added, and even driving a nail into them required special equipment.

The concrete complexes were ill suited for villages, and they could not satisfy the impatient demand for housing in cities. Thus, many people, losing the hope of state-supplied housing, began to build homes with the help of private artisans.[12] Between 1971 and 1975, 44.2 percent of all homes were built by the private sector (KSH 1981, 191). From the 1960s on, the fastest growing segment of the private sector was residential construction.[13]

Finally, the crusade against the private sector aggravated the already pitiful state of services, especially in the countryside. The demand for services was on the rise. New homes, outfitted with electricity and plumbing, as well as old ones that had deferred maintenance for many years, increased the need for electricians and plumbers. The widespread acquisition of consumer durables produced an ever-growing market for appliance and car repair. According to one study, the average car spent 30 work hours in repair shops each year. The most troublefree car was the Trabant, an outdated vehicle with a two-stroke engine that averaged 19 hours of repair annually. The most troublesome automobile was the Dacia, designed by Renault and manufactured in Romania. This car, the most sophisticated of the lines produced in socialist countries, required 54 hours of repair each year (Békefi 1984). Personal services were equally deficient. Except in large cities, there was a shortage of hairdressers, beauticians, and photographers.

It was not profitable for large state companies to provide services such as these in small villages, and private artisans and tradesmen were discouraged by the seesawing of official tolerance and hostility. Few people were willing to take out licenses, although some would provide services off the books. The number of self-employed in the countryside was declining slowly, as old artisans gradually closed down their shops. But the services they offered, albeit in waning numbers, were of the old type—shoe repair, well digging, or smithcraft. A wide spectrum of other needs went unmet. By 1976, the increasing discontent in the countryside over the lack of services and the ghost of a burgeoning shadow economy had persuaded the leadership to adopt a more favorable position toward private services in small towns and villages (MF/2448/1979).

The meat and housing shortage and limited services pointed to fundamental weaknesses in the one-nation-one-factory model. Factory production requires, and therefore imposes, a rigid internal division of labor. This rigid organization is tailored to suit special-purpose machinery and architecture, which, in turn, requires substantial investment. As a result, large-scale production is inflexible and resists alterations in its products or procedures (Piore and Sabel 1984; Hirst and Zeitlin 1991). Large-scale production achieves its spectacular success under conditions where such changes are unnecessary, where on one end of the process incoming materials arrive on time, and where on the other end there are enough reliable buyers for the products so that they can be safely placed. Large Western corporations developed by investing in suppliers and distribution, thus minimizing uncertainty on both ends (Chandler 1984).

In the state-socialist ideology, flexibility carried no theoretical weight. Flexibility assumes emergencies and unforeseen circumstances. In a world where the future can be mastered and even planned, flexibility was considered a tactical but not a strategic virtue. Indeed, shortage economies all but eliminated one factor of uncertainty: since demand was overgrown, the ability to find buyers for a product was rarely in question, even in the consumer market, as long as people were willing to accept products that were not exactly what they wanted (Kornai 1980).

Still, flexibility played a paramount role in certain areas of the economy, and in those the large-scale model was unable to deliver. The private sector flourished wherever large-scale methods proved to be inappropriate, mainly in areas where labor could not be rigidly organized. Labor in household farming, for example, was able to adjust to the capricious demands of tending certain plants and livestock, while large farms could not cope well with such irregularities. Growing and harvesting wheat, flax, or alfalfa could be mechanized; growing peaches or tomatoes, or raising chickens or pigs, remained highly labor intensive but intermittent in its demands. By including farming among other domestic chores, household farmers were able to attend to irregular tasks quite effectively. In construction, too, there is a need for flexible labor combined with the ability to deliver customized products. Construction crews, especially those building single-family homes, typically are small, they must work on site, they have to adapt their work schedule to the vicissitudes of the weather, and they have to follow unique instructions since they build private homes to order. A last important area in which large-scale production proved ineffective was consumer services, where an elaborate division of labor is rarely required since a single provider usually can deliver the service. Most services must be performed on short notice and according to the whim of the customer. By the late 1970s, the private sector was flourishing in the cracks of large-scale production. Confined mostly to the consumer economy, the private sector offered an alternative venue for making money, an autonomous social space with its own rules and logic.

As soon as the new social order crystallized it began to expose its internal contradictions. The leadership first shifted its ideological position somewhat and tried reforms to decentralize the economy without ever entertaining the idea of reversing the main achievements of the socialist Great Transformation: the nearly complete elimination of the private sector and the creation of universal state employment. The institutional structure evolved, the leadership proceeded by trial and error, but their learning was severely circumscribed not only by the keen attention of the Soviet leadership, but also by their own fundamental ideological beliefs. They were also restricted by the dynamic of societal interests—most importantly the interests of large companies—shaped by the institutional order growing from those ideological beliefs.

CHAPTER 6

The Private Sector: The Economy of the Weak

Introduction

The HSWP's approach to the private sector was a roller-coaster ride of liberalization followed by suppression, of qualified encouragement suddenly giving way to loud denunciation. These erratic swings reflected the tension between the regime's dual commitment to raising living standards and maintaining a large-scale economy, even when the latter was unable to deliver and was riddled with internal problems. Whenever the private sector received support from the state, it was to ease consumer hardship, to fulfill the government's "provisioning responsibility" (*ellátási kötelezettség*). Turning to the private sector as a source of goods and services was a temporary, if ideologically embarrassing, necessity. More problematic was the fact that the private sector was also a source of income for those who toiled in it. This was a direct assault on the state's monopoly on employment, as it undermined the edifice of universal state employment, the chief source of the state's economic control over the population. The ability to earn money from the private sector weakened state employees' dependence on the state. Buying a new car was no longer conditional on getting a bonus or a promotion from one's boss. One could earn the same amount by moonlighting or raising a few extra hogs. But for being able to disregard the tyranny of state bosses private sector participants did not exchange fetters for shackles. The whims of the market were mitigated by the basic security of guaranteed state employment. One was not forced to undertake any private activity at any price. Serving two masters, one became a slave to neither. It was this increased independence that fed the leadership's obsession that the private sector was the embodiment of evil, the virus of moral decay, the easy road to undeserved affluence, the ultimate threat to social equality and justice.

In this chapter I argue that, contrary to the regime's obsession and the anecdotal evidence that was used to nurture it, the private sector of the late 1970s was an economy of needs, a consolation prize for those who were unable to maintain a sufficient income from the socialist sector. As a whole, those who labored in the private sector lived no better than those who drew their entire income from the state, despite the extra time these private-sector workers put in after hours. Unlike the situation in capitalist countries, where state intervention provides the primary cushion to soften social inequalities generated in the private sector, at this stage of socialism the socialist state and private sector acted in mirrored opposition (Manchin and Szelényi 1987).[1] Overall, the private sector now reduced rather than exacerbated social inequalities generated in the state sector.[2]

But precisely because it was a consolation prize, the private sector mobilized groups that occupied lower positions in the hierarchy of universal state employment, groups with little political weight. Policies oscillated between tolerance and rejection because the interests of private-sector participants could be disregarded with little risk of serious repercussions. Similarly, the inconsequential nature of the groups that undertook private activities made it easy to rally members of dominant groups—Party members, managers of various ranks, white-collar workers, and blue-collar workers in large industrial enterprises—against this sector in the early 1970s. The dominant group members' only stake in the private sector was the stake of the consumer.

This chapter begins with an overview of the full-time and part-time segments of the private sector at the end of the 1970s. The latter are then separated into four categories: household farming, artisanry and services, contract labor, and renting real estate. Finally, the chapter turns to an analysis of the social composition of the private sector based on a representative survey taken in Hungary in 1981.[3]

The Private Sector in the Late 1970s

To provide an overview of the private sector, one first has to draw its boundaries clearly. The private sector of the 1970s was composed of income-earning activities people pursued outside the institutional framework of universal state employment. These activities were self-initiated and were not organized by the central authorities (Kornai 1992b, 433–60). The private sector was not a social group but a set of pursuits involving certain social groups. Full-time artisans and traders who had activities only in the private sector were a meager 3.8 percent of the labor force by 1981. A much larger number of people, about 27.9 percent of the labor force, mixed socialist and private-sector activities regularly, participating in the private sector part time while maintaining a job at some socialist company (see table 6.1).[4]

The Full-Time Private Sector in the Late 1970s

The full-time private sector was highly regulated. As not having a legal job was normally a criminal offense, there were few people who survived in the full-time private sector without a formal license. Local authorities were charged with dispensing licenses. For some occupations, such as carpenter, locksmith, and tinsmith, special training credentials were required; for others, such as car mechanic, pastry chef, electrician, and elevator repairman, a special examination was sufficient; and for a third, including such trades as bookbinder, upholsterer, and shoemaker, experience was the only condition stipulated as necessary for a license. There were other occupations with no particular skill requirements. Yet before 1982, even if an applicant met the requirements, the final licensing decision rested with the state bureaucracy. Bureaucrats could deny any permit application on purely whimsical grounds. They could simply deem the issuance of a new license "unnecessary."

Until 1982, a license for private commerce was a privilege the bestowal of which was left to the complete discretion of local authorities. These licenses were allotted with even less generosity than were other permits. The number of people in small trades remained unchanged for decades, standing firmly at around 10,000 in both the 1960s and 1970s; most ran tobacco shops, small groceries, pubs, food stands, and boutiques.

License holders automatically became members of the National Association of Artisans (Kisiparosok Országos Szövetsége) or its sister organization, the National Association of Small Traders (Kiskereskedök Országos Szövetsége). These bodies were part of the state bureaucracy and were charged with supervising the self-employed. The leaders of both organizations were carefully selected by the top Party leadership, and they were members of the *nomenklatura.*

TABLE 6.1. Prevalence of Different Forms of Participation in the Private Sector and the Gender Composition of Each Form in 1981

Private Sector Activity in the Category	Percentage of Participation	Proportion of Males
None	68.3	0.5298
Part-time	27.9	0.6283
Household farming	21.3	0.5945
Nonagricultural labor	5.0	0.7867
Labor contracts	2.5	0.7432
Renting	1.0	0.4507
Full-time	3.8	0.7044
N	7,190	

Source: Social Stratification Survey 1981.

In the 1960s and 1970s, many people moved back and forth between self-employment and state employment, trying their luck in each. The self-employed stratum became more open. By the late 1970s, most of the full-time self-employed were recruited from the ranks of state employees. The traditionally high rate of inheritance among the self-employed dropped, and by the early 1980s only 18 percent of the self-employed came from families in which the father had been self-employed, compared with 27 percent in 1973 (Andorka 1982, 93–94). A study of 389 self-employed artisans and tradesmen in the eastern part of Hungary in 1982 found that only 14 percent had inherited their workshops and professions.[5] The same percentage had chosen self-employment because of conflicts at a previous workplace. Half had decided to become self-employed because they believed that their dreams would be better realized this way. Only 17 percent reported having chosen self-employment simply as a route to material gain.[6] Most of the respondents believed that skill was the most important ingredient for success. Entrepreneurship was rarely mentioned. Given the acute consumer shortages, there was little competition; marketing strategies and advertising campaigns were nonexistent (Kuczi 1984).

Being a licensed member of the full-time self-employed meant higher visibility and more harassment from the authorities. Normally licensing carries the benefit of extending legal protection to the licensed business, and the business can rely on the muscle of the state in enforcing contracts. Paradoxically, in the private sector under communism, licenses made the self-employed not less but more vulnerable. The license was a scarlet letter attracting the distrustful attention of authorities, a pass to legal prosecution rather than a ticket to the courts as a plaintiff. The other usual benefit of a license is that it restricts competition by limiting entry. Indeed, functionaries of the two associations overseeing the full-time private sector in Hungary often presented licensing to their members as a service to them, preventing unqualified entrepreneurs with cheap but shoddy products and services from driving honest, licensed operators out of business. This claim was disingenuous; demand for most goods and services was so strong that there was little danger that any of the self-employed would be left without customers.

The Part-Time Private Sector

The legal full-time private sector may have been small and weak, but the part-time private sector was large and robust.[7] People kept their jobs in the socialist sector, waiting until after hours to go their own ways to earn extra income. This kind of schedule was made easier by the reduction of the official work week, which had begun in 1968 (see table 6.2).

The decision to retain one's state employment even when private-sector employment paid much better made sense for a number of reasons. In an interview, a railway man explained why he held on to his state job:

> How big is your vineyard?
> Less than three acres. My parents work on it with my son and his wife.
> Wouldn't they need you at home [full time]?
> For the time being they can carry on, but if my son stopped I would have to go home. With paid labor it would be expensive. A day's labor starts at 150 forints.
> How much income does [the vineyard] produce?
> I keep two kinds of grapes and they can be harvested every two or three years. In an average year we make 60,000 forints.
> Only that much?
> In good years, more.
> How much do you make at the railways?
> Three thousand a month.
> But then the railway gives you only pocket money. Have you not considered leaving your job?
> Well, in the summer I could use a couple of days off instead of the money they pay, but I will not leave my job of 18 years. Now there are specialized cooperatives, and they let us work, but if they change their minds and we lose the land to the cooperative or the state farm, what can I do then? (Moldova 1978, 28)

The ideological hostility of the authorities made it more prudent not to cut the umbilical cord to state employment. This cord provided more than security, however. A state-sector job often gave people valuable access to

TABLE 6.2. Number of Hours Worked in the Socialist Sector without Overtime and Number of Vacation Days in Socialist Industry in Selected Years

Year	Number of Hours per Week	Number of Vacation Days per Year
1967	47.9	
1974	44.6	18
1980	43.8	
1984	41.0 (42.7)[a]	21

Source: Timár 1985.
[a]With overtime.

materials, tools, information, and clients for their private economic pursuits.

In the novel *Do It Yourself!* the fictitious hero decides to build his house with the help of the private sector. He explains the advantages of hiring a part-time unlicensed craftsman this way:

> The difference between a [licensed] private sector operator and a moonlighter is deep and significant. The private sector entrepreneur is fully licensed, has to render invoices and has to pay tax. The moonlighter is probably as good at the job—maybe better—but keeps no records and doesn't pay any tax. . . . Over and above the saving of tax, we anticipated further cost-savings too. The private sector operator has to charge for purchasing and preparing materials and supplies, the time factor getting and transporting these—if we were to do these things ourselves, we would be making a net gain. . . . However, there is an even greater potential gain from the careful selection of a moonlighter. The real treasure is the one who brings supplies and materials from their regular workplace. . . . [The carpenter] and his mate worked from Friday afternoon to Monday midday. They brought with them a large circular saw from the theatre workshop without which they probably wouldn't have undertaken the job. Private sector carpenters can't usually afford such equipment. They use hand saws which puts up their prices, for they take longer. (Kenedi 1982, 46)

Part-timers could use some of the resources of their socialist company. They could borrow tools, vehicles, and materials, or they could use the office phone or the factory shower.

Part-time private-sector activities can be subdivided into the categories of household farming, nonagricultural labor entrepreneurship, part-time labor contracting to socialist companies, and the renting of property. Income in the first three groups was based primarily on work; in the fourth it was the result of some private entitlement.

Commercial Part-Time Household Farming

In the 1970s, the most thoroughly studied part of the private sector was commercial household farming. A little over 21 percent of the work force participated in this area part time.[8] Most of those raising crops or livestock for sale took advantage of the household plots (*háztáji*) that agricultural cooperatives provided for their members and the auxiliary plots supplied by state farms and other companies to their workers. By the late 1970s, the standard size of the private plot was 0.54 hectares.

Household farming was within the reach of any family that did not live in an urban environment (Lampland 1991). The shortage of urban housing forced many workers to live in the countryside and commute to their industrial jobs in the urban centers. Thus, many industrial workers participated in part-time farming because having a single member of the family in the local cooperative was sufficient for obtaining a plot. Even the most advanced plots were variations on primitive forms of household production, wherein the most important input expected from the farmer was time and peasant common sense (Gonda 1979). The strength of household farms was that the family was able and willing to absorb the uneven demands of growing tomatoes, raising chickens, or keeping pigs or cows, as farming the plot could be flexibly included among other household tasks. Household farming as a labor organization was flexible from the other direction as well. Those farming tasks that posed no urgency, for instance, plucking goose down or weeding the plot, could be completed in small segments whenever the farmer had time. Other jobs, such as shelling corn, could be carried out while watching television.

Not everyone eligible for household plots took advantage of this opportunity. By the early 1980s, many agricultural cooperative members considered plots a burden. They took their allotted land only to rent it back to the cooperative for cash or in-kind compensation. Through this circuitous route, ownership of household plots became little more than a way for members to increase the income they received from the collective. Fifty-four percent of all the land in household plots was cultivated by the collective rather than the individual members. Almost 40 percent of those who had household plots preferred this arrangement (Oros 1983).

Most of the household-based production was traditional, and very few people bothered to calculate costs and benefits. Household farming was not an easy, or even an efficient, way of making money for most who undertook it. As one of the participants who made 24,000 forints by selling 4,000 liters of milk, two bulls, and ten pigs in 1974 noted ruefully:

> This is the profit of our labor. . . . If we calculated the number of hours I had to work for this, it would become clear how little an hourly wage we worked for. But we say this: time would pass even if we were just to sit in an easy chair after working for the collective. (Cserkúti 1975)

The average household that farmed in 1982 spent 4.9 hours each day on this activity (Oros and Schindele 1985, 970), yet the calculated hourly wage in part-time private farming was a very low 14 forints. In 1982, the average hourly wage of a semiskilled farmhand was between 17 and 23 forints

(KSH 1985). Not only was this less than the average hourly pay in the socialist sector; it was far below the incomes other private activities could provide.

A small segment of the private farmers could be identified as entrepreneurs. Intensive, specialized, private farming began to emerge in the 1970s when fodder, especially corn, and other farm inputs began to appear in stores. Previously these items had been available only as in-kind benefits paid by the collective (Juhász and Magyar 1984). The institutional restrictions and protections that had developed over the years brought about an internal polarization in part-time private farming. Many farmers let their household plots fade into kitchen gardens or become a part of their wages, but another segment of part-time farmers chose to intensify their small-scale production (Juhász 1988). Because these specialized minifarms emerged in the face of restrictive regulations on land size, machinery, and credit, even the more advanced ones were primitive. People used considerable mechanical ingenuity, fabricating makeshift egg incubators, sprinklers, and corn grinders from space heaters, waterpipes, and electric motors removed from other appliances. Once inexpensive transparent plastic sheets became available, the countryside was dotted with hothouses: plastic sheets mounted on aluminum scaffolding. Many households started to specialize in chicken or goose breeding, beekeeping, pig and rabbit husbandry, vegetable and fruit growing, or cattle raising and milk production. The meat, eggs, goose down and liver, honey, tomatoes, peppers, apples, and milk were usually bought by the cooperative or the appropriate state monopolies on a contract. Some of these products were sold to private small traders as well. In 1982, 3 to 4 percent of rural households were engaged in specialized, high-volume, agricultural production (Szelényi 1988, 86–87).

However, the link between entrepreneurship and market orientation was less than straightforward. An analysis of the life histories of 145 commercial part-time farmers from a village in eastern Hungary found that entrepreneurship and market orientation were inversely related (Kovách and Kuczi 1983). The older, more traditional farmers, mostly of peasant background and with agricultural occupations in the local cooperative, were the ones more likely to sell their produce at peasant markets, but they were less specialized and they operated on a smaller scale. They would accumulate wealth by building their own homes and buying livestock. They invested in equipment only rarely. On the other hand, younger people, often with nonagricultural occupations, were more willing to borrow money and try nontraditional lines of highly specialized production, but they sold their produce through fixed annual contracts with their cooperatives or some state agency, and thus they faced no market risks.

Part-Time Artisanry and Services

Part-time artisanry and services mobilized 5.0 percent of the labor force. In this domain of heterogeneous pursuits, some people held private licenses.[9] The part-time licensees could feel much safer than their full-time counterparts could because the irregularity of their operations made state supervision more difficult. When part-timers sensed that the authorities were about to crack down, they would simply suspend their activities. In the 1970s, the number of part-time licenses more than doubled. But why did a person need a license at all? Being caught without a license carried only a nominal fine, a maximum penalty of 5,000 forints (a little more than the average monthly wage) and the confiscation of one's tools and products. The population clearly supported unlicensed activities. Each year there were no more than six to eight reports denouncing unlicensed practitioners to the authorities.

There were certain jobs that could only be done by a properly licensed professional, however. A newly built home, for instance, could not receive electrical service until the owner provided proof that the electrical work had been carried out by a licensed electrician. Some jobs required materials and parts that were difficult to procure without the proper license. Others, such as transportation, involved activities so visible that undertaking them without a license would have been foolish. Visibility also was an important factor for professionals. Doctors, for example, would always register their private practice if it grew beyond a certain size. Nevertheless, these types of jobs comprised only a small portion of the activities conducted in the private sector. Part-time license holders were vastly outnumbered by moonlighters working informally. These unlicensed craftsmen were often referred to as botchers (*kontár*), though the quality of their work was by no means worse than average.

Part-Time Labor Contracts with Socialist Firms

Until 1981, the state was eager to keep all private activities out of the socialist sector. Their experience with semiprivate businesses had made the leadership very cautious. The tolerated forms of the private economy had to take place outside the spaces occupied by the socialist sector, and the services or finished products they supplied were to be for individual private customers rather than socialist companies. While the first stricture was often violated and moonlighters often worked on their private tasks at their workplaces, where they could pilfer time, machinery, and materials, the prohibition on state firms' use of private contractors was more successfully enforced. Still, there was a small group of state employees who in their spare time contracted with other state companies and worked for them as private labor contractors rather than employees, blurring the boundaries of the private-socialist sector divide.

Part-time private labor contracts usually were undertaken for occasional jobs that required a high level of expertise. Employees of research institutes and universities often received such contracts from state companies to consult or develop and test products. Writers, translators, and typists were given private part-time contracts.[10] Unlike the case with state employment, here the labor process itself was beyond the control of the state, and only the final product appeared in front of the supervisor. The state's capacity to set the pay of contractors was also limited. The cost of contract labor usually was paid not from a firm's wage fund but from its general expense account, which left more room for direct negotiation between the firm and the contractor. From the vantage point of the immediate boss, contracts were flexible, as they lasted only as long as the services of the contracted worker were needed. In 1981, only 2.5 percent of the labor force reported having worked on contract for any socialist company.[11]

Income from Property

The form of private-sector income the Communist leadership considered most loathsome was rent. Rent did not even have the mitigating quality of being earned with labor. It was undeserved income, social injustice par excellence. Yet the leadership tolerated the renting and subletting of housing because the housing shortage, especially in urban areas, was so severe. Thus, some people who owned a house or apartment rented subdivided segments, rooms, or even beds to others for a monthly fee. One did not have to be an owner to collect rent. Having rental rights enabled principal renters to sublet their apartments to others. Accruing additional income through rent often meant the inconvenience of sharing living quarters with strangers, since measures limited the number of real estate properties one could own to two pieces, a place of residence and a vacation home. Vacation homes in a coveted resort area were frequently rented to others. Renting to tourists or friends, through informal arrangements or the state travel agency, was a common way to recoup the expenses of building a home.

Rent collectors were the smallest of the four groups, comprising only 1 percent of the work force.[12]

The Social Composition of the Private Sector

The private sector gave individuals an opportunity to improve their lot. It would be reasonable to expect that people who decided to risk undertaking full-time private-sector activities or those who put in long hours after their socialist-sector shifts would be living more comfortably than those whose only source of income was their state employment. Indeed, as we have seen, the Party leadership was keenly concerned about people getting rich quickly in the private sector and was obsessed by the idea that a new elite might emerge outside the system of universal state employment.

These fears were highly exaggerated. People who worked in the private sector did not live better. If anything, they lived worse (see table 6.3).[13] The household income per capita of those who worked only in state jobs was 280 forints higher than those who also worked part-time in the private sector and 260 forints more than the incomes of full-time private artisans and traders. Those wholly dependent on state employment lived better. One may object that household income is an unreliable indicator because even though it contains income earned on the side, it surely underestimates it, as people did not truthfully report their earnings from the private sector.[14] Yet, if we look at other indicators of material living standards, we find the same picture.

An index of housing quality was constructed as the unweighted sum of 12 components such as the presence of running water, electricity, bathroom, flushing toilet, gas, telephone, and other conveniences. People earning income only from the socialist sector had on average over 8.3 of these 12 items, those working part time in the private sector had 6.6, and the full-time self-employed had 7.4. Those relying solely on their earnings from the state not only reported having more money to spend, but they also lived in better housing. They ate meat more often than did part-time private-sector participants. Nine percent of the socialist-sector workers owned a vacation plot or home (still a luxury) compared with only 5.4 percent of those who worked in the private sector after hours. Private artisans and tradesmen were similar to the first group.[15]

Automatic washing machines were a novelty in 1981, and only 13.9 percent of those not participating in the private sector owned one. Again, full-time private-sector participants were equally likely to have this convenience, but part-timers lagged behind. The same scenario applied to expensive electronic entertainment equipment. In the early 1980s, acquiring a stereo radio, stereo record player, color television, or movie camera required a major investment. Thirty-two percent of those not active in the private sector had one or more of these items, compared with 22 percent of part-time private-sector participants. The difference between the first group and full-time participants was within the margin of error of the survey.

Ownership of automobiles showed a slightly different breakdown. Cars, symbols of power in the 1950s and the epitome of consumer extrav-

TABLE 6.3. Measures of Material Well-Being by Participation in the Private Sector in 1981

Private Sector Activities	Average Household Income per Capita	Housing Quality (average number of 12 conveniences)	Meat Consumption (days per week)	Proportion with Vacation Home or Plot	Proportion with Automatic Washing Machine	Proportion with Expensive Electronic Entertainment Equipment	Proportion with Automobile
None	2,985.0799	8.2752	4.2792	0.0917	0.1385	0.3186	0.3820
Part-time	2,705.0281	6.5695	4.0788	0.0538	0.0887	0.2222	0.3996
Full-time	2,724.7710	7.4088	4.2527	0.1058	0.1423	0.2737	0.4927
Total	2,896.9889	7.7661	4.2223	0.0816	0.1248	0.2900	0.3911
F	21.1182***	232.3509***	9.7243***	14.7818***	16.6715***	32.5955***	7.1168***

Source: Social Stratification Survey 1981.
*$.05 > p > .01$ **$.01 > p > .001$ ***$p < .001$

agance in the early 1960s, gradually came within reach of the broader population with the introduction of new East German and Soviet models beginning in the mid-1960s. The most popular car was the Lada, designed by the Italian company Fiat but manufactured in the Soviet Union. By 1981, 39 percent of the work force lived in a household that owned an automobile. Here those in the private sector had an advantage, regardless of whether they pursued private activities full or part time. For private-sector participants, cars were not just consumer items to enjoy; they were often an indispensable tool for executing their private-sector activities. Some used cars to provide transportation services. Some, such as household farmers or moonlighting plumbers, needed their cars to ship goods (e.g., fodder) or to reach their clients (e.g., a distant customer with a broken water pipe).

Since consumer durables are accumulated over the life course and older people are more likely to have these possessions, one may question whether the older age of people with no activity in the private sector explains their relative affluence. This is clearly not the case because overall this group was younger than the other two (see table 6.4). Age may explain some of the differences between part-time and full-time private-sector participants, but it sheds no light on the difference between those who did and did not participate.

If working in the private sector improved people's living standards, and those standards were still similar to or even lower than what state employment provided, private-sector participants must have started with a handicap. In fact, those who participated part-time in the private sector were paid 226 forints less in their state jobs than were other state employees.[16] People joined the private sector because in the system of state employment they were marginal and comparatively poorly paid. The private sector gave them a chance to catch up.

A different explanation for the finding that people active in the private sector earned less in their state jobs might be suggested. Wages in socialist companies were not very responsive to achievement, but neither were they totally indifferent to it. Perhaps private-sector participants earned less in the socialist sector *because* of their private activities. Might it be that their low incomes from state employment were the consequence rather than the cause of their private-sector activities? If people who saved their energy for after-hours private jobs put in less effort in their state jobs and were paid less accordingly, and each worker randomly decided where to focus his or her energies, one would expect to see similar results. In that case, the social composition of people who did participate in the private sector could be identical to that of those who did not.

Let us assume that every worker was paid the average income a per-

TABLE 6.4. Characteristics of Individuals by Participation in the Private Sector in 1981

Private Sector Activities	Average Age	Average Wage from First Job in the Socialist Sector and No Private Activities	Average Wage in the Socialist Sector Given One's Occupation	Average Years of Education Completed	Average Number of Subordinates	Proportion of Party Members
None	36.3805	4,434.1210	4,428.2317	10.2096	3.0691	0.1495
Part-time	38.5685	4,208.0764	4,270.5358	9.2297	2.6492	0.1131
Full-time	41.8796		4,041.1644	9.0292	0.9526	0.0365
Total	37.2008	4,369.9373	4,377.1742	9.8911	2.8712	0.1350
F	51.5311***	16.0400***	12.6602***	91.2789***	3.0386*	20.0323***

Source: Social Stratification Survey 1981.

*.05 > p > .01 **.01 > p > .001 *** p < .001

son without private activities earned in his or her occupational group in the socialist sector. Thus, no monetary difference is allowed to exist among a self-employed electrician, a part-time private electrician who took moonlighting jobs, and a third electrician who worked only for his socialist factory. This figure can be seen as the income one could expect to earn as a loyal state employee given one's occupation. In this scenario, the socialist-sector worker would still be best off. He would still make 158 forints more than the part-time private-sector participants. The difference would be smaller, as one might expect, but it would still exist. People who worked full-time in the private sector would have made 387 forints less than those who never dabbled in the private sector.[17] To put it simply, people who did not participate in the private sector were not just better paid. They were also in occupations that were better paid in the system of universal state employment.

A closer look at the social composition of the private sector reveals some of the reasons why its participants occupied weaker positions in the system of universal state employment. People in the private sector were in worse paid occupations partly because they had less formal education. The system of state employment prized formal education; the private sector was less demanding. Those who worked only within the socialist sector had over 10 years of education on the average. In the Hungarian educational system, this meant some middle-grade education. Those in the private sector had a year less, barely completing elementary school. State employees had similar authority at their workplace, regardless of whether they participated in the private sector (though we will take a second look at these figures later). As private entrepreneurs were limited in the number of employees they could hire, they had fewer people to supervise. Finally, private-sector participants were less likely to have joined the Communist Party. Eleven and 4 percent of part- and full-timers joined, respectively, compared with 15 percent of those active only in the socialist sector.

The observed differences between those with and without private pursuits are even more accentuated if we separate men and women (see table 6.5). Since the most important asset in the private sector was time, and women disproportionately shouldered the burden of housework, they were much less likely to participate in the private sector. At the same time, as state employees, they were worse paid than their male counterparts, had fewer subordinates, and were less likely to become Party members. They were as marginal and ill paid as was the typical private-sector participant, but they could not work outside the home after hours because they had to cook, clean, take care of children, and do other domestic chores. Separating the sexes shows even larger differences between private-sector participants and loyal state employees. The overall pattern remains the same, however.

TABLE 6.5. Characteristics of Individuals by Gender and Participation in the Private Sector in 1981

Private Sector Activities	Average Wage from First Job in the Socialist Sector	Average Wage in the Socialist Sector Given One's Occupation and No Private Activities	Average Years of Education Completed	Average Number of Subordinates	Proportion of Party Members
			Men		
None	5,077.0448	4,851.0350	10.2887	4.7505	0.1980
Part-time	4,715.0182	4,585.5590	9.5289	3.3957	0.1459
Full-time		4,197.7238	9.2176	1.3005	0.0466
Total	4,957.1332	4,751.4543	10.0015	4.1650	0.1746
F	23.5977***	27.7916***	34.4345***	4.9212**	19.6815***
			Women		
None	3,710.2088	3,954.2511	10.1205	1.1742	0.0949
Part-time	3,217.4312	3,708.8860	8.7239	1.3874	0.0576
Full-time		3,655.7873	8.5802	0.1235	0.0123
Total	3,600.8059	3,895.1789	9.7483	1.1978	0.0839
F	45.0374***	8.4731***	74.0572***	0.9855	7.8895***

Source: Social Stratification Survey 1981.
*$.05 > p > .01$ **$.01 > p > .001$ ***$p < .001$

Breaking up the part-time private sector into its four segments, we find the same overall picture of the private economy as the economy of the weak, except in one segment, where we find the opposite (see table 6.6).[18] Socialist companies gave private labor contracts to people who were better educated, supervised more people in their regular jobs, were more likely to have joined the Party, and worked in occupations that were better paid. Their small number gives this subgroup little weight in the overall picture. Nevertheless, it is because of their high level of authority that the previous table shows virtually no difference between the number of subordinates of part-timers and those solely dependent on the socialist sector. Once we remove labor contractors from the part-time group, we do find a difference.

Even though labor contractors made up only a small fraction of the labor force, their existence is important. They highlight the initial disintegration of the boundary separating the private from the socialist sector. Opening even a small crack in the iron curtain that had been drawn between the two provided opportunities to become less dependent on state employment for those who carried the primary burden of maintaining it. A small group of highly educated Party members with management responsibilities became interested in colonizing a segment of the private sector, a segment adjacent to the socialist sector, a segment into which they

TABLE 6.6. Characteristics of Individuals by Participation in Forms of Part-Time Private Activity in 1981

Private-Sector Activities	Average Wage in the Socialist Sector Given One's Occupation	Average Years of Education Completed	Average Number of Subordinates	Proportion of Party Members
None	4,428.2317	10.2096	3.0691	0.1495
Household farming	4,136.9209	8.7220	1.7829	0.0929
F	46.0493***	316.4901***	9.6412**	31.9769***
Nonagricultural activities	4,473.3573	9.7729	2.1551	0.1330
F	0.3084	7.4116**	1.2741	0.7293
Labor contracts	4,996.1801	11.7158	8.2404	0.2459
F	21.8609***	45.1566***	19.1604***	12.6737***
Renting	4,387.8199	10.9155	4.2535	0.0986
F	0.0496	4.0129*	0.4338	1.4332

Source: Social Stratification Survey 1981.

*$.05 > p > .01$ **$.01 > p > .001$ ***$p < .001$

Note: The *F*-statistic indicates the statistical significance of the difference between those with no private activities ("None") and each form of participation.

could easily slip to augment their state incomes. Private labor contracts with socialist firms had never suffered the same violent denunciations from the leadership as had all the other forms of private activity. Attacking this aspect of the private sector would have meant turning on their own friends, colleagues, and immediate subordinates.[19] In 1982, this segment of the private sector burgeoned, as new forms of private labor contracts were introduced. As a result, the social composition of the private sector was dramatically transformed.

As growing size was the driving force of the socialist sector and private artisans were allowed to employ only a few workers, it comes as no surprise that, while people in the socialist sector worked in establishments of about 2,000 people on average, most artisans worked alone. But it is less obvious why people who participated in the private sector part time worked during the day in smaller socialist companies (see table 6.7). This was partly because larger firms paid better but also because creating oversized giants was more difficult in such areas as service, agriculture, and construction, precisely those in which the private sector flourished. Oversized as these companies became in areas where size was a distinct liability, they were still smaller than firms engaged in manufacturing, energy production, and mining. Worse paid, and with skills and access to resources from the workplace (such as the circular saw), which could be put to good use directly in the private sector, people working in smaller establishments were more likely to venture outside the limits of state employment.

Conclusion

In all state-socialist countries, the inflexibility of large-scale production left a vacuum to be filled by small private entrepreneurs (O'Hearn 1980, 1981; Korbónski 1981; Łos 1990; Brezinski 1985; Grossman 1977; Samp-

TABLE 6.7. Average Company Size of Nonparticipants and Part-Time Participants in the Private Sector in 1981

Private-Sector Activities	Average Size of Company (number of employees)
None	2,236.1917
Part-time	1,356.1674
Total	1,978.8811
F	74.9197***

Source: Social Stratification Survey 1981.
* .05 > p > .01 ** .01 > p > .001 *** p < .001

son 1986, 1987). In all these countries, the private sector was suppressed and severely limited. A series of measures made full-time participation in the private sector risky. Thus, most people participated part time while holding a job in the socialist sector. In most cases, the private sector was confined to the consumer economy (Åslund 1985, 66, 169; Berend 1990, 189). Private entrepreneurs were restricted to selling goods and services to consumers and had to buy their tools and materials in the retail market (Kornai 1992b, 507).

To separate the socialist and the private sectors, the state restricted the flow of material resources, labor, and skill between them (Gábor 1989). Private enterprises were forced to remain small, labor-intensive, often informal, and largely confined to a local market of households. Thus, the private sector developed in areas that required little cooperation, capital, or organization.

The division of labor in the private sector was rudimentary. Ideological concerns that identified private employment with exploitation limited the number of staff a self-employed individual could hire. The authorities conceived of small private production in terms of traditional artisanry and imposed this model on the private sector.

Private enterprises stayed labor intensive, partly because the tools and machinery they might have used were not available; in other instances, the use of particular machines and tools was prohibited. Moreover, private entrepreneurs had no access to bank loans. Given the uncertainties of the political climate, most people did not want to make large investments in a business that might be forced to shut down should the political winds shift. As there was little point investing in one's private business, people spent their money on improving their standard of living. Thus, the restrictions on the private sector fed consumerism in a back-handed way.

Confining the private sector within the boundaries of the small, traditional enterprise had another unintended and ironic effect: it made the private sector accessible to everyone on equal terms. The restrictions eliminated any pursuit with high barriers to entry. As little capital was allowed and highly specialized skills were of little use given the confined market and limited division of labor, virtually anyone who had extra time to work could participate. The restrictions made the private sector most attractive to social groups with the worst position in the official economy. These groups were in greatest need to complement their meager state sector incomes. They had the most to gain by shifting effort from state employment to a private sector job, and they were the ones who were used to the kind of jobs the private sector could offer. With some notable exceptions, the private sector at this time was the economy of needs, the economy of the weak, and the economy of the politically marginal.

The private sector in Hungary in the late 1970s was not very different from private sectors in other socialist countries in the late 1970s or 1980s. Faced with similar pressures, all the Eastern European countries reluctantly made similar small concessions to their private sectors. Some countries were more generous, others less so; some took liberalizing measures earlier, others took them later. Yet all aimed at harnessing the existing private activities of individuals or families in order to improve the consumer economy. In the 1980s, Hungary took a new approach, which profoundly altered its private sector and made it unique in Eastern Europe (excluding Poland).

CHAPTER 7

The Private Sector: The Economy of the Strong

Introduction

The year 1982 brought a radical turn in the development of the private economy in Hungary. Before the reforms the private economy grew slowly from below, forcing the state into cycles of repression and concession, loud condemnations fueled by ideological fury, and grudging tolerance born of tactical pragmatism. The 1982 reforms created a profound break with this pattern. The Party-state decided to take the initiative. Rather than simply giving its blessing to already existing private economic activities, it opened up a new institutional space for private enterprise. With the private sector no longer rigidly contained, the boundary between private and public became hopelessly blurred and was eventually redrawn. This bold step, at that time unique in socialist Eastern Europe, contradicted previous policies, and its consequences later seriously undermined the power of the leadership. It locked in the gains of the private sector and made future retrenchment impossible by enticing dominant social groups into the private economy.

Why the leadership was willing to make an about-face and embark on a course that proved to be the undoing of whatever economic grip it still held over society through the system of state employment is a question that needs to be answered before we assess the social and political consequences of the reforms.

The Genesis of the 1982 Reforms

The final years of the 1970s brought to an end a period of slowly increasing prosperity in Hungary. The full impact of the oil crisis that shocked the world economy in the first part of the decade reached Hungary with a five-year delay. Prices in the Soviet trading bloc, the Council of Mutual Economic Assistance (CMEA), were adjusted to world market prices on the basis of a five-year moving average. After this cushion disappeared, Hungary, heavily dependent on foreign sources for raw materials, began to feel that the terms of trade had changed to its disadvantage. Its balance of trade and balance of payments slid into a deficit that required substantial borrowing from abroad (Berend 1990, 232). Between 1975 and 1979, the net hard currency debt of Hungary grew from 1.5 to 7.1 billion dollars and its hard currency debt service jumped from 19 to 37 percent of its exports (Zloch-Christy 1987, 36, 41). This was further exacerbated by rising interest rates on international financial markets. These peaked in 1981. Subsequently, in response to the disintegration of the Polish economy during the Solidarity period, a credit squeeze and capital flight developed in the entire region.

These external problems explain the timing of the crisis, but they by no means caused it. Their role was simply to reveal the deep internal inadequacies of the country's economic structure. The economic model of extensive growth that expanded production by increasing input still had not been overhauled, despite the efforts of the New Economic Mechanism of 1968. In the first part of the 1970s, the effects of poor quality, low productivity, inert production profiles, and outmoded technologies, as well as mistaken investment decisions, were all temporarily hidden by an inflow of Western credits and loans and by the money the country earned by being competitive on the world market as a result of getting oil and raw materials from CMEA at less than world market prices.

By the end of the decade this veneer had worn away. In 1979, for the first time in two decades, real wages in the socialist sector began to decline (see table 7.1). The rapid transformation of economic tensions into pressing social and political concerns presented the leadership with a dilemma. In order to maintain economic growth, the Party-state either had to carry out far-reaching reforms in the socialist sector, reforms that would move far beyond the changes proposed in 1968 and would radically loosen state control over the entire economy—with the hope that such reforms would result in higher efficiency, increased productivity, and a better industrial structure—or it had to follow its earlier path of extensive growth and attempt to increase production by drawing new resources into the economy.

Radical reform in the socialist sector was politically unfeasible. In the political backlash against the liberalizing economic reforms of 1968, the position of large state companies had strengthened dramatically (Szalai 1990). Top management in these enterprises would have resisted radical changes even had the leadership been willing to pursue this option.

Following its own inclinations and moving in the direction of least resistance, the regime chose the second alternative. The new resources needed to keep the economy going could not come from foreign sources. The state thus decided to extract these resources from the population in the form of labor and goods. This was very difficult. Virtually everyone who could work was in the labor force; moreover, the overall size of the work force was declining (Galasi and Sziráczky 1983). Political considerations precluded increasing working hours. A temporary cut in consumption would have undermined the bedrock principle of the Kádárist compromise and would have created political tensions. Under these circumstances, expanding the private sector seemed a possible solution. Although reluctant to work longer hours in their state jobs, people were willing to work to the point of self-exploitation in the private sector.

Both the political and economic situations offered the leadership strong incentives for exploiting the private sector. In addition, by the late 1970s, an ideology existed for framing liberalization in a politically acceptable way. In the early days of socialism the private sector had been viewed in terms of class struggle. It had been vilified as a remnant of the capitalist past, an obstacle to modern large-scale production. As the foundation of the political order shifted from coercion to economic domination, the private sector, still destined for the scrap heap of history, came to be conceived of more as an ethical than a political problem. It embodied the menace of the petty bourgeois mentality. This new perspective moved the discussion from classes and laws of history to individuals and morality. From the mid-1970s on, thinking about the private sector underwent yet another shift. The campaign against petty bourgeois values had been led by poets, writers, philosophers, and bureaucrats responsible for ideological instruction. The new concept of the private sector was developed mostly by economists (Seleny 1994).

The language proposed to describe the private sector kept its focus on the individual, but now rationality replaced morality. What used to be

TABLE 7.1. Real Wages in the Socialist Sector over Time

Year	Real Wages per Worker (1978 = 100)
1978	100.0
1979	98.3
1980	96.7
1981	97.8
1982	97.1
1983	94.0
1984	91.7
1985	92.9
1986	94.7
1987	94.3

Source: Calculated from Baló and Lipovecz 1988, 665.

greed and selfishness, disregard for the common good, and lack of moral character became no more than rational calculation and optimizing behavior. Slacking off on the job was not laziness, irresponsibility, or a plot to undermine socialism. It was a clever redistribution of work effort from one's state job to private economic pursuits; the workers were simply attempting to maximize their material well-being. To the extent that such actions had undesirable consequences, those ill effects were not the fault of the workers. They arose from shortcomings within the system of economic incentives and, ultimately, within the structure of the socialist economy (Gábor 1979). The private sector, now called the "second economy," was discussed in the scholarly literature along three dimensions. Each broke an important taboo without directly engaging the official ideology. Activities in the private sector were classified by whether income was earned solely from labor or from some combination of labor and capital. Presenting rental income as something other than the yield of the exploitation of others broke the first ideological prohibition. The second dimension was the extent to which private activities were integrated into the socialist economy. Some activities, such as household farming, were linked closely with the operations of socialist enterprises. The suggestion that there need be no wall between the state and private sectors was heretical.[1] Finally, private-sector activities varied in their degree of legality. Suggesting that rational action can lead to breaking the law skirted advocacy of lawlessness, for the authors argued that whenever rational action results in illegality, laws of economics should take precedence (Gábor and Galasi 1981, 27). They quickly dissociated themselves from such odious practices as corruption and embezzlement, but they provided no theoretical rationale for doing so. Source of income, level of integration, and legality were suggested merely as descriptive dimensions useful for classifying the many forms of rational private action. The new approach was challenged (Héthy 1980; Erdélyi 1979) and defended (Köllő and Pete 1980; Vági 1980). Over the course of the debate a new language emerged, one which made it possible to think and talk about the private sector without reference to troublesome questions. The private sector now could be discussed as an economic rather than a political issue.

As the state apparatus geared up for the Sixth five-year plan, to be inaugurated in 1981, the leadership was very much aware of the difficult times ahead. They were in no position to expend resources on first fighting and then replacing the private sector in areas where it already had become a significant provider of goods and services (Belyó and Dexler 1985). The most important ones, agriculture and consumer services, were perceived as major influences on the public mood. Any decline in these areas was considered highly undesirable. The main lesson of the period since 1976 was that loosening control in these areas had no perceptible political side effects. In fact, some argued that the private sector added to stability by eliminating potential sources of discontent.

The bureaucrats responsible for monitoring and studying the private sector in the different ministries and offices were churning out reports full of facts and figures, hedging their modest policy suggestions with proposals that alternated among calls for more and less state intervention, support, and criticism. These reports either avoided making any general political assessment or they suggested that the private sector generally was performing up to expectations.[2] In a detached and cautious way, most bureaucrats, both younger ones who had not yet committed themselves to any contrary political positions and many of the older warriors of the 1968 reforms, were sympathetic toward change in their area of responsibility. They understood that their own importance and careers were to some extent tied to the importance and longevity of their field of expertise.

In September 1978, the National Planning Office began to work on a report concerning issues of income distribution (Fekete 1987). The topic reflected one of the chief political concerns of the leadership: the private sector as an independent force in shaping the structure of society. In early 1979, a commission was formed, which consisted of a group of social scientists, experts on the topic of the "second economy." Most of these experts were sympathetic to the private sector. Originally, they were wary, fearing that their ideas would be turned inside out and used in an upcoming conservative campaign against the private sector, but the composition of the commission reassured them. The Planning Office also let them know that liberalizing measures were under consideration.

The experts agreed that the private sector should first be seen as a source of useful services and goods for the rest of the population; its influence on income inequalities should be treated as a secondary issue. Beyond this general agreement, there were profound differences among the participants. Some believed that the private sector would smoothly blend in with the socialist sector, while others suggested that the private sector would always be in friction with the first due to contradictions inherent in socialist economies.

From the beginning it was clear that the commission was to supply ideas to pragmatic members of the leadership.[3] For the first time, some politicians, planners, and top advisers acknowledged that the problems created by the immense concentration of production had to be addressed. They recognized that large-scale production, while still probably the inevitable destiny of economic development, was unable to operate efficiently in many areas of the economy. As breaking up state firms would have met with tremendous resistance from managers, they turned to small enterprises in the private sector as temporary solutions.[4]

The project was conducted with caution and secrecy. The expert commission was linked to the Planning Office by means of a single, low-level bureaucrat who acted as a liaison. In December, after only two meetings, the commission submitted its report and promptly disbanded. The Economic Workgroup, a permanent advisory body to the Central Committee, discussed the report and sent its own recommendations to the Economic Policy Committee, which in turn submitted its own proposal to the Politburo, the highest level of power. The Politburo discussed, deliberated, and approved the rejuvenation of the private sector on February 19, 1980.

Thus, in a coup-like fashion,[5] sponsors of the reform measure rushed through their proposal in two months. They took the shortest possible route to the Politburo, circumventing ministries, the state bureaucracy, and Party offices. In March the Twelfth Party Congress endorsed the Politburo's decision, which cast the reform in the concrete of top-level approval.

The original intentions of the top leadership were announced in a decree issued at the Politburo's February meeting (PIA/288.5/793/1980b). The document hastened to point out that the cure for the country's economic ills ultimately rested with the performance of the socialist sector, and thus the interest of the socialist sector had to be protected above all. It was deemed a mistake, however, not to take advantage of the "second economy"—or *secondary* economy, as the Party preferred to call it—since more than three-quarters of Hungarian families already participated in it.[6]

The document spelled out five goals for the private sector. First, it should help satisfy the need for consumer goods and services, and it should help in the protection and expansion of residential housing stock.

Second, the private sector was expected to help create small units of production. As the leadership now acknowledged, the socialist sector was overcentralized and burdened with too many large firms. The most important question posed by this second goal was left unresolved: were small units needed temporarily or were there segments of the economy in which the small would always prevail? This ambiguity is reflected in a strictly confidential internal memo prepared for the Politburo meeting by the Economic Policy Commission, which first explained that

> [t]he basis for the presence of the secondary economy is those real and differentiated needs that come with the rise in living standards [and which] cannot be met—or cannot be met with proper efficiency—by the socialist economy within the framework of large-scale production. (PIA/288.5/793/1980a)

This wording still left open the possibility that the problem was a fundamental incompatibility between certain "real" needs and socialist production. In a later section the memo made a clearer statement:

> A segment of needs can be met properly only by small organizations, often with a few members. *Currently,* organizations of this kind rarely exist in the socialist sector; small firms more or less have disappeared. (PIA/288.5/793/1980a, emphasis added)

Socialism will eventually somehow create small companies. At this point, though, the ideological conviction that large-scale production and progress were synonymous seemed to have dissipated. Giving up the last remnants of the Marxist-Leninist vision of the one-nation-one-factory model was an important and necessary step for carrying through the reforms.

Third, the leadership foresaw that the necessary restructuring of the economy away from loss-producing, inefficient industries and toward dynamic, modern, competitive firms would result in the reorganization of workers.[7] The private sector would then help by absorbing frictional unemployment, just as it had been expected to do in 1968. Restructuring was seen as a one-time effort rather than an unending process of adaptation to change. The private sector was envisioned as a temporary holding place for labor during this transitional period, after which time people would be reabsorbed into the general system of state employment.

Fourth, the leadership expected the private sector to draw more labor into production. The decree was vague about mobilizing capital through the private sector, but the confidential internal memo made this need explicit (PIA/288.5/793/1980a).

Finally, the new measures were to help integrate the private sector into the socialist economy as a whole. The measures were touted as allowing better visibility and thus more control over these activities. As the resolution put it:

> We have to make it explicit, that recognizing private activities politically does not mean that we widen their realm at the expense of the socialist sector but that we connect them better into our entire economic system, *into the reach of the planned economy.* We wish to make the spontaneous economic activities of the population better serve our goals of economic policy, and we make an effort to *make them more socially organized.*[8] (PIA/288.5/793/1980b, sect. 9, emphasis added)

Illegal and invisible activities were supposed to decline as a result and gradually become amenable to a comprehensive system of regulation and planning.

As to the social effects of these measures, the decree, echoing the report of the expert commission, suggested somewhat ambiguously that the private sector was "more *usefully* approached from the angle of the needs it serves than from that of the incomes [it generates]" (PIA/288.5/793/1980b, sect. 2, emphasis added). Incomes earned proportionate to work were to be acknowledged. Again, the confidential internal memo was more blunt. It estimated that as of 1980 there were less than a few tens of thousands of people with very high incomes derived from the private sector. Besides, very high incomes existed in the first economy, too. The memo also gave estimates about the participation of different social groups in the private sector. Consistent with the picture presented in the previous chapter, that the private sector of the 1970s was the economy of the weak, the memo estimated that the lowest rate of participation was for managers. Moving down the socioeconomic ladder, the rates increased. The memo made it clear that income earned from the private sector helped those worse off (i.e., people in need of housing, young couples, people with large families, and the elderly), thus relieving political tensions. Consequently, the leadership should anticipate no significant change in income inequalities as a result of these measures. It was the compensatory nature of the private sector that made widening its scope politically acceptable.

The fact that the private sector was compensatory precisely because of the restrictions that were about to be lifted most certainly occurred to many in the leadership. The lingering nervousness about growing inequalities was addressed by the action plan written by one of the chief institutional sponsors of the reform, the Finance Ministry. Trying to further ease these fears, the document presented the following reasoning in a discussion of the tax measures that had to accompany the new law:

> [I]nitially the measures . . . will increase inequalities within the secondary economy because of competition, on the one hand, and will increase differences between the secondary economy and those . . . living on wages and salaries [on the other]. Because of the cutting back of internal consumption, incomes in this latter group will fall and for this same reason incomes from the second economy and the numbers of its participants will rise. . . . Labor power will be drawn into this area as that is where differentiation will seem to occur according to performance. . . . [I]f we do not obstruct this process by administrative measures, increasing competition will weed out many. Not everyone

> will be able, then, to earn high income from the secondary economy. . . . All this will equalize incomes . . . (MF 1980, 9)

This is the classic liberal argument for equality through market competition. Ministry bureaucrats were far ahead of the cautious leadership.

Clearly, at this time the leadership envisioned a socialist economy controlled by the state, with small private units helping out only as long as necessary.[9] The new laws were to enhance economic performance, which, in turn, was expected to increase the legitimacy of the regime. The political leadership, aware of possible dangers, kept pointing out that the umbrella term "second economy" was too inclusive. As they put it in the decree:

> The Politburo regards the comprehensive treatment and the aggregation of different activities appropriate only under exceptional circumstances. . . . As these are diverse activities, which cannot be treated in a unified manner, it is more useful to review and legislate individual areas separately. (PIA/288.5/793/1980b, sec. 10)

This caveat was designed to give leaders maximum flexibility with which to tailor regulations according to their interests and forestall the possibility of undesirable activities creeping in on the backs of desirable ones.

The new laws adopted in October 1981 took effect the next January. Until 1981, the private economy had been completely atomized. To put it more precisely, there were no legal provisions for cooperation of any sort among its participants.[10] Only licensed artisans could join forces, and even they were constrained to small units. In services, only up to five persons could work together; in all other areas, the maximum was two persons. The new set of laws was designed to open up a restricted but institutionally protected space for the private sector.

The novelty of these laws was that for the first time they allowed, and even encouraged, the organization of small private work partnerships,[11] and at the same time they liberalized the operating conditions and licensing of small artisans and tradesmen working alone or with their families. The new laws somewhat relaxed the limitations on the number of people that could be employed in the private sector. One of the most fateful innovations proved to be the introduction of company work partnerships (*vállalati gazdasági munkaközösség* or VGMK) (Stark 1989; Sziráczki 1989), associations of workers employed by the same company.[12] Company Work Partnerships were not considered until very late in the drafting of the legislation. By devising a form specifically intended to allow industrial workers to participate in the private sector, the drafters wanted to avoid the debacle of 1972, when hard-liners were able to mobilize these workers against the New Economic Mechanism.[13] Overall, the crucial concession in the 1982 laws was that they allowed the private sector to engage in business with state companies.

There were restrictive conditions as well. None of these partnerships could become a legal entity on its own, a limitation that constituted discrimination in a legal and administrative system that favored corporate actors. They were excluded from health care, child care, most educational and legal services, and wholesale trade and advertising, since these areas were open only to legal entities.[14] The law did not allow for members not actually working in the partnerships, and therefore no one could become a member through investment only. Members of the police, military, and judiciary were excluded from the "second economy."

The reform had profound effects. On the one hand, the forms in which people participated in the private sector changed. People who stayed with the old forms, based on individual or family participation, began to alter the ways in which they operated. At the same time, the new forms of business partnerships allowed people to work together with others under a formal contract and develop rudimentary, small organizations in the private sector. On the other hand, the reform brought about dramatic changes in the social composition of the private sector. Throughout the remainder of this chapter, I draw on a second Social Stratification Survey taken in 1986 (SSS–1986) to illustrate this change.[15]

The New Face of the Private Sector

Old Forms of Individual and Family Participation

The reform had the smallest impact on private artisans, whose number increased only modestly. The occupations that provided for most of the increase in the late 1970s, all of which were construction related, leveled, and among masons and carpenters there was even a small decline. Full-time participation would have declined had it not been for the new policies that allowed private transportation services in the form of small truck rentals and taxis and an increase in the number of small shops, pubs, and restaurants (KSH 1987, 177, 208–9). SSS–1986 found that 4.3 percent of the labor force was in the full-time private sector, a little higher percentage than in 1981 (see table 7.2).

The small change in the number of full-time private participants revealed the lack of trust in the leadership's commitment to the private sector. At the same time, it concealed the facts that full-time participants could work under improved circumstances and that the face of the full-time private sector was changing. A study conducted in 1988 found that those who took out full-time private licenses after 1982 were better educated and had enjoyed longer and more successful careers as state employees. They also were more likely to have left managerial positions to join the private sector (Kuczi and Vajda 1990). In addition, the study found that, while the most common complaints in the private sector continued to be about taxes, the difficulties involved in getting supplies, and bureaucratic hurdles, post-1982 entrepreneurs also complained more about competition, insufficient demand, uncertainty, and lack of information. Having had more socialist companies among their customers, more recent entrepreneurs were more dissatisfied with their relationship with the socialist sector. Moreover, they assigned greater importance to the role of advertising and personal networks in their success. The full-time private sector was gradually becoming less traditional and isolated and more market driven.

If the overall size of the full-time private sector grew only a little, there was a vigorous increase in the number of part-time licenses. Although a large informal part-time sector persisted, the number of part-time licenses rose as changes in the laws encouraged people to legalize their informal activities. The largest increase here, too, was in transportation.

The 1982 reform did not specifically address agriculture. The general change in the political climate, however, resulted in new opportunities for commercial farming.[16] Household farms continued their polarization between a small number of more and more specialized commercial farms and an increasing number of hobby gardens. Some individual labor contractors formed partnerships; others took advantage of the widening con-

TABLE 7.2. Distribution of Respondents in the Labor Force in 1986 by Participation in Private Forms Created or Directly Affected by the New Legislation of 1982

Private Forms of Labor	Sample	Percentage Number
None	2,390	64.1
Part-time	940	25.2
Full-time	161	4.3
New forms, total[a]	238	6.4
Semi-independent forms (VGMK and ISZSZCS)	198	5.3
Independent forms (GMK and PJT)	47	1.3
Total	3,729	100.0

Source: Social Stratification Survey 1986.

[a]The next two rows do not add up to these totals because there were a few people who participated in both semi-independent and independent forms.

tract opportunities alone. According to SSS–1986, about 25 percent of the labor force participated in the part-time private sector, not counting those who took advantage of the new forms of business partnerships.

New Forms of Collective Participation

The new business partnerships formed the fastest growing segment of the private sector. By 1986, small partnerships were producing one-tenth of the national income (PIA/288.5/996, 31). There were 447,041 people registered as participants in these new forms, even though only 51,658 were participating full time (see table 7.3). Had every person registered only once, this would have been 9.1 percent of the work force.[17] These new so-called entrepreneurial forms fell into two general categories. The first category included partnerships that were completely private and were independent of any organization in the socialist sector. The second contained semi-independent forms, organizations that operated under the auspices of a socialist firm.

TABLE 7.3. Number of Participants in Small Business Enterprises Filing Tax Forms at the End of the Year, 1983–87

Partnerships	1983	1984	1985	1986	1987
Business partnerships (GMK)	27,647	47,999	60,303	72,541	74,793
Full-time	6,623	10,962	14,096	16,818	16,876
Part-time	18,734	31,554	41,342	49,499	51,171
Employee	2,290	5,483	4,865	6,224	6,746
Company work partnerships (VGMK)	103,864	201,085	241,945	266,917	241,461
Full-time	1,944	4,430	4,447	3,754	3,695
Part-time	101,520	195,644	237,012	262,907	237,499
Employee	400	1,011	486	256	267
Specialized work partnerships (ISZSZCS)	42,193	75,651	89,147	102,223	86,224
Full-time	10,951	24,641	28,360	28,402	19,762
Part-time	30,553	49,114	59,598	72,374	65,413
Employee	689	1,896	1,189	1,447	1,049
Other work partnerships	6,636	8,472	10,587	5,360	9,302
Full-time	2,104	3,518	3,619	2,684	4,023
Part-time	4,267	4,302	6,259	1,346	2,863
Employee	265	652	709	1,330	2,416
Total	180,340	333,207	401,982	447,041	411,780

Source: Baló and Lipovecz 1988, 696–97.

Independent Forms

Economic work partnerships (*gazdasági munkaközösségek* or GMKs) soon became popular. GMKs were excluded from commerce, but they could undertake service and production activities as diverse as developing computer software, desktop publishing, matchmaking, funeral services, and office cleaning. As in all partnerships, members were obliged to actively work in the GMK. Part-time members had to inform their primary employers and receive written permission to participate. The maximum number of members was set at 30. To avoid the possibility of linking several GMKs in a single chain, through overlapping membership, no individual could belong to more than one of these partnerships. The GMK could hire employees in proportion to the number of its members, but not more than 10 people. It could hire an unlimited number of close relatives of members (except siblings). Under certain conditions apprentices could also work for these partnerships in limited numbers. GMK members bore complete financial responsibility for their business, and all the assets had to come from the members (table 7.4).

The second independent partnership form was called a civil legal association (*polgári jogi társaság* or PJT). The PJTs were intended to cover small traders in retail business. The PJT was the only form that theoretically permitted association between corporations and private persons (e.g., the state distributor and the private grocer) but was not itself a corporate entity. Its size was more limited: at most four members could join. Because the tax laws governing the PJTs were very unfavorable, these partnerships had little appeal initially. In 1987, restrictions on other forms and minor changes favoring PJTs made them more attractive.

Semi-independent Forms

The partnership form with the greatest impact was the semi-independent company work partnership or VGMK. The VGMK was under the legal patronage of its parent company. The company manager had a decisive voice in the founding contract, and he could disband the VGMK at will. The firm employing the workers was supposed to serve as an "institutional base." This meant that the parent firm provided resources for the jobs and was liable for any failure to fulfill a contract undertaken by the VGMK.

Most—but not all—VGMKs were engaged in industrial manual labor. In 1984, about 20 percent of the VGMKs involved intellectual work organized mainly by employees of research or policy institutes taking outside commissions (Laky 1984, 47).

The other newly introduced partnership forms legalized existing practices in the private sector. The VGMK had a unique genealogy. Introduced as a last-minute political ploy, it represented the triumph of the erosion of state employment from within. Formally, and keeping with the original intent of the new laws, the VGMK was an extension of the part-time labor contract. However, the VGMK can be traced back to the hidden shop floor bargaining that had been taking place within socialist firms for a long time (Héthy and Makó 1978; Sabel and Stark 1982). The distribution of overtime lay at the heart of this bargaining. Since wages were inflexible, the usual way of increasing workers' income was to assign them overtime jobs with higher hourly pay. In many respects, the VGMK was an extension of this practice. Instead of each person, or strategic

TABLE 7.4. Number of Small Business Partnerships (Filing Annual Tax Forms at the End of Each Year), Average Value of Their Assets, Average Value of Assets per Capita, and Average After-Tax Annual Income of a Part-Time Participant (in current forints, thousands)

	1983	1984	1985	1986	1987
Business partnerships (GMK)					
Number	4,629	7,340	9,314	10,941	11,185
Assets per enterprise	191.8	247.1	262.8	312.7	394.1
Assets per participant	32.1	37.8	40.6	47.2	58.9
Net income per part-time participant	40.3	54.1	54.5	56.5	69.4
Company work partnerships (VGMK)					
Number	9,837	17,775	20,267	21,490	19,117
Assets per enterprise	65.9	75.1	69.4	76.8	39.6
Assets per participant	6.2	6.6	5.8	6.2	3.1
Net income per part-time participant	28.9	35.8	36.9	37.9	42.6
Specialized work partnerships (ISZSZCS)					
Number	1,276	2,243	2,523	2,768	2,337
Assets per enterprise	454.8	570.7	554.8	621.9	752.3
Assets per participant	13.8	16.9	15.7	16.8	20.4
Net income per part-time participant	27.3	33.9	34.5	36.4	42.9
Other work partnerships					
Number	463	622	833	1,484	2,199
Assets per enterprise	266.6	284.9	222.8	178.7	528.9
Assets per participant	15.8	20.9	17.5	49.5	125.0
Net income per part-time participant	17.9	38.6	19.7	22.3	25.8

Source: Calculated from Baló and Lipovecz 1988, 696–97.

alliances among a few persons, forcing the management to give them overtime work, the VGMK allowed workers to join in a formal group and contract a job after hours for two to three times the hourly wage they earned in their regular jobs (Stark 1989, 146; Sziráczki 1989, 45). Within these work groups, control over the work process was almost completely in the hands of the members. Workers could organize the labor process in any way they wished. They were free to discard the division of labor designed by the firm for the same tasks and reinvent a new and more flexible work organization.

The VGMK had been envisioned as a work association that would subcontract jobs from any state firm that needed its services. These partnerships were supposed to bid on contracts competitively, squaring off against other VGMKs and outside firms. Only a few VGMKs followed this path, however. Most subcontracted with their own employers.[18] As a result, the internal organization of the firm and the VGMK became closely intertwined. The VGMK was always interested in having among its members people who had an "in" with the management hierarchy, were informed of the deadlines management was facing, knew how to keep books, were able to calculate costs, and had a general understanding of all the firm's activities.

Internal contracting turned out to be advantageous for management as well. Managers found that they were able to circumvent the strict regulations limiting wages because VGMK work was not paid out of the wage fund but from the firm's expense account. The VGMKs allowed companies to keep their best workers and provide others with incentives to work hard.

A cousin of the VGMK, the specialized work partnerships (*ipari és szolgáltató szakcsoport* or ISZSZCS), was very similar, except that it existed in cooperatives. If ISZSZCSs were more entrepreneurial than were the VGMKs, that difference was due to their location in the economy. Nonagricultural cooperatives were overrepresented in the service sector, where it was much harder to give ISZSZCSs internal contracts, as most of the work had to be delivered directly to customers. Agricultural cooperatives, on the other hand, seized upon ISZSZCSs as a replacement for the semiprivate side businesses that had created such a scandal in the early 1970s. Following the tradition of side businesses, these ISZSZCSs were usually launched in small manufacturing and services.

Despite the rapid growth in the number of small partnerships, the general mood was cautious. Most people kept their jobs in the socialist sector; in fact, for the ISZSZCSs and the VGMKs this was a requirement. Prohibitive social security taxes also proved to be a disincentive for full-time participation in the private sector.[19] Another sign of caution was how little capital was invested. The value of the per capita assets of these new partnerships was small, generally less than the annual net income of a part-time member, though it was slowly increasing. The GMKs remained small. Even by 1987, less than seven partners were joining on the average, far below the 30-member limit, and they employed only one person for every 10 members.

Participating full time in the private sector was still too risky for most people. The deterrents were not so much the incalculability of demand or competition, even though there were areas where demand was getting saturated and competition had begun to appear. Taxi services in major cities, for instance, seem to have reached this point by 1987 (Gábor and Horváth 1987). The real risks lay elsewhere. There were several factors that made full-time private enterprise insecure. First, there were the long-standing difficulties involved in procuring supplies. This pushed entrepreneurs in the direction of services that required little material input and more labor or skill, inputs the entrepreneurs could supply themselves. Second, the unlimited liability of small artisans, tradesmen, and GMK members left them open to the loss of all their property in the event of bankruptcy. Those who went bankrupt did not do so because they failed to compete: the lethal blow to private enterprise was not getting reimbursed in time by state companies. The third factor was the absence of an insurance system to cushion the effects of unforeseen disasters. The state-run insurance companies did not provide business insurance, and private insurance companies were not allowed. The fourth factor was the instability of the legal environment. Any reform or institutional change creates a measure of instability; institutional reforms inevitably proceed by trial and error. Frequent changes in the tax laws and in other regulations made it very difficult to plan ahead. The instability of the legal environment crushed those who did not have the sophistication to find their way around the ephemeral regulations. The fact that the larger political environment was also in constant flux only worsened matters. This was the fifth and most important factor. In transitional periods, political trust in both the intentions and the competence of the leadership becomes crucial.[20] In Hungary in the mid-1980s, it was difficult to trust in either, given the past record and continuing ambivalence of the Party-state.

Ideological suspicions aside, the state had strong reasons to be ambivalent about the private sector. With respect to its original objectives, the reform legalizing the small private sector proved to be a failure (PIA/BB.1/VB–1986/2). The first objective, the creation of a private sector that attended primarily to the needs of consumers, remained unmet. The majority of the new enterprises were semi-independent partnerships founded in firms or cooperatives by employees who used the resources of their mother companies to fulfill internal subcontracts. In 1983, only 2 percent of partnership receipts came from consumers (KSH 1984), and these figures did not substantially improve as the decade wore on (Róna-Tas 1995). Those who pursued independent work partnerships also quickly discovered that business with state companies was more lucrative than peddling to individual consumers. As a result, while the supply of consumer goods and services improved somewhat overall, in many places it actually deteriorated as private entrepreneurs abandoned consumers in favor of the more promising opportunities to be found among state companies.

The second objective, while also unmet, did not fall as far short of the mark as did the first. The predominance of large firms did decrease following the 1982 reform. Most of that was due to the multiplication of small private enterprises, however, rather than to the creation of small companies in the socialist sector. The state firm proved resilient in keeping its bloated size; only in a few cases did local plants become autonomous subsidiaries and form "small enterprises."[21] To the extent that decentralization in the socialist sector succeeded at all, it was only in the cooperative segment. Cooperatives shrank by spawning "small cooperatives," ones with less than 100 but more than 15 members. The number of cooperatives of the old type declined as well (see table 7.5).

The government's third goal for the private sector, to absorb unemployment, turned out to be medicine for an illness never contracted. The economy was not restructured, and no unemployment occurred. In fact, internal reports to the leadership claimed it as an achievement that private enterprises did not siphon off labor from state firms as they had done in the late 1960s. This was hardly surprising, for most participants in the new ventures kept their state jobs and engaged in their private activities part time. If anything, the reform impeded a restructuring of the work force.

TABLE 7.5. Distribution of Firms in the Socialist Sector by Size in 1982 and 1988

	1982	1988
Companies and trusts	1,782	1,986
Number of companies with more than 1,000 employees	752[a]	723
Number of employees (thousands) in companies with more than 1,000 employees	2,280[a]	2,126
Number of subsidiaries/small enterprises	25	391
Cooperatives	4,132	3,772
Small cooperatives	145	3,100

Source: Calculated from KSH 1989; and KSH 1990b, 120b, 120d.
[a]In 1981.

Internal subcontracting made it possible for state firms to keep their workers, even if these companies were piling up losses. What attracted workers to a firm was not that it was profitable, and therefore able to pay its employees better, but that it was able to provide subcontracting jobs and thus higher pay.

The success of the fourth objective, mobilizing extra labor, was also ambiguous. The amount of time a person worked in 1986 was exactly the same as in 1977 (table 7.6). Time spent in the private sector increased, but this was counterbalanced by a two-hour cut in the work week in 1981–82.[22]

Yet this constancy in the number of minutes and hours counted obscures underlying differences. The cut in work time in the socialist sector was two hours per week across the board; the increase in work time in the private sector was distributed very unevenly. Thus, those who worked in the private sector worked more in 1986 than in 1977, and those who didn't worked less. As the free time of those working in the private sector shrank, they increasingly began to use their workplace time to do things they should have done after work. They studied for evening classes, went home to receive the repairman, or ran private errands. This, of course, gave others license to do the same. In 1983, a survey of 8,400 clients of various service outlets and government offices found that about half of them were there on private business at a time when they should have been at work (Tímár 1988, 115). Half of those had permission from their bosses. Clearly, the extra labor input in the private sector came at the expense of cutting effort in the socialist sector. In other instances, people did work hard during regular hours, but what they worked on were jobs for their private partnerships. This was especially common among professionals, such as engineers and architects, who could not be supervised by means of factory-style methods (Laky 1984). The 1982 law did not

TABLE 7.6. Time Budgets of Hungarians in 1977 and 1986 (number of minutes spent on an average spring day)

Activity	1977	1986
Primary occupation	217	191
Conferences	1	2
Secondary nonmanual work	0	3
Secondary manual nonagricultural work	2	9
Household farming	60	74
Occasional agricultural work	1	2
All income-earning activities	281	281

Source: Falussy and Harcsa 1987, 13.

result in more labor drawn into the economy; it resulted only in a redistribution of effort.

The reforms did not mobilize much capital, either. None of the VGMKs needed capital of their own, as they used their company's machines and premises. People in other types of private enterprises were reluctant to invest because of the lack of matching credit, legal limits on the size of the operation, and, most importantly, distrust of the intentions of the Party-state to keep its political promises.

The reforms did not make the private sector easier to control. The proportion of illegal activity in the gross domestic product did not diminish. In fact, it was estimated to have risen from over 15 percent in 1980 to around 20 percent by 1987, the year before personal income tax was introduced. After that, this figure almost doubled in two years (Lackó 1991).

Where activities were the easiest to oversee, that is, in internal subcontracting partnerships, very serious—and unanticipated—difficulties arose. As early as November 1982, the State Office of Wages and Labor decried the practice by which firms circumvented wage regulations by subcontracting with their own workers. Subcontracts paid out of the expense fund enabled managers to pay their workers more than the rate prescribed by the central authorities. Although workers performed efficiently while working on internal subcontracts, their total production on the job also included their inefficient and "undisciplined" regular work hours. Taken together, their overall labor output was not proportionate to the overall income they received from their firms in two installments: as regular wages and as subcontractor fees. The memo sent to the Party's Economic Policy Commission deplored the resulting loss of control over wages and purchasing power as a serious blow to macroeconomic balance and a spur to inflation (SOWL/1976–1/1982, V/21).

If, indeed, the 1982 reform did not live up to original expectations, why didn't the leadership terminate the experiment? It was not for want of trying. In 1984, for the first time in several years, Hungary had a foreign trade surplus. This generated a new optimism in top circles. Believing that the recession was over and economic growth was back on track, the leadership now felt sufficiently confident to roll back the most undesirable features of the private sector.[23]

In March 1985, the Thirteenth Party Congress was held. The Congress endorsed new, stricter policies designed to tighten the leadership's control over the economy, but then the unexpected occurred. Breaking a decades-long tradition of sitting silently through interminable speeches, applauding enthusiastically, and then dutifully voting according to plan, the floor balked. A long and sharp debate developed over work partnerships. Some argued that partnerships eroded work discipline because they encouraged people to devote all their energies to them rather than to their regular jobs, ruined workers' solidarity, and enhanced materialism and petty bourgeois morality. Saving their harshest attacks for VGMKs, they pointed out that if management had done its job correctly there would have been no need for partnerships. But, delivering a strong defense, a surprisingly large number of delegates countered that VGMKs were tools that managers could use effectively to motivate workers, that solidarity within partnerships was high, and that people were not materialistic but simply trying to make ends meet.[24] Nevertheless, when the Congress was over, new regulations slapped extra taxes on contracts between state companies and work partnerships designed to cut down on the outflow of wages. Even though the initial targets were the VGMKs, the extra tax was applied across the board. The leadership, which in 1980 was fully aware of the importance of handling parts of the private sector separately, must have realized that penalizing VGMKs alone would simply turn them into other forms of private business partnership. In the absence of an elaborate bureaucratic system of regulations and enforcement, only across the board measures would succeed. The extra tax had climbed to 20 percent by 1987.

The leadership decided to attack the private sector on a second front as well. In October 1985, in a draft of an action program designed to "defend labor time," the State Office of Wages and Labor lamented:

> In the last years several signs have suggested that labor discipline is deteriorating, and considering the last three decades it can be stated that it is at its lowest point. (SOWL/79–1/1985.V/31, 1)

In the summer of 1987, *Pártélet* (Party Life), the official organizational journal of the HSWP, published a roundtable discussion with the telling title "On Fundamental Social Order." The participants bemoaned what they considered to be the complete breakdown of order, the lack of labor discipline, poor management and organization at the workplace, corruption, and the absence of discipline in society in general. The representative of the State Office of Wages and Labor put it this way:

> We even encouraged people: work at six [different] places! Take a second job, join the VGMKs, work on Saturdays and Sundays! This is how it happened. But scattered effort, exhaustion, and the fact that one could make more money in the second economy led to the decay of respect for the first job. *There is a loosening of a solid value system, which linked people's material success to the clockwork precision of labor in large-scale industrial organizations,* [i.e.,] *to conformity to traditional work culture.* (*Pártélet* 1987, 44, emphasis added)

By 1986, the Council of Ministers issued a secret decree mandating a clampdown on undisciplined workers.[25] This program, which was in many respects similar to earlier disciplinary campaigns (Makó and Gyekiczky 1987), turned out to be the last of its kind. It fizzled out within a year, never having achieved its goals. The assessment prepared by the State Office of Wages and Labor in July 1987 admitted that ". . . this year the unfavorable tendencies continued, occasionally strengthened . . ." (SOWL/2741–1/1987.V/5, 1). Power was slipping away from the state.

Social Consequences

Why did the leadership not assert its will with more force? The reason is to be found in some unforeseen social and political consequences of the reform. The new laws were intended to integrate the private sector into the economy as a whole. By providing a legal and institutional infrastructure, the state brought the "second economy" somewhat closer to the first. At the same time, the socialist sector was changing as well. Socialist enterprises were increasing their autonomy, and market mechanisms were taking on a more prominent role. Thus, the socialist sector was moving slowly further away from the original socialist model. At this point, the private sector took on a new social character. It began to lose its compensatory function and became aligned with the forces generating inequalities in the first economy.

Our guide to these social changes, SSS–1986, shows a clear picture of a radical transformation (see table 7.7).[26] In 1981, those who had participated only in the socialist sector had the highest per capita household income. In 1986, they could spend 688 forints less than those who participated part time within the old forms and 1,440 forints less than those who took advantage of the new opportunity to form business partnerships. People relying only on state employment were now the worst off.

Selected consumption measures show the same shift. In 1981, those without private-sector pursuits had had more meat in their diets than did part-time private-sector participants; now they comprised the group least likely to eat meat. In 1981, they, along with those who worked full time in the private sector, were the ones most likely to own a vacation plot or home. Now those in partnerships were the most likely to relax in their own weekend houses. Other part-timers, working alone or with their families, were doing as well everyone as else, except partnership members. In five years they had caught up.

Consumer durables, such as automatic washing machines, color televisions, and cars also had become more common since 1981. The differences in ownership showed the same pattern for all of them, a pattern quite

TABLE 7.7. Measures of Material Well-Being by Participation in the Private Sector

Private Sector Activities	Household Income per Capita	Meat Consumption (days per week)	Proportion with Vacation Home or Plot	Proportion with Automatic Washing Machine	Proportion with Color Television	Proportion with Automobile
None	4,014.4868	3.8486	0.1213	0.2659	0.2682	0.4418
Part-time	4,702.7653	4.1651	0.1138	0.2907	0.2926	0.4936
Full-time	3,913.3007	4.6429	0.1118	0.4845	0.5280	0.7267
F	48.0129***	13.7960***	0.2218	18.1428***	25.3280***	26.5261***
New business forms	5,454.3192	4.0295	0.1723	0.3866	0.3782	0.5462
F[a]	132.5593***	1.4034	5.1059*	15.8169***	13.0869***	9.5501**

Source: Social Stratification Survey 1986.

[a]The *F*-statistic indicates the statistical significance of the difference between those with no private activities ("None") and those participating in new business forms.

* $.05 > p > .01$ ** $.01 > p > .001$ *** $p < .001$

different from the one seen five years before. By any of these measures, people without private-sector incomes and activities were falling behind. Those working full time in the private sector were the best supplied, followed by partnership members.

By 1986, those involved in the private sector in their spare time were also better paid in their socialist-sector jobs. Across groups, partnership members received the largest income from state employment (see table 7.8). Partnerships, especially VGMKs, were extended to the most valued workers of the company; not surprisingly, these individuals were better paid as employees as well. If everyone earned the average income of those in their occupation with no private pursuits, partnership members would have made 451 forints more than employees who did not dabble in the private sector. Those involved in the old forms of part-time private activities were between these two groups. Full-time private-sector participants, though they had the highest living standards, would have had the lowest income had they abandoned the private sector entirely and switched over to the socialist sector.

The people in the private sector were not just relatively well off. Socially they were a very different group from those who had participated in the private sector five years earlier: partnership members were the best educated, had the highest number of subordinates at their workplace, and were almost twice as likely to be members of the Communist Party as were others in the socialist sector. But those who were involved in part-time activities in the old forms were also better educated and did not differ in workplace authority and Party membership from state employees without private-sector incomes.

The new partnership forms and the more liberal regulations, especially the ones opening up the socialist sector to private contracting, suddenly brought into the private sector the people who were the main beneficiaries of the socialist economy. The 1982 reforms had accelerated the process that made first-economy assets convertible and useful in the second.

Political Consequences

The changed composition of private-sector participants had serious political consequences. In 1983, when the Ministry of Finance was preparing its next report on the status of the second economy, it asked for external opinions from all over the country. The first secretary of a northern county, Károly Grósz,[27] submitted an 11-page study that was generally supportive of the second economy. Yet he also made the following observations:

TABLE 7.8. Measures of Social Status by Participation in the Private Sector

Private Sector Activities	Average Age	Average Wage from First Job in the Socialist Sector	Average Wages in the Socialist Sector Given One's Occupation	Average Year of Education Completed	Average Number of Subordinates	Proportion Party Member
None	37.1799	5,061.19	5,067.65	10.7410	3.9328	0.1410
Part-time	37.2766	5,365.60	5,345.34	11.2064	3.4067	0.1574
Full-time	37.8634		4,683.47	10.9752	0.8019	0.0621
F	0.2968	12.0644***	10.3379***	6.5754**	3.2360*	5.1635**
New business forms	36.0126	5,978.06	5,518.23	12.1303	6.4873	0.2647
F[a]	2.4025	31.1336***	14.4760***	40.3608***	4.6969*	25.9005***

Source: Social Stratification Survey 1986.

[a]The *F*-statistic indicates the statistical significance of the difference between those with no private activities ("None") and those participating in new business forms.

*.05 > p > .01 **.01 > p > .001 *** p < .001

> It is our conviction that these new opportunities can contribute to the strengthening of consumerism. It distracts a portion of people interested and potentially active in public affairs, it reduces the pool of potential cadres, and raises doubts in people who are unselfishly working for the public good. (MF/MP/Ui.2596/83, 6)

Moreover, the private sector ruined the socialist brigade movement and eroded trade unions.

> Many rightly see a contradiction in the fact that until now the trade unions had fought for shorter working hours, a reduction in unhealthy jobs, [lowering of] the retirement age, etc., and now the workers in the new enterprise forms completely ignore [these achievements]—in pursuit of higher income—and they do not want them. In the long run this can have undesirable effects for the workers and [bad] consequences for companies and society. (MF/MP/Ui.2596/83, 6)

The National Council of Trade Unions submitted a report in which it voiced the same concerns Grósz had about unregulated incomes and working conditions in partnerships. It underscored not only the fact that partnerships created tensions within the socialist work movement but that the "political activism" of the members of these partnerships was weakened as well, for they were neglecting to go to union and Party meetings (MF/MP/Ui.2598/83).

The Patriotic Popular Front, the official umbrella organization of all social organizations, pointed out half a year later that:

> The new enterprise forms provide the chance for upward mobility to two strata: one is the progressive force of our society, the creative manual workers and intellectuals; the other is that stratum that is unable to pass onto others the burden of inflation and must work extra in order to maintain its standard of living. (MF/HI/1984, 2)

This "progressive force" was precisely the base from which the Party had drawn its membership since the 1970s (Szelényi 1987). These people could take advantage of their connections to find good contracts with socialist firms,[28] knew how to negotiate with bosses, and had organizational skills. Very soon the Party found that many of its formerly most committed activists had become deeply involved with the private sector and now had little time for public affairs.

Acutely aware of this problem, the Party conducted a series of studies in Budapest between 1984 and 1986. The main focus was on VGMKs and ISZSZCSs, but other forms were also discussed. Just as they did after the New Economic Mechanism was introduced, local Party bosses had to submit reports. Party officials at the district and factory levels were asked to provide figures about Party members' participation rates in private-sector activities and to submit their own evaluations of the situation. The Party officials of the Csepel Steel and Metal Works, who in the early 1970s had helped spearhead efforts to dismantle economic reforms, this time were warmly supportive of VGMKs and had few critical comments. They also revealed that 62 percent of the Party membership and 64 percent of Party officials were working in VGMKs—35 and 8 percent, respectively, of all those in the partnerships. The rest of the reports—with a few exceptions—were equally supportive. All noted that Party members were vastly overrepresented in VGMKs. The Fifteenth District reported that about 35 to 40 percent of those who participated in VGMKs or ISZSZCSs were Party members and 15 percent were Party officials, much higher than their proportion in the work force, which stood at 15 and 5.9 percent, respectively (PIA/BB/1f/1984–89/GPO/8, 99).

Among the many favorable comments there were a few hints of trouble: maintaining organization among Party members who were scattered across many small units was not easy (PIA/BB/1.f./1984–89/v./110, 52–57); it was hard to get people to enroll in Party schools and other political training courses; and it had become difficult to recruit young people to the Party (Székács 1987, 40). Finally, some people felt that the private activities increased inequalities between those who could and did participate and those who couldn't or didn't, and others complained that private activities resulted in undeserved incomes (PIA/BB/1.f./1984–89/330, 36).

The report writers' effort to put the best possible face on the new economic forms was obvious. The original district- and company-level reports still contained a few criticisms, partly because some Party bosses were more hard-nosed than others. Yet, in the summary report produced by the Budapest Party Committee, even those few critical remarks were toned down. One example was the undeniable problem that the extra time people spent working after hours prevented them from participating in political activities. Some of the original reports lamented the fact that Party members were skipping Party meetings. In the final report to the Politburo, however, this issue was given an ingenious spin:

> The activities of work partnerships—according to the experiences of the meetings of local Party organizations—made leisure time more precious and placed higher demands on the quality of political and community activities. (PIA/288.f.5/945/PB/1985, 41)

The private sector was just what the Party needed to invigorate its political life.

The second unanticipated consequence was the behavior of company managers in the socialist sector. This group's power had increased considerably in past decades. Company managers had played an important political role in reversing the New Economic Mechanism, and with increased concentration of production in the 1970s, they further enhanced their power. Their resistance to reform played an important part in postponing radical measures in the late 1970s, a delay that led to the 1982 laws expanding the private sector. In 1984, company managers took another significant step in advancing their autonomy from the Party-state. A new law that took effect in 1985 introduced company councils into each enterprise and delegated to them all rights previously exercised by the state through the ministries.[29] The Company Councils were given full responsibility for their company's by-laws, production profile, investments, income distribution, and labor issues. Most importantly, the councils decided on changes in the legal form of the company, controlled mergers and acquisitions, and elected the chief executive. The composition of the Company Council assured that the actual power was held by top management. Half of the council was elected by the employees, the other half by management. Selection of up to a third of management's half was at the discretion of the chief executive, who could choose anyone except a close relative, regardless of whether the person worked for the company. Only one member of the council, with a single vote, represented the state. Since managers depended much less on the Party and the state than before, they no longer felt an obligation to follow the Party line unwaveringly.

Initially company managers were skeptical about work partnerships, but most quickly became strong supporters. They soon realized that VGMKs were highly efficient and kept the best workers satisfied. They also recognized that they could improve the economic performance of their companies by contracting with capable outside private partnerships. Company managers resented the state's decision to levy an extra tax on contracts with work partnerships.

Managers also resisted the disciplinary campaign. Despite all the complaints in the media about increasing chaos and subsequent pressures to restore workplace discipline, the number of disciplinary actions remained steady. There were a little more than 7,000 actions per year during the early and mid-1980s, with a slight increase occurring in industry.[30] Either company managers were reluctant to address the issue or they solved the problem of workplace disorder in other ways. The State Office of Wages and Labor report that evaluated the results of the disciplinary campaign observed that

> the execution of the decree—in certain respects—was met with the disagreement of workers and company managers. This is also related to the fact that in certain cases central regulation was taken as limiting the autonomy of the company. In our opinion the new regulation helps to bar the management from granting certain, sometimes unprincipled, concessions in the process of labor market bargaining that are not in harmony with the spirit of the law. (SOWL 2741–1/1987.V/5)

The 1982 reform presented the more adventuresome managers, especially those in the cooperative sector, with an opportunity to split off the better-functioning parts of their firms and start small companies. Not surprisingly, top company managers threw their political support behind small enterprises. They established a special Small Enterprise Division within their political organization, the Chamber of Commerce. This division was the organized political voice of small companies and work partnerships until 1988, when the National Association of Entrepreneurs was founded.

The reforms of 1982 created a social constituency with a vested interest in preserving—and even extending—the new economic arrangements. Worse yet, this constituency was recruited from among the company managers and activists, the people the Party depended on most for its local presence. The private sector was now the economy of the strong, the domain of dominant groups. To discontinue the reforms would have required the leadership to turn against its own cadres.

Shifting Boundaries of Private and Public

The reforms shifted and blurred the boundaries of private and public. Until 1982, the private and socialist sectors of the economy had been carefully kept apart. Private activities had taken place in private spaces—one's workshop, the customer's home—and in private time—after work and on the weekends. Private activities had been confined to the consumer market. Private had been the individual, the household, consumption, leisure, and friendship networks. Public had been the state, the factory, the office, production, authority, credentials, and political organization.

It was with respect to these divisions that the VGMKs created the most confusion. Workers engaged in internally subcontracted jobs not only worked in the same shop, using the same tools alongside the same colleagues as in their state jobs, but sometimes they did the subcontracted job during regular hours. In one factory, management set the parameters of the workers' state-sector tasks not in terms of time but in terms of a production quota: the workers had to fulfill 130 percent of what the quota used to be. Once workers had achieved this higher quota, they were considered to be working as members of their VGMKs and not as employees of the firm. As a result of lax labor discipline in the past, the quotas were unrealistically low. Many workers could deliver the 130 percent in five hours, leaving the rest of the day free for VGMK work (Ternovszky 1987, 54; Szmicsek 1986, 66).

The long-standing separation between public and private had afforded little opportunity for people to subordinate public goals to their private pursuits. Corruption had been easy to identify. With the shifting boundaries of private and public, this clarity was diminished. The 1982 reforms prohibited top managers from joining VGMKs formed and subcontracted by their own firm. This restriction was more vague for managers of cooperatives. It was far from obvious, however, where the dividing line ran between top managers, who were supposed to attend to the public interest, and the rest of the employees, who could pursue private gain. It was impossible to devise inviolate criteria for determining who should be excluded from these work partnerships. If a GMK working for a state firm needed supplies to do the job and one had to pull strings to get them, was that any different from trying to do everything for the state firm? Was it private or public interest that was served when the GMK got those supplies?

In the first years of reform, the State Office of Wages and Labor was inundated with requests to evaluate the legality and appropriateness of particular cases. Recognizing how difficult it would be to develop a legally coherent position, the Office simply refused to give opinions. It routinely directed applicants to a public memorandum published in 1976, five years before the reforms were announced (ML/2718/82.Ui–7/1982).

The normative void created by the sudden shift in the boundary between private and public led to general condemnations of corruption—the private misappropriation of public (i.e., state) property—but resulted in very few cases of actual prosecution (Szamel 1989).

The End of the Reform Period

As a result of the 1982 reforms, the "private sector of needs" was transformed into the "private sector of opportunities." With the opening of the rusted iron curtain that separated the private and state sectors and the releasing of private businesses from their traditional mold, new social groups set foot in the private sector (Szelényi and Kostello 1996). Reform, initially an attempt to avoid substantial changes in the state sector, instead inadvertently weakened the power of the Party-state. By redrawing the boundary between private and public, the 1982 reforms uncoupled the interests of company managers and the Party membership from the power interest of the Party. Worse yet, since the Party had initiated the reforms, managers and Party members could argue that in following their new interests they were also following the Party line. This paralyzed conservatives in the Party from the inside and made it impossible for them to engineer the sort of successful retrenchment that had occurred in the past.

Responding to mounting pressure from state enterprises, the leadership began trying to stimulate economic growth in 1984. It abandoned its obsession with balancing the books and allowed investment-hungry companies to expand, gambling that the country's economic difficulties were over. They weren't. In the end, large parts of those investment projects were underwritten by Western loans. In 1985, Hungary increased its hard currency debt by over 25 percent (Zloch-Christy 1987, 42–58; Obláth 1993, 202), and in subsequent years foreign debt grew rapidly.

In May 1986, a group of reform economists from various research institutes started drafting a document that outlined ideas for radical economic reform (Lengyel 1987). The document was written for consideration by the leadership (Antal et al. 1987). Published in 1987 under the title *Turning Point and Reform,* it called for fiscal restrictions, deregulation, and decentralization. It proposed the breakup of large, monopolistic companies and urged property reform that would introduce new types of enterprises. The document endorsed a larger role for private enterprise in the economy, but most of its suggestions revolved around the idea of state holdings that concentrated the shares of several companies.

Economic reform gained new impetus in 1987, partly because real wages again began to decline (KSH 1994, 109) and partly because foreign debt escalated rapidly. In many respects the country was at the same point it had been in in 1980 (Fekete 1987, 316). A report by three ministries to the Party leadership reiterated the objectives set in 1980. This time, however, the ministries proposed more radical solutions without which they feared "small-scale organizations may undergo a process of slow atrophy and exclusion from the economy" (MF/1–00107/1987, 4). The suggested changes included introducing private limited liability companies and joint ventures between state and private enterprises and liberalizing the rules regulating private investment.[31] In 1987, bank reform commenced. A two-tiered banking system was established, dividing financial services between the National Bank and newly created commercial banks (Bartlett 1995). The next year, tax reform inaugurated the general sales and income taxes.

These were the first steps in the transition to a market economy, which continued with the drafting of the new Enterprise Law. Introduced on January 1, 1989, the law created the legal framework for a market economy. Limited liability companies now could be formed by any private individual willing to put down 1 million forints (about 13,000 dollars at that time). Other new forms of business were approved and old forms were recast to conform to the requirements of a capital market so that their assets could be traded. The law also—for the first time—embraced the principle that the private and state sectors must be equal players in the economy.

The Enterprise Law was soon complemented by the Law on Economic Transformation, which specified the process by which state companies could reorganize as joint stock or limited liability companies. This kind of transformation required locating outside buyers who would purchase at least a 20 percent share in the company. The law put the entire process into the hands of the Enterprise Council, that is, into the hands of management. Managers could select the outside investors—usually another, similar company—and they were also in charge of preparing their own company valuation. The law referred to a special agency that would manage state property and oversee enterprise transformations in order to prevent managers' opportunism, but this agency was to be created at an unspecified later date. With these legal changes, the last bastions of universal state employment gave way. Top managers and high Party officials now could readily cross the increasingly blurred boundary between the socialist and private sectors.

Institutions are always resisted by some, and openly questioned by others, yet institutions tend to be durable. Institutions may withstand internal contradictions, even serious challenges as long as social groups entrusted with articulating, monitoring, and enforcing its rules are willing to sanction violations of its norms. Once those whose task is to guard the norms of the institution groups begin to defect—most importantly, party officials, party activists, managers, and intellectuals—the institution is put on a downhill slope.

CHAPTER 8

The Collapse of Communism

The year 1989, often referred to as *annum mirabilis,* brought sweeping political change to Eastern Europe, stunning Western experts and Eastern European dissidents alike. What was most astounding was how quickly the regimes gave way, one after the other. The secret was suddenly revealed. Their seeming strength and normalcy was a facade mounted on supports both hollow and brittle. Yet the countries of Eastern Europe neither toppled the same way nor fell independently. Some regimes collapsed peacefully, as the old leadership negotiated its way out, surrendering power voluntarily, if reluctantly. Other regimes resisted, with their leaders clinging to their positions until they were dislodged by mass demonstrations or, in the case of Romania, by armed insurrection. Significantly, the two countries with "negotiated revolutions" (Bruszt 1990)—Poland and Hungary—were the first dominoes to fall. The relative peacefulness of the power shifts in these two states, along with the Soviet Union's declared unwillingness to intervene, encouraged mass protest elsewhere and signaled to East German, Czechoslovak, Bulgarian, and Romanian leaders that they were in deep trouble. Thus, negotiated revolutions did not happen because successful insurrections in other countries scared elites into voluntary submission. Instead, insurrections in some countries succeeded partially because leaders in Poland and Hungary had already begun making fundamental concessions.[1] Negotiations started the bandwagon rolling. This raises two questions: why were elites willing to yield power in Poland and Hungary, and why were the other countries so quick to follow?

The answer I propose, and demonstrate in the Hungarian case, is that, although all Eastern European countries had suffered from serious economic problems that undermined their system of universal state employment, only Hungary and Poland had developed a private sector, which provided an easy exit for the political elite.[2] In these two countries, the private sector had not been squeezed to the margins of the economy. Instead, it was allowed—sometimes even encouraged—to grow beyond the traditional, individual, or family-style organization. Thus, the private sector in Hungary and Poland was well positioned to make inroads into the once exclusive domain of the socialist sector. This made it easier and more lucrative for elite groups to convert their assets for use in the private economy and at the same time made the boundary between private and public increasingly less distinct.

In the other countries, where the private sector did not develop to the same extent, elites had no easy way out. With the erosion of the system of universal state employment, they lost their economic grip on the population and had to resort to force to preserve their power. Yet escalating the use of force beyond a certain point without military support from the Soviet Union, and in the face of almost certain international ostracism, was a gamble only Romanian leader Nicolae Ceauşescu was willing to take.

In previous chapters I have demonstrated how Hungary's private sector grew, attracting new and more dominant social groups in the process. The presence of these highly skilled industrial workers, professionals, and Party members ensured the irreversibility of private-sector reforms. The final phase of the collapse did not begin, however, until top managers and the *nomenklatura* decided to abandon the socialist sector and reinvent themselves as private entrepreneurs.

The Dissolution of the Party

By 1989, the leadership was in disarray. Kádár had been eased out of his all-powerful position as general secretary in May 1988. Károly Grósz took his place. Beginning in January, heated public debates erupted over the legacy of the 1956 revolution, pitting one Party leader against another. The debate quickly widened, dragging into question the most fundamental principles of Communist rule. The original guiding vision of history was now fully eclipsed. One Politburo member, entrusted with canvassing the opinions of the rank and file on political reforms, reported on March 29 that the membership, especially highly skilled workers and the technical intelligentsia, strongly supported reform (S. Kosztricz et al. 1993, 629–30). Such change would entail both political and economic decentralization because

> Today there is an almost unanimous agreement in the sciences investigating economic and social organizations that the star of hierarchically built, strongly centralized organizations is waning. The future belongs to those enterprises and organizations that are also able to operate a network of smaller units of great autonomy and responsibility. (631)

This new vision, in which small was beautiful, raised an uncomfortable question: what role, if any, could the Party play in the future? Opinion was divided sharply over whether the Party should share its power with other political forces. Some thought it was desirable, some argued that it was impermissible, and others maintained that, desirable or not, it was inevitable. The leadership, resembling nothing so much as a group of feuding generals, began to notice that its troops had silently defected. Universal state employment, the system of organized dependence through which society had been regimented for three decades, had lost its commanding strength. Now the private sector was open to everyone, with state jobs functioning merely as a safety net. Even people highly placed in the power hierarchy no longer felt that their careers and well-being depended on the socialist system.

By 1989, the private sector included some members of the *nomenklatura.* Data from a survey taken in 1993 of a representative sample of those who belonged to the Hungarian *nomenklatura* in 1988 confirm this movement (Social Stratification Survey 1993, 1988 Elite Sample, SSS–1993/1988ES).[3] Among this sample, 8.5 percent reported having been involved in the private sector during 1988. For managers of large companies still under central control, this figure was twice as large (see table 8.1).

At a Central Committee meeting held in April, one speaker lashed out at his comrades for their willful disregard for the disintegration of the Party, warning them that

> the experiences of recent days have proven to me that there is a strange illusion among high officials—both within and outside the Party apparatus—as if the HSWP is dancing its "*danse macabre,*" but their situation remains untouched. As if this already had no consequence whatsoever as far as their personal existence or jobs are concerned. (S. Kosztricz et al. 1993, 828)

TABLE 8.1. *Nomenklatura* Participation in the Private Sector in 1988

	Nomenklatura Company Managers	*Nomenklatura* without Company Managers	*Nomenklatura* (total)
Percentage participating in the private sector in 1988	17.6	7.2	8.5
N	102	710	812

Source: Social Stratification Survey 1993, 1988 Elite Sample.
Note: $\chi^2 = 12.56$, $df = 1$.

This impassioned indictment fell on deaf ears. At the same meeting, the Central Committee accepted a resolution abolishing the *nomenklatura* system. The Party had ceded its right to select most company managers in 1985; now it relinquished its power to handpick or even veto managers of those last strategic companies as well. The Party also surrendered its prerogative to appoint the leaders of social, cultural, and political organizations. The laconic explanation prefacing the resolution merely noted that: "Changes in society and in political life made it necessary for the Party to modify the practice of its authority in cadre selection" (S. Kosztricz et al. 1993, 902). This meeting also decided to follow Poland's example and initiate roundtable negotiations with dissident political groups.

Spontaneous Privatization

Abolishing the *nomenklatura* system cut the last strings tying managers to the state, but as owner the state still had certain legal rights over its companies. Most importantly, any major change in a state-owned company, such as starting a new venture or getting rid of unprofitable operations, required prior approval by the proper state agency. Plant closures were an especially thorny issue. The potential political and economic costs of laying off workers made the state bureaucracy reluctant to close down any plant. This reluctance was understandable: it was the large industrial enterprises with strong Party organizations and huge annual losses that were most often targeted for closure. Moreover, in the distorted world of socialist prices, many unprofitable operations were actually fulfilling vital needs in the economy. Closing them down would have resulted in shortages and the demise of other companies.

Under these circumstances, company managers had to find a way to reorganize their enterprises without ownership title and in the absence of a capital market. The Enterprise Law and the Law on Economic Transformation were intended to address this problem. Enterprise managers, however, had found their own solution by the time the laws were enacted.

The pioneer was Medicor, a manufacturer of medical instruments. The company was in trouble owing to large debts that it had accumulated in the mid-1980s (*HVG,* April 16, 1988; *HVG,* October 22,1988). In 1987, well before the new laws were proposed, using an obscure 1875 law still in effect, company managers transformed various divisions of the enterprise into separate joint stock companies. Medicor's plant manufacturing X-ray machines, its factory that constructed hydraulic hospital beds, its research and development department, its service division and marketing division, and five other units became 10 independent companies, all owned by Medicor. The latter became only a holding company, managing the shares of its 10 offspring and engaging in no production of any kind. Medicor was replaced with 10 new companies and an empty shell, Medicor Holding Company, which had just a few offices and a couple of dozen employees. The top managers divided the 10 companies among themselves. The few who stayed with the holding company were given well-paying positions on the boards of directors of the new companies. Probably the most important part of the maneuver was the division of assets and liabilities. As a selfless parent, Medicor kept all debts. The descendant companies thus started with clean slates.

During the creation of the new companies some shares were sold to other state firms, mainly Medicor's suppliers, buyers, and lenders, but they held only a minority interest in the newly formed enterprises. As the shares were not traded, Medicor could pick and choose its partners. Later, as other companies undertook similar reorganization schemes, Medicor bought their shares and, in exchange, those newly spawned companies bought shares in Medicor. The exchange of shares created a bewildering complexity of cross-ownership patterns (Stark 1990, 1996; Böröcz 1993), further loosening the ties between the ultimate owner—the state bureaucracy—and enterprise directors. In 1988, the year before the new laws went into effect, at least 15 other large companies began to follow in Medicor's footsteps. Many were among the 50 or so large enterprises that had enjoyed special treatment since the early 1970s.[4]

With the introduction of the Law on Economic Transformation and the Enterprise Law in January and June of 1989, respectively, managers began to take full advantage of their powerful positions, moving their companies out of the socialist and into the private sector—and securing ownership for themselves in the process. ÁPISZ, the largest office supplies chain and the holder of a virtual monopoly on school supplies and office products, created one of the most public scandals (*HVG,* September 9, 1989; *HVG,* October 12, 1989). ÁPISZ was very successful, earning a net profit equivalent to 37 percent of the value of its assets in 1988. In April 1989, the firm's managers, with some outside help, established a joint stock company with start-up capital of 40 million forints. The three top managers of ÁPISZ bought a small share in the new company. As the next step, the property of the state firm, mostly inventory and real estate (worth 700 million forints) was transferred to the newly established joint stock company. The state firm was given shares in exchange. A third of these shares were bought by Citibank Budapest and another part by an Austrian firm. The new company then issued bonds with modest returns of 15 percent over a 10-year period, and offered them to ÁPISZ, which purchased them using the money it had got for the stocks. The bond money was used to run the company's operations rather than for investment. Then the owners announced that they would reduce the value of the capital stock to 100 million by repaying shareholders most of their money. Now the newly formed company had a small capital stock in shares and a large inexpensive loan in the form of bonds, courtesy of ÁPISZ. For an expenditure of 100 million forints, the owners came to hold property worth 700 million. At the end of the day, the bank, the Austrian firm, and the managers had roughly a third of the chain and ÁPISZ was left with only a very small share. The new owners had acquired a successful retail chain by using very little money of their own, borrowing from the seller, ÁPISZ, at a cheap rate. Because of the uproar in the media, however, the ÁPISZ deal eventually was reversed.

Managers finagling their companies into the private sector faced risks other than touching off public scandals. The Dél-Budai Vendéglátóipari Vállalat (DBVV), a company operating restaurants, bars, and small hotels on the southwest side of the capital, tried to replicate ÁPISZ's success while avoiding public indignation and government intervention. On the last day of November 1989, DBVV created a joint stock company called Budavár, with the participation of three other firms, two of which, Technomark and Zoto, belonged to an Austrian citizen. The top management of DBVV contributed 100 of its hospitality establishments, including many elegant and well-known restaurants, to the new company. Eighty of these units were brought into the deal for free. Thus, property and rental rights worth over 2.5 billion forints were transferred at a value of 250 million. DBVV retained 50 percent of the shares, enough to control Budavár; the remaining shares were deliberately sold to the outside investors in order to make it difficult for the state to reverse the deal without trespassing on private property. By contributing another 250 million forints, the outside owners acquired the other half of the 2.5 billion forints' worth of property. The director of DBVV assumed the directorship of Budavár and thought he was safely outside the reach of the state. And so he would have been but for two fatal mistakes.

The director's first mistake was that he gave a commercial credit of 250 million forints to Technomark. His second mistake was to exchange a large portion of DBVV's stocks for bonds, as the top management at ÁPISZ had done. The bonds carried no voting rights, though they did promise a high yield. The stocks DBVV gave up went to Technomark. When Technomark was slow to repay its debt, the director of Budavár decided to go to court to recover the value of the credit. Now however, Technomark, in conjunction with Zoto, possessed the necessary number of voting shares to fire the litigious director, and so they did. The state eventually became involved because of the fury of the local managers of the restaurants included in DBVV's deal. The spontaneous privatization designed to benefit the top managers of DBVV had preempted the local managers' right to buy from the state the diners, bars, and inns they had been running for many years. Their anger propelled the government into action, but, as DBVV had foreseen, this time it was impossible to reverse the scheme (*HVG,* July 27, 1990; Parliament, July 3, 1990, 1252–55; *HVG,* September 1, 1990).

Both ÁPISZ and DBVV had been successful state enterprises. Their managers' actions were motivated primarily by the desire to reap private benefits from their companies. More frequently, however, managers were spurred into similar sweeping reorganizations by the threat of bankruptcy, as happened in the Medicor case.[5]

The Party Enters into Spontaneous Privatization

The public outrage prompted by the spontaneous privatization of firms like ÁPISZ and DBVV paled in comparison with the outcry that followed the top Party bureaucracy's entry into the privatization process. The first to move state property into the direct ownership of a political organization were clever bureaucrats from the Party's youth organization, the Communist Youth League. Beginning in the fall of 1988, the league laid claim to several pieces of real estate that housed offices and training centers. Responding to this news, a member of Parliament proposed legislation to prevent such actions. Despite considerable resistance, he managed to push through legislation prohibiting social organizations from taking possession of real property belonging to the state. The law was passed in early June 1989, effective July 1.

On June 23, the Central Committee of the Hungarian Socialist Workers' Party created a limited liability company named Next 2000 to hold onto 30 pieces of valuable real estate—Party hotels, school buildings, and garages (*Népszabadság,* August 29, 1989; *Magyar Nemzet,* August 31, 1989; *HVG,* September 2, 1989). Circumstances worked against the Party, but had their plan succeeded over a billion forints' worth of real estate would have become the private property of the Party's Central Committee, and the top Party leadership would have presided over a company that ran hotels, restaurants, and conference centers. Within days of the creation of Next 2000, local Party organizations followed suit. The transactions were perfectly legal because they took place before the new law went into effect. The emerging political opposition, intent on preventing the Party from turning itself into a business empire by appropriating state property, had to dig out a paragraph of the Civil Code on "abuse of rights" in order to mount an effective attack on the Party's forays into privatization (*168 óra,* September 26, 1989). The Party's response was an assertion of its right to do whatever it pleased with property bought with the membership dues it had collected over the years. The Ministry of Finance soon revealed, however, that the vast majority of the funds the Party had used to develop its property came not from members' pockets but from the state budget.[6] In the end, Next 2000 was prohibited from receiving the real estate because the registry court found some technical errors in the application. This forced the Party to resubmit the paperwork, and by that time the new law was in effect. The Next 2000 debacle did not, however, shut the door on enterprising cadres. The law prohibited direct transfer of property from the state to the Party, but the Party could form state companies for meeting its own needs, providing such services as printing, catering, and holiday lodging. These companies were permitted to establish other companies, just as ÁPISZ and Medicor did, in effect serving as an intermediate step in the process of laundering state property. By October the Party had eight newly founded enterprises.[7]

The Party's feverish efforts to secure its own property were an unambiguous signal that its leaders were preparing for life after communism. The fact that the once omnipotent Communist Party was unable to assert legal ownership over the property involved in the Next 2000 scandal revealed how weak the HSWP had become.

The Roundtable Negotiations

The Party's machinations would likely have gone unnoticed had it not been for the newly organized political opposition and the increasingly independent press. From the spring of 1989 on, dissident political organizations had been pressuring the Communist leadership for organized dialogue. Originally interested only in discussing the details of radical political reform, the dissidents insisted on excluding economic issues from the negotiations. Following developments in Poland, the HSWP maintained that economic matters must be part of the dialogue, hoping to implicate the opposition in future austerity measures (which both sides knew to be inevitable). The opposition was eager to avoid taking responsibility for the fiascoes of the socialist economy, but at the same time it viewed privatization with increasing alarm. Many opposition leaders feared that the Party, and individual Party members, would gain private property rights over a large or strategic segment of the economy and would be able to marshal formidable economic power even after being ousted from political office. Economic issues thus were strongly tied to political ones, and it was impossible to ignore the former and attend only to the latter.

After much haggling, the roundtable negotiations began on June 13, 1989, nine days after the Polish Communist Party suffered a crushing defeat in legislative elections. Iván Pető, an economic historian and one of the leaders of the newly formed liberal party, the Alliance of Free Democrats, gave a speech in which he carefully disavowed any responsibility on the opposition's part for the future consequences of the economic crisis. He painstakingly reiterated the reason for the opposition's decision to discuss economic issues, namely, its alarm over the Law on Economic Transformation, which allowed the Communist leadership to distribute rights over state property gratis. This threatened to cast in stone existing monopolies and unhealthy linkages among companies, thus preventing the development of a real capital market. The law, Pető argued, "gave an opportunity to transform positions attained for largely political reasons into economic power" (Richter 1990, 308).

The opposition was not, however, unanimous in their negative reaction to spontaneous and *nomenklatura* privatization. Some economic experts in the opposition argued that spontaneous privatization was not wholly bad. After all, it was happening without direct state intervention, while all alternative options would have involved returning control to the state apparatus. Spontaneous privatization occurred as a result of the weakness of the state, and it made the state weaker still. It was this ebbing of its power that had brought the state to the bargaining table. Any measure that strengthened the state would put the negotiations in jeopardy. Moreover, for the opposition, a weak state was not just a temporary political convenience but a long-term, ideological goal. It envisioned the society of the future as one with a minimalist state.

Spontaneous privatization was also beneficial to the extent that it broke up giant, monopolistic companies into smaller ones and thus stimulated competition. Four decades of overconcentration were now being rectified. The economy was moving away from swollen giants to nimble small and midsized firms.[8] Moreover, spontaneous privatization brought in outside capital (Matolcsy 1989). Managers usually sought a Western investor in order to gain access to new capital and take advantage of the tax exemptions granted to joint ventures. A foreign partner also ensured that privatization would be irreversible. The leadership, keen on attracting and pleasing foreign investors, could not afford to offend these financiers by renationalizing the companies in which they had shares. The number of joint ventures increased sixfold in 1989 (Pichler 1994).[9]

Márton Tardos, one of the chief economic experts of the Alliance of Free Democrats, and a long-time advocate of economic reforms, argued that spontaneous privatization was the lesser of two evils. There was no good way to privatize, and any state bureaucracy would have done a worse job. Oddly enough, on this particular point the experts of the liberal opposition took a somewhat more permissive approach than did the HSWP itself. The latter suggested setting up a state property fund, which would administer, but not control, privatization. The representative of the HSWP added a political reason for not interfering too much with the process. He pointed out that a hands-off approach was the only way to secure the cooperation of company managers. The rest of the opposition disagreed and loudly demanded strong measures to stop spontaneous privatization, though they were divided over how best to achieve this goal (Szalai 1994, 44–53).

The events of the second half of 1989 completed the political disintegration of the Party. At its extraordinary Fourteenth Congress in October, the HSWP split into two groups. The reformists, who by now controlled most of the state apparatus, founded the Hungarian Socialist Party (HSP), deliberately dropping the word *workers,* while hard-liners formed another party under the old name. The majority of Party members deserted, and less than 80,000 of the original 765,000 members bothered to re-enroll in one of the two successor parties. Those who did re-enroll most often chose the HSP. A nationwide referendum in late November further humiliated the political leadership. People voted in favor of ousting Communist Party organizations from the workplace, disbanding the Party militia, engaging in a public reckoning with respect to all property controlled by the Party, and postponing presidential elections until after the parliamentary elections scheduled for March.[10] With the exit of workplace Party organizations, the linchpin of universal state employment was pulled.

As one of its final measures before the spring elections, the government passed legislation to create a State Property Agency as of March 1, 1990, leaving it to the next legislature to determine what exactly this new agency should do. By this time about 100 firms had transformed themselves into joint stock or limited liability companies (Kocsis 1992). The value of state property brought into these newly spawned companies was estimated to be around 110 billion forints, or about 6 percent of the estimated pool (*Privinfo* 2/16, 4).[11]

The two rounds of the legislative elections on March 26 and April 8 brought humiliating defeat for both successors of the Communist Party. The Hungarian Socialist Party garnered less than 9 percent of the legislative seats. The hard-line Hungarian Socialist Workers' Party failed to get any. Six parties gained representation. The winner of the elections was the Hungarian Democratic Forum, followed by the Alliance of Free Democrats, the Independent Small Holders' Party, the Hungarian Socialist Party, and, tying for last place, the Alliance of Young Democrats and the Christian Democratic People's Party. All six parties, including the Socialists, endorsed a greater role for the private sector in the economy.

The Dynamics of the Collapse

Observers of the collapse of communism in Eastern Europe typically have focused on one of two processes as precipitating the fall. Earlier works paid attention to the "silent revolution from below," the "revolt of civil society," and the development of a "second society," that is, processes involving the social structure of state socialism. Later works concentrated on the role of internal decay at the top, the development of corrupt and weak elites that had lost their will to rule. My own explanation, developed in this and earlier chapters, seeks to link the two processes.

Several students of Eastern European state socialism have noted the rise of a civil society opposed to the almighty Communist state. Impressed by the experience of the Solidarity movement, which emerged in 1980 as the political representative of Polish "civil society," scholars built various theories about the erosion of socialist rule from below. Civil society was seen as the realm of freedom, an arena of natural and organic social life that stood in contradistinction to the oppressive, artificial, and externally imposed state. The definition of civil society encompassed the private economy, political dissent, alternative culture, family life, friendship, even religion and the church (Arato 1981; Keane 1988; Hankiss 1988; Skilling 1988; Hann 1990; Frentzel-Zagórska 1990; Rau 1991; Hirst 1991). The concept of civil society proved to be important for two reasons: it provided a general framework for describing symptoms of the disintegration of state socialism and it made it possible to articulate a leftist-liberal political agenda. On the other hand, the concept was weakened by its exclusive focus on the conflict between civil society and the state. The very real internal conflicts and differentiation that characterized civil society—and the state itself—were ignored. Political dissent, for instance, was diverse. Some opposed the regime on the basis of leftist syndicalism, others wished to replace communism with a conservative nationalist regime, and still others proposed a new system built on the principles of Western European liberalism. These differences got full play after the collapse. The different elements of civil society also contradicted one another. While both political self-organization and private entrepreneurship were rooted in liberal ideals, in reality private entrepreneurs did not show much interest in overtly political action. In fact, they tried to keep a low political profile (Manchin 1988). The civil society approach overemphasized the coercive elements in the rule of the Party-state. The state was more than simply the machinations of a clique of cadres backed by strong police and military forces. Through universal state employment, Communist regimes were able to co-opt civil society, even though the power of state employment to sustain the socialist order was declining all over Eastern Europe.

Szelényi proposed that Hungary was undergoing a "silent revolution" (1988). As socialist large-scale production faltered in many sections of the economy, petty commodity production was reemerging, continuing a long-term historical trend of commercialization that had been interrupted by the socialist experiment. Exploring small-scale private farming, Szelényi demonstrated that some 30 years after communism set out to eradicate the private sector, private entrepreneurship had reemerged among part-time household farmers in the Hungarian countryside. These agricultural entrepreneurs were often carrying on a family tradition of small private production, returning to the embourgeoisement trajectory of their parents.

Yet, if the history of the Hungarian private sector under socialism began as a "revolution from below," it ended as a "revolution from above." From 1982 on, the hermetic seal between the state and the private sector began to loosen. The elite of the socialist sector started defecting to the private sector, often without giving up their state employment. Thus, this group was able to combine the advantages of both sectors.

Since 1989, a large literature has developed regarding the role of communist elites in the collapse of communism. Some observers emphasize the importance of "moral rot" and loss of self-confidence, contending that revolutions become inescapable once elites lose their sense of mission (Chirot 1991, 9; Kornai 1992b, 563; Przeworski 1991, 6).

Elemér Hankiss suggests that by the end of the 1980s, after a long and gradual erosion of the political elite's power, a "grand coalition" formed in Hungary (1990, 240–65). This coalition consisted of four social groups: the younger members of the Party elite, technocrats in the state bureaucracy, enterprise managers, and successful private entrepreneurs. According to Hankiss, these groups were strongly linked by informal ties, and people could move easily from one group to another. Communism folded in Hungary peacefully, Hankiss argues, because the old elite realized it could convert its political power into advantages in a market economy based on private ownership.[12]

Murrell and Olson propose that the decay of Communism was the result of increasing collusion among high- and middle-level bureaucrats and enterprise managers (1991). Socialist economies were successful initially because, even though they had eliminated market competition, they had replaced it with bureaucratic competition. Drawing on Olson's earlier work, which claimed that in stable environments collusive type activities increase over time (1982), the authors argue that bureaucratic competition abated as time passed. Managers, overcoming the difficulties of collective action, joined together to promote their own partial interests at the expense of the common good. This resulted in poor information flow from bottom to the top, the leadership's loss of control, and, finally, economic slowdown and crisis.

The weakest link in Murrell and Olson's argument is their assertions that classical state socialism can be characterized by bureaucratic competition and that bureaucratic competition was responsible for the early successes of socialist industrialization. Even if one accepts that state socialism had early economic successes, there is little evidence that bureaucratic competition existed in that initial period or, if it did, that it was a major force in these accomplishments. The absence of collusion among enterprise directors in the early years did not result in better information flow.[13] Managers were intimidated and unable to organize, but distorting information did not necessarily require much cooperation among them. *All* managers were interested in reporting the best possible results, hiding resources, hoarding labor, and cooking their books. Documents show that the leadership had much less and more distorted information about the economy in the early phase of Hungarian communism than they had later and that the leaders were aware of this problem. They were able to accomplish what they did because they focused on a few projects at the expense of everything else, including the common good. Moreover, they had resources—most importantly labor, capital goods plundered from their owners, and natural resources—that they could exploit and abuse.

The histories of Eastern European countries show that economic slowdown was not the result of collusion. Instead, slowdowns enhanced opportunities for reform. These changes, in turn, often increased the autonomy of managers. As I have demonstrated, autonomy was granted precisely because the center was overwhelmed and incapacitated by the complexity of its tasks. Managers then used their newly gained autonomy to collude. It is here that Olson and Murrell's theory is most useful: it draws attention to the center's gradual loss of economic control and the growing power of managers.

Nee and Lian offer a formal model of how opportunism slowly devoured the power of the Communist Party (1994). Unlike Olson and Murrell, they do not believe that the erosion of Communist power caused economic decline. They argue that the causes of the decline were exogenous: a shift from large-scale manufacturing toward flexible specialization and craft production (Piore and Sabel 1984; Hirst and Zeitlin 1991) made communist states lose their global competitiveness. Thus, economic reforms became necessary—specifically, the introduction of market elements into a redistributive, bureaucratic economy. For such a reform to succeed, the leadership had to reduce the cost of transacting across the borders of the redistributive (state) and marketized (private) sectors. The lowered cost of crossing this border created opportunities not only for the citizens at large but for cadres as well, as they were now free to combine the advantages of the two sectors.

Now the Party began to unravel in earnest. The first few defectors were followed by a steady stream of new ones. With each defection the Party became weaker and less able to monitor and sanction new defectors. It was caught in a downward spiral that was both self-reinforcing and constantly accelerating. Nee and Lian's model captures the basic dynamics I have outlined in previous chapters. Once cadres began to defect to the private economy, the state became less and less able to retreat from reform. The presence of a positive feedback loop "locked in" the private sector (Arthur 1990). Spontaneous and *nomenklatura* privatization were the final steps in a process begun in the early 1980s.

This model is not fully satisfactory, however. It cannot explain why communism survived in China—a country with a strong market economy—and fell in other places, like the Soviet Union, where the market was weak. Nee and Lian counter this objection by pointing out, first, that in the Soviet Union political reform proceeded too quickly, further undermining the Party's monitoring and sanctioning capacity; and, second, that reform brought no real improvement in economic performance. The first part of this explanation ignores countries such as Bulgaria, Czechoslovakia, and Romania, where no political and few economic reforms occurred and yet the Party-state still collapsed. The second part suggests that had these countries been more successful economically in the 1980s they would still be run by their communist parties, as in China. I concur that the economic failures of these countries account for their political demise. But what causal role then remains for the dynamics of cadre defections in the Communist collapse?

I propose that the collapse in Eastern Europe occurred because of the prolonged commitment, despite growing signs of crisis, to an economic model that sought to construct the entire economy on the principle of large-scale production. The crisis engendered by the ultimate failure of that model created the disintegration of state employment in all of these countries and the development of an autonomous private sector. Although in most countries this private sector remained small, traditional, and weak, it was nevertheless strong enough to challenge the social order built on state employment.[14] The quickness of the collapse of Eastern European state socialism was due to the tensions that accumulated as a result of adhering to a late nineteenth-century modernistic vision long outdated. As Chirot suggested, communism had produced the most advanced late-nineteenth-century economies in Eastern and Central Europe by the 1960s (1991, 5–6). Eastern European communism's success was its undoing. China has never been as successful in realizing this model as the European communist countries were, so concentration has never succeeded as much and state employment has never attained as pervasive a role as it did elsewhere. China has always had a more decentralized economy and its own Small Transformation has created less of a shock to its social and political order. Much of its current spectacular economic growth is due to the gain in productivity that results from the shift from agriculture to industry, a gain European state socialist countries had already pocketed by the 1960s as a result of their Great Transformation. China's inability to carry through its own Great Transformation may have given the country the opportunity to develop a new model of industrialization.

In countries such as Hungary and Poland, where economic reforms fostered the limited development of the private sector, a self-reinforcing cycle of elite defections began.[15] Elites give up power voluntarily when the means by which they exercise their power—in this case the institution of universal state employment—have eroded, when elite members no longer have their ideological convictions, and when they have reasons to expect that individually they will not lose, and may even gain, in case they have to step down. Their participation in the private sector persuaded key segments of the Hungarian and Polish communist elites that they had a promising future after communism.

The private sector existed in every state socialist economy. Universal state employment was crumbling everywhere. But only Hungary and Poland gave opportunities to members of their communist elites to participate in legal private enterprise. In other communist countries, if elite members became involved in private business at all, their pursuits were either outright criminal or skirted legality, but more importantly, their ability to engage in private enterprise directly depended on their continued membership in the political elite.

If Hungarian and Polish elites were disinclined to fight for the survival of a system they had already chosen to leave behind, other private-sector participants were similarly interested in a safe and orderly exit from communism (Sik 1994). Ordinary people who had already embarked on some form of private enterprise did not wish to see the fruits of their earlier efforts erased by revolutionary upheavals. Thus, in these countries the farewell to communism happened early and it was a negotiated and peaceful process. The dynamism Nee and Lian account for is not the collapse of communism but the way communism fell.

The unraveling of the Party and the development of a strong private sector had important consequences for the subsequent course of privatization and the postcommunist economic transformation. The social groups that came to dominate the private sector after 1990 were formed by these two processes.

CHAPTER 9

The Private Sector Unbound

Introduction

With the fall of Communist rule in Hungary, the stage was set for sweeping institutional reforms designed to usher in a new economic order. Although these changes were less wrenching than the ones that had preceded the imposition of state socialism, they necessarily upset the stability of everyday life by dismantling the core institutions of state socialism. Just as in the early days of socialism, sweeping changes required a strong ideological framework with a compelling vision of an imagined future. Once again, ideology set the agenda for building a strong private sector, undoing the effects of the Great Transformation and finishing the work of the Small.

The Ideology of the Small Transformation

The ideology that framed the early years of postcommunism, and lingers today, is a neoliberal one. It was developed in contrast to Marxism-Leninism, and much of its coherence and focus has stemmed from its attempts to engage and refute that ideology. Internally this new vision has proven much less uniform, consistent, and comprehensive than its predecessor. Despite these internal divisions, it has withstood challenges from an array of different ideologies and remains the compass for elite actions. The new vision was founded on a strong rejection of Marxism-Leninism, but it shares ironic similarities with its loathed predecessor. Just as communist ideology saw socialism as a transition between failed capitalism and unblemished communism, so neoliberalism views postcommunism as a transition between two historical stages. Failed state socialism and its practices must be extirpated. As that happens, society will move ever closer to a highly efficient free market delivering material prosperity to all and to a highly democratic free polity offering both justice and human rights. Much as with the transition to a communist utopia, the transition to a market economy and democracy includes a pronounced historical vision. It supplies a conception of the future, so necessary in times of rapid social change.

In Hungary the neoliberal vision of history developed during the last decade of state socialism. It argued for the existence of a readily discernible trajectory of embourgeoisement, one that the nations of Western Europe have been following for many centuries. Among the many clear markers of this trend are the separation of state and church, the balance between state and society, the presence of free towns, the contractual nature of social relations, a culture of individualism, and protection of local autonomy, privacy, and private property.[1] Hungary, the argument continued, has struggled to keep to this trajectory, but a series of historical accidents repeatedly has diverted the country from this path. Central Europe, that is, Poland, Hungary, Czechoslovakia, and the western parts of Yugoslavia, has gained its particular character by being suspended between this Western model and an Eastern European one, represented by Russia and the Balkans, where such institutions never developed (Garton Ash 1989, 179–213). Thus, incomplete embourgeoisement at once represents the curse, the challenge, and the future hope of Central European societies (Szelényi 1988; Gerő 1993; Gyurgyák 1991; Kovách 1991).

Although in its original form the incomplete embourgeoisement thesis made no historical predictions, it did offer a picture of a future deemed both desirable and possible. In fact, it suggested two contending visions. The first, resting on sounder principles, was rejected; the second, built on weak reasoning, was embraced. Advocates of the first vision contended that the incompleteness of embourgeoisement created a qualitatively new kind of society, one that neither could nor should imitate the Western model. Each Western nation had its own path of development: Italy, England, Spain, and Holland all evolved differently, uniquely shaped by the legacies of their individual histories. By definition, the diversity of development in the West precluded the imitation of a single Western model. Moreover, proponents of the first vision cautioned, institutions enabling countries to attain economic prosperity and power should not be confused with institutions that had resulted from and sustained such wealth and might. Thus, even if a single Western model did exist, copying contemporary institutions would be a mistake. Postcommunist countries should chart their own way, just as every other nation had done. This new road would not be either Western capitalism or Eastern state socialism. It would be what its advocates called the Third Way, a road as yet untraveled.

Today there are few people who would disagree that five years after the end of communism, Eastern and Central Europe are quite different from the western part of the continent. Nor would many people deny that these countries wander on previously uncharted territory, that they are de facto on a Third Way—or rather on several Third Ways. Why, then, was the ideological appeal of the Third Way so limited? Why did it never become the guiding vision of the postcommunist transformation?

The principal failing of Third Way ideology was that its vision of the future was too fragile to sustain the burden of underpinning radical institutional change. When a version of this ideology was first proposed in Hungary, in the 1930s, the future it depicted was "Garden Hungary," a developed country of smallholding farmers, bypassing industrialization. In the short period after 1945 and before the Communists took complete control, the Third Way stood for a future that encompassed neither capitalist individualism nor socialist collectivism (Bibó [1945] 1982). Its supporters were more committed to a particular ethical stance than to a clear vision of the future. More recent advocates of the Third Way similarly failed to deliver a compelling historical vista. Some offered muddled rhetoric, others cautious suggestions laced with historical contingency and uncertainty.[2] It was an approach doomed to failure. Broad institutional change requires a strong ideology tied to a specific vision of the future.

The ideology that won out against the Third Way argued for following the Western model. Here the future had to be asserted, but it did not need to be argued at great length, since anyone could experience it simply by taking a trip to Austria, West Germany, or Switzerland. The problematic nature of the premise of a single Western model was conveniently ignored by this largely ostensive argument. Focusing on current structural similarities in the most successful countries in Western Europe allowed advocates of this ideology to overlook or dismiss completely the experiences of countries like Portugal, Greece, and Ireland. Similarly, considering Western Europe as the natural historical trajectory permitted them to exclude from the discussion lessons from the economies of the successful newly industrialized countries of Southeast Asia and to discount as irrelevant cautionary tales from Latin America.

The chief protagonist of this embourgeoisement trajectory was the urban burgher or *polgár* (the Hungarian term means both citizen and bourgeois). The *polgár* was the attractive cousin of the repulsive petty bourgeois, or *kispolgár* (petty *polgár*), vilified in the 1960s and 1970s. The *polgár* was acquisitive but with taste and moderation. Not at all the kind of citizen portrayed in Manage the Smart Way! (whose life revolved around acquiring the next consumer durable), the *polgár* considered material comfort as a means not an end. He valued his privacy, but, far from being bound up in misanthropic egotism, he was a family man and a loyal friend. Neat and clean, punctual, polite, he was a man of his word. He was independent minded but considerate of others. He was courageous but tolerant, competent in his narrow specialty but broadly conversant with the ideas of Western European high culture (Szelényi 1988; Konrád 1993).

Like the hero of the "second economy," he was given to rational calculation but was also law abiding. He was an entrepreneur and a democrat. The figure of the *polgár* thus reconciled rationality and morality, acquisitiveness and culture, market and democracy, making him an icon acceptable to intellectuals and entrepreneurs as well as to ordinary folk and to most of the Party faithful.[3] The *polgár* seemed like a real entity rather than an ideal type because in countries like Denmark, West Germany, and Britain this kind of person existed and provided the foundation for a prosperous democracy.[4]

Thus conceived, the *polgár* more closely resembled the members of the comfortable middle class of the West than its hustling entrepreneurs or obnoxious *noveaux riches*. Nevertheless, there was general agreement that private entrepreneurial activities fostered the *polgár*'s many good qualities.[5] Others argued that without a private sector the *polgár* would remain hopelessly dependent on the state. The characteristic *polgár* mentality cannot develop under the paternalism of universal state employment.

But it was not just the existence of the friendly *polgár* that made the transition to a market economy based on private property seem the best choice. The fiasco of state socialism and the failures of experiments with market socialism had convinced many that the market has no historical alternative and that private property is a precondition of a well-functioning market (Kornai 1992a). Moreover, the example of Western countries was also convincing. In addition to having built their economies around private property, these countries—especially Britain and France—had also launched privatization programs to curtail the state sector.

The Post-Communist Dilemmas of Privatization

All political parties supported privatization as the primary means of expanding the private sector. This choice, however, was not the only way to strengthen the role of the private sector. In theory, at least, another alternative was to elevate existing or newly born private enterprises to a level where they could compete as equals with state companies. As private companies drove state enterprises out of business, the private sector would expand and the state sector would shrink. But, to create a level playing field, the state would have had to provide fledgling private firms with low taxes and easily available business loans. It also would have had to reduce the cost of doing business by improving the infrastructure. Most importantly, it would have had to take draconian measures to force state companies to play by market rules.

This alternative scenario was never seriously entertained. Some leaders were apprehensive about the political consequences of not destroying the state sector, not driving a stake through the heart of Communist rule. Others feared that the private companies that would be best able to compete with state enterprises would be foreign-owned ones. Unless the country was willing to erect economic barriers to exclude foreign competition, the contest would be between foreign multinationals and Hungarian state enterprises—with the budding domestic private sector left out in the cold. Ultimately, though, what vitiated this option was the same problem that had undercut the Third Way ideology. By acknowledging uncertainty about the proper future economic role of the state, this option failed to deliver the commanding vision necessary for strategic action in times of institutional change.

If there was strong ideological consensus that privatization was the best path, it was still a road with forks, demanding further decisions. The new leadership had to decide whether state property should be treated as property belonging to the state or property belonging to its original owner, who had lost it in nationalization (which many now viewed as organized theft). Taking the second position meant advocating restitution: giving property back to its pre-Communist owners or their heirs. Restitution was a way of reaffirming the sanctity of private property. It was a means of generating confidence in the ultimate stability and reliability of the legal system as one that always eventually dispenses justice.

This logic, however, assumed that private property rights had been violated once, during nationalization, but not earlier. In Hungary, as in other socialist countries, this was scarcely true. There had been several serious violations of property rights immediately before the Communists took power. Jews were dispossessed during World War II. At the end of the war, the country was occupied first by the Germans and then by the Russians, both of whom destroyed and looted property. After the war, land reform dispossessed large landowners, violating their centuries-old property rights by distributing their holdings to hungry, landless peasants. Finally, also before the Communist takeover, ethnic minorities, Germans and Slovaks, had been shipped out of the country—as collective punishment in the first case and population exchange in the second—carrying with them only what they could squeeze into a few suitcases. Clearly, determining what "original state" of property relations constituted the proper one to be restored was difficult.

Nevertheless, given the wave of anticommunism, restitution of owners disappropriated by nationalization seemed a logical solution to right the wrongs of an evil Communist system. Yet, once the legalistic argument was framed more broadly and invoked moral principles, a new question arose: Did people who had worked to maintain state property also deserve restitution, regardless of their ownership status in the pre-Communist period? After all, they had suffered low wages to allow for more capital investment; improvements to state property were financed by money wrung from everyone. Righting this wrong would require the original owners to share the property with all those who had worked in the company and thus contributed to its capital stock. That was not all, however. In a socialist economy, where investments are centralized, the development of one company often is financed by income from others. In the one-nation-one-factory model, companies were linked much as various plants of large corporations are. Therefore, an equitable restitution program would require giving all workers a property share, at which point reprivatization would have lost its original meaning. From a legal perspective, it was not difficult to oppose such an expansion of property claims, but supporting these claims politically was hard to resist.

If, however, the state was the legal owner of state property, even if it was neither the morally nor the economically correct one, restitution was not the proper solution. Much of the existing property had been created under socialism. Many companies had not existed prior to Communist rule and thus had no original owners. The new government then had to decide whether to sell state property or give it away. Selling it had the advantage of bringing revenue into the state's coffers at a time when the government was deeply in debt. Moreover, selling companies conformed to the idea of a market economy where goods are distributed on the basis of purchasing power. Selling state property would also create real owners who, many argued, would invest in their newly bought companies and therefore would be motivated to do their best to make or keep their firms prosperous. There was, unfortunately, one insurmountable obstacle. Few individuals in Hungary could afford to buy state companies. Given the Communist regime's preoccupation with social inequalities, accumulating large fortunes had been difficult under socialism. Furthermore, the relative economic security provided by the system of universal state employment made saving as insurance against future economic misfortune unnecessary. During the 1980s, those who were active in the private sector typically chose to spend most of their income rather than save it, since there was no way to know how long the regime would keep its friendly attitude toward private entrepreneurs. If people saved, they did so mostly to buy housing or more expensive consumer durables, just as players did in Manage the Smart Way! In 1990, net household savings were only one-sixth of the official book value of all state-owned enterprises to be privatized (Mihályi 1993, 107). Moreover, the purchase price was only the first expense for the new owners, who subsequently would have to find additional resources for investment if they were to make their companies profitable.[6] Thus, the most likely buyers of state property would be foreigners. Since foreigners were showing only modest interest,[7] and even that created a barrage of political charges that the government was selling out the country and displaying a callous disregard for its citizens, sales could not be the only way to privatize.

Disposing of state property by means other than selling it would not eliminate controversy since the leadership would still need to decide how best to distribute state assets. It could give all citizens vouchers for a token sum, and then citizens could choose for themselves whether or not to turn their vouchers into ownership shares in state companies. Alternatively, the state could hand over the companies (in some form) to the people who worked in them. Or the state could select individuals who seemed the best equipped to operate the companies profitably and cede the firms to them for as long as they continued to run the companies successfully.

Concealed behind the competing versions of development plans for the private sector were diverging visions of the country's future economic system and differing ideological constructions of the private sector. Advocates of reprivatization envisioned a private sector with individual and family ownership. How nationalized joint stock companies would be reprivatized was an issue never raised. Property rights were assumed to be sacred, indivisible, and absolute. Property was construed as objects, things; property rights over intangible possessions, such as stocks, organization, copyrights, and goodwill, were largely ignored. The focus was on land and real estate—the "real" property that had in the past belonged to individuals and families.

Those who wanted to sell state property held a different view. For them property included both tangible and intangible possessions. The state was to sell companies, not simply the factory building, grounds, and machines. Preferably, ownership would be concentrated in one hand, but it did not have to be a family or an individual. Private corporations were seen as legitimate owners as well. Selling state property through a public offering of stock was also a possibility, though not a priority. The sale of state property was justified on the grounds that it would create an active owner, who, having paid for the company, would be actively involved in its operation.

Various giveaway schemes were based on yet another notion of the private sector and private property. By extending ownership to collectives of workers, to municipalities, to the social security fund, or to society in general, giveaway plans sought to create a collectivistic private sector. Here ownership and control would have been divorced.

The final course of privatization was not decided by argument, however. It was decided by politics, which in turn was shaped by the way the private sector had evolved during the Communist era. The important constituencies were already in place, steering privatization in the direction best suited to their own interests. Nor was privatization the only force driving the growth of the private sector. It played a significant role in the development of the new elite within the private sector, but it had less impact on smaller private enterprises.

Charting the Course of Privatization

Charting the course of privatization fell to the new government, formed by the Hungarian Democratic Forum (HDF) in coalition with the Independent Small Holders' Party (ISHP) and the Christian Democratic People's Party (CDPP). Prime Minister József Antall, a historian by profession, presented the political program of the new government on May 22, 1990. In a lengthy discussion of the economy, Antall promised a go-slow approach, explaining that Hungary's relatively developed economy made taking a "big jump" more dangerous. The final goal was a "strong, social market economy based on private property and private enterprise" where the less fortunate would be protected by a social safety net (Parliament, May 22, 1990, 192). Privatization was at the heart of the new government's economic program. It was to achieve two goals: a shift in the economy in favor of the private sector and a division of oversized companies into small and medium-sized firms. Antall announced that with the important exception of land, property appropriated by the Communists would not be returned to its original owners.[8] Admitting that the new government as yet had no privatization plan, he promised as a first step the rapid privatization of small shops, restaurants, bars, and local services. He hinted that the government intended a special role for employee share ownership plans. At the same time, he pledged to weaken or eliminate enterprise councils, the main guarantors of managers' autonomy, and to conduct a legal review of cases of spontaneous privatization. He made clear, however, that the government was not prepared to create legislation with retroactive provisions. Cases in which the parties were in formal compliance with the law at the time would stand. Overall, the new government was poised to lead the country back to its "European heritage," to end the "broken unity of the continent" (Parliament, May 22, 1990, 194).

In his response to Antall's address, Péter Tölgyessy, the parliamentary leader of the Alliance of Free Democrats (AFD), deplored the absence of a privatization plan in the new program. He noted that his party was for a faster transition and that it opposed land restitution. He claimed that returning the land to those who had been its owners in 1947, as the government planned, would devastate Hungarian agriculture. In the plenary debate, representatives of the HDF reiterated the need for the elimination of enterprise councils and the removal of enterprise managers left by the old regime. Speakers of the ISHP hammered away with single-minded zeal at the importance of land restitution, vowing that private farmers would rejuvenate Hungary's sclerotic economy. The CDPP, while supporting Antall's program, registered its preference for a larger role for communal property forms in the economy.

Among members of the ruling coalition, the most critical address was delivered by János Palotás, a leader of the National Organization of Entrepreneurs. Himself a private entrepreneur, Palotás had built several successful enterprises since 1982. In 1985, he became the cochair of the small enterprise section of the Chamber of Commerce, the organization that had played an important role in defending private entrepreneurs in the 1980s. Palotás demanded that the government give special treatment to domestic private entrepreneurs, shielding them from both foreign competition and large state companies. He was seconded by János Petrenkó, an HSP member and owner of a large steel factory.

Everyone cast the private sector as the source of economic salvation, with the private entrepreneur in the role of savior. When disagreement occurred it was over who should have the opportunity to play this role. It took one of the AFD legislators to point out that even though private entrepreneurs were mentioned on nearly every page of the government's economic program, employees—who still constituted the overwhelming majority of the electorate—were almost completely ignored (Parliament, May 23, 1990, 291–92).

The first measures of the new government, designed to slow down spontaneous privatization, were in response to reports that local councils were selling or writing long leases on prime real estate on the cheap. Legislation was proposed to halt real estate deals and create county-level oversight, which would provide exemptions from the ban on an individual basis. The ISHP, ever vigilant regarding land, expanded the bill to cover agricultural cooperatives' land. In the end, a separate law, freezing land deals by co-ops, was accepted.

As the next step, the State Property Agency (SPA) was refashioned into a new, strong bureaucracy responsible for exercising the state's ownership rights. The previous head of the SPA, who had represented the HSWP at the economic negotiations at the opposition roundtable, was dismissed, and a new political appointee was put in charge. By recentralizing ownership rights through the SPA, the government hoped to tighten its control and put an end to spontaneous privatization. The SPA was charged with initiating privatization of companies and supervising deals initiated by companies and buyers. Entrepreneurs in the private sector backed the government's efforts. Many of them had been managers themselves until recently. Now their interests lay in preventing company directors still on the other side of the fence from using their insider advantages in the privatization process.[9]

The opposition worried that the SPA would slow down privatization too much. It was also concerned that local councils would lose their ownership of property, which was necessary for carrying out their duties. In the parliamentary debate, a representative of the HDF, in a burst of impatience, charged that the opposition favored uncontrolled, spontaneous privatization. In response, Márton Tardos, the leading economist of the AFD, explained that his party was not against social control of privatization, but in the absence of a well-functioning capital market there was no way of telling exactly what a company was worth. The SPA would have to weigh many, potentially contradictory criteria. For each company, it would need to evaluate how much the state would profit from the sale, how much it would save by getting rid of a loss maker, and how much income it would forego by selling a profitable company. Clearly, the SPA's bureaucracy would face a nearly impossible task. Rapid privatization would make social control very difficult to exercise.

The opposition was cornered. Spontaneous privatization inflamed the popular sense of justice, and it had begun to stand for the failure to eliminate Communist rule. Private entrepreneurs were clamoring for action. Moreover, there was agreement that the state, deeply in debt, needed the proceeds from selling state property, and spontaneous privatization brought in little revenue. On the other hand, recentralization threatened to raise old ghosts. Although the state was still far from reclaiming its old role of directing production, turning the entire process of privatization over to a state agency was courting trouble. This would allow the government to handpick managers and reward its own party faithful with well-paid sinecures as representatives of the state on supervisory boards and boards of directors of fully or partially state-owned firms. The occasional chore of casting a vote on matters previously decided by the government bureaucracy earned obedient legislators, for each board on which they served, a salary greater than the average income.[10] Most importantly, working through the SPA, the government could use political discretion in awarding state property. Recentralization thus provided the governing coalition with the opportunity to build a political clientele. Given the short history of the coalition parties, the temptation to use privatization to fabricate a solid social base for themselves proved irresistible.

Understandably, the opposition coupled its demands for more rapid privatization with calls for more accountability (Parliament, July 3, 1990, 1231–32). In the final vote, the government prevailed. When the new SPA was formed, the opposition was offered seats on its supervisory board. The party leaders declined. The board was to have little power to influence specific transactions, and the opposition did not want to share responsibility by participating.[11]

Having slowed privatization, the government issued a challenge to company directors. In order to "clean house" and "give greater legitimacy to difficult decisions ahead," it ordered enterprise councils to reelect their top directors by September 15 (*HVG,* August 18, 1990; *Figyelő,* August 2, 1990; *Figyelő,* August 23, 1990). It was an awkward campaign. Enterprise councils had been first introduced in 1985, and the managers they elected took their positions for five years. When the government called for new elections, most directors had only just begun to serve their terms. Undoubtedly under pressure from enterprise directors, the previous government, as one of its last measures, issued a decree requiring that these elections take place by June 30. No one was surprised when most of the directors were reinstated. Dissatisfied with this outcome, the new government ordered a second round of elections. This time, in 20 percent of the cases the directors were dismissed (Szalai 1994a, 95). The government also replaced many directors in the few large firms that had remained under state jurisdiction after 1985.

Privatizing Small Business (Preprivatization)

In August, the Antall government introduced its first bill to get privatization moving again. Following the scenario Antall had outlined in his speech in May, the government began with the privatization of small shops with not more than 10 employees and restaurants, hotels, and service outlets with less than 16 workers. Only Hungarian individuals or their associations were allowed to bid. As the minister of industry and commerce explained when he submitted the bill to the legislature, the program, called preprivatization, was aimed at developing a domestic bourgeoisie (*polgárság*) (Parliament, August 27, 1990, 2325–30).[12]

Speaking for the CDPP in support of the bill, Béla Csépe, who had worked for the National Organization of Small Artisans for 20 years, put the new legislation in historical perspective:

> The economic structure of the last 40 years, which so many of us have criticized and condemned, was a centralized and plan-directed economic system essentially based on monstrous companies, and the private sector represented a very small proportion. However, the special feature of our country, compared with that of our neighbors, is that

> here the private sector was not eliminated completely by administrative measures, and this gives us a base, so we don't have to start from absolute zero.
>
> This small private sector has fought an enormous battle for its survival in the last 40 years, and not even today is it properly legislated—a task for future legislation. But when we have to change the previously described nature of the economic structure, the main steps at long last must be taken in the direction of strengthening the already existing small private enterprises and dismantling the gigantic state sector with them and with new ones. (Parliament, August 27, 1990, 2332)

Iván Szabó, an engineer who had begun running a small cooperative in 1985 and was now the HDF chairman of the Economic Committee, disclosed the government's political concerns:

> When the ÁPISZ scandal broke, the presidium of the HDF threatened to leave all negotiations at the opposition roundtable unless the [Communist] government promised to take action to stop such practices effectively. And, yes, this is when we heard from the lips of some representatives, currently in the opposition, that the important thing is not who is the [private] owner but that there is a [private] owner. Well, this I cannot dispute economically, this is true in pure, laboratory economic sense, but I don't think this principle is suitable to bring back the abated enthusiasm of the people.
>
> In a certain way and in a certain sense, you must accept, regardless whether we like it or not, regardless of whether it fits certain economic doctrines, [that] in this country there is a peculiar class struggle going on, class struggle in the sense that the people of the single Party [*hatalompárt*] were defined as a new class by Milovan Djilas 40 years ago. . . . I heard it in my youth from the leader of the Social Democrats between the two world wars, Károly Peyer, who talked about the fledgling [Communist] Party bureaucracy, that a new bourgeoisie is evolving in Hungary that is different from the old one only because it is more stupid and immoral. Well, today Peyer's observation is not true in all respects. This new bourgeoisie wised up in the last 40 years; it was unable to lead a country, but it was able to line its own pockets. What remains unchanged is its immorality, and this is what the struggle is against now. (Parliament, August 27, 1990, 2340–41)

Despite the political rhetoric that found its way into the explanation published with the final law, preprivatization affected only a very small fraction of state property. As the government made clear, privatizing an establishment meant selling its furniture, inventory, goodwill, and the rental rights to its premises. It did not involve the premises themselves: the buildings and land were not part of the deal. Initially, the government resisted giving anyone an advantage in the bidding, but, responding to pressure from its own legislators, it allowed workers from small shops an edge in the case of equal bids. This was justified, legislators argued, because many of these small businesses were already operated on lease by private traders. The law took effect in September 1990, but auctions did not begin until the following April because it took that long to appraise the businesses. By the end of 1991, only 2,120 of the 10,000 eligible small businesses had been sold (ÁVÜ 1991).

There were several reasons why the aspiring small bourgeoisie was only modestly interested in preprivatization. Paying a large sum and not getting much tangible property led many people to protest that the government was "selling the air." Banks required high collateral for those who thought "buying the air" was worth it. And, finally, financially strapped local governments, the owners of the premises, recognizing an opportunity to collect revenue, doubled or tripled the rent. Shopkeepers found it more advantageous to begin their shops from scratch, opening grocery stores in their own garages and buying furniture and merchandise as their finances permitted.

Privatizing Medium and Large State Companies

In conjunction with the passage of the law on preprivatization, the government announced its First Privatization Program, putting up for sale 20 large companies with a combined estimated worth of 33 billion forints (ÁVÜ 1990). The goal was to mobilize both foreign and domestic investors, the latter to be assisted with special loans funded through a new program. The companies were to be privatized through a public offering of shares, competitive tenders, and employee-share ownership plans (ESOPs). The last of these was little more than an empty political gesture to employees. ESOPs were not a real option because they had no legal definition. Almost two years passed before the legislature formulated laws pertaining to ESOPs.

The government's gesture was nevertheless necessary because the privatization of large companies was the first frontal assault on universal state employment. The transformation of the first 20 companies was expected to result in layoffs for large numbers of workers, ending decades of employment security. Moreover, many of these large firms provided welfare services such as housing loans, vacations, and meals for their employees. Many retired workers survived on their low pensions only because they retained their company dining privileges. Companies also supplied inexpensive day care, and they participated in professional training for high school students. Large firms contributed to their local communities as well. Many funded community projects, including paving roads and building public parks. All these services were jeopardized by privatization. The government hoped that ESOPs would sweeten this bitter pill.

The First Privatization Program embodied the new, centrally directed approach to privatization. The state was to be fully in control. By reining in managers, the government expected to stem the tide of spontaneous privatization.[13] The program's designers anticipated that the outside investors who bought these companies would install new technology and initiate new management practices. The program failed. By the spring of 1991, not one of the 20 companies offered in the program had been privatized.[14] The SPA explained the debacle in a straightforward manner in its annual report (ÁVÜ 1991). It was not so much the undesirable social effects that thwarted privatization but the lack of cooperation on the part of company managers.[15] Bypassing managers meant that the agency, with its limited staff and resources, had to assume an enormous task. More importantly, though, the SPA had to contend with the active resistance of managers, whose inside knowledge of their companies gave them a decided advantage. By manipulating inventory and production figures, dragging their feet, and scaring off potential investors who were not to their liking, managers won the cat-and-mouse game against the agency. Offering shares to the public on the stock exchange was no solution, either. Most Hungarians did not understand this new form of investment, and those few who did knew that in a stock market with a handful of companies in an uncertain economy the risks were too high.[16]

Thus, in the summer of 1991, the government conceded defeat and introduced self-privatization for small- and medium-sized companies.[17] This was a modified version of spontaneous privatization. Companies were allowed to initiate privatization deals with the help of small private agencies licensed by the SPA. These small private agencies sold companies without any interference from the SPA, which had to accept all sales unless they violated some law. If the State Privatization Agency was dissatisfied with any private agency, it could withdraw its license. Altogether, 81 private agencies were licensed. Most were small accounting firms with staffs of one to five, which received a commission based on a percentage of the sale price.

Self-privatization was a success. By the end of 1993, 255 companies had been privatized (Pichler 1994, 78–88). The first ones to sell were companies in the food processing and consumer goods manufacturing businesses.[18] Self-privatization was a boon for two powerful groups. First, it gave managers back their control over their companies. Now they could find outside investors themselves, often becoming partial owners in the process. Second, self-privatization was a gold mine for those who ran the private agencies, since they received around 3 percent of the sale price on each transaction. Many of these agencies were run by ex-officials from ministries and economic policy institutes who happily abandoned their ill-paid and insecure jobs for these new ventures.

To speed up privatization, new financing techniques were announced. Property that was to remain in state ownership in the near future was transferred to the newly created State Holding Company, thus unburdening the SPA from managing those businesses. Belatedly, employee-share ownership programs were introduced in July 1992. Many of the ESOPs were thinly veiled forms of management buyouts. This form was also explicitly allowed and regulated in order to keep privatization moving. From January 1993 on, companies could be leased with an option to buy at a low price after six to eight years. This rent-to-own technique allowed people to take control of companies without putting up money of their own. Finally, more and larger government loans were made available. In 1992, the average loan[19] approved was around 250,000 forints; a year later the typical loan was several million. By 1994, only 25 percent of the income from privatization was in cash; the rest was in the form of loans and compensation vouchers (see table 9.1).

TABLE 9.1. Revenues of the State Property Agency and the State Property Holding Company (to December 31, 1994)

	1990	1991	1992	1993	1994	Total
Yield of assets	n.a.	0.94	8.25	6.63	4.46	20.28
Sales						
Foreign exchange	0.53	24.61	40.98	110.64	11.36	188.12
Forints (cash)	0.14	4.82	17.51	15.92	16.53	54.92
Total cash sales	0.67	30.37	66.74	133.19	32.35	263.32
Credit	n.a.	1.01	9.07	22.60	31.13	63.81
Compensation vouchers	n.a.	n.a.	2.38	19.54	64.21	86.13
Total	0.67	31.38	78.19	175.33	127.69	413.26
Percentage noncash	n.a.	n.a.	14.64	24.03	74.67	36.28

Source: ÁVÜ 1995, 6–7.

Missing Forms of Privatization: Mass Privatization and Reprivatization

Two methods of privatization popular in many other Eastern European countries were notably missing in Hungary: mass privatization and reprivatization. The former method was only briefly discussed and never with serious intent. During the debate in early 1991 on restitution and reprivatization, the AFD suggested giving each citizen a token voucher worth 20,000 forints. This proposal contradicted the AFD's previous positions. It was an effort to score points with the voters—the party was well aware that their suggestion would be rejected by the governing majority. The AFD abandoned its proposal but not before being forced to make a convincing argument to support it. Its representatives made the case that mass privatization was quick and popular and possibly the only way to privatize unwanted companies.

The leader of the AFD faction also pointed out that rapid privatization accomplished through sales would hand state property over to three groups:

> The first [group] is the people of the past administration who were able to convert their political capital to real, material capital. . . . The second group is profiteering [*ügyeskedő*] entrepreneurs. A very large portion of Hungarian entrepreneurs acquired wealth in a limited market with all sorts of business tricks. . . . The third group consists of honest entrepreneurs, who can easily become legitimate and productive owners in a new Hungarian market economy. (Parliament, February 11, 1991, 5897)

Therefore, citizen vouchers were a good solution. They would speed up privatization while leaving enough property for honest entrepreneurs to purchase. The AFD leaders' uncharacteristically confused argument made much more sense in reverse: a comprehensive citizen vouchers program would have preempted these groups' bid for state property.

Reprivatization had more sincere and forceful advocates. Nevertheless, the government decided early that it would not provide restitution. It offered instead a heavily discounted compensation, capped at 5 million forints, for property appropriated by the Communist regime after June 1949.[20] The strongest support for reprivatization came from the ISHP, which promised its constituents the return of lands taken during collectivization. The ISHP was backed by some representatives of the other coalition parties. Though their rhetoric waxed with each utterance of the word *land,*[21] they presented an argument based on the sanctity of private property in general. Private entrepreneurs were divided on the issue of reprivatization. Artisans joined the small farmers represented by ISHP to support reprivatization. Many were continuing their parents' trades and stood to benefit from getting their shops back. The artisans' largest organization, the National Association of Industrial Guilds (Ipartestületek Országos Szövetsége), endorsed reprivatization.[22] Bigger entrepreneurs, organized by the National Association of Entrepreneurs (Vállalkozók Országos Szövetsége), were strongly against it.[23] The first time the issue was discussed in the legislature, their representative, János Palotás, voiced strong opposition to reprivatization of any kind (Parliament, May 23, 1990, 277).

These entrepreneurs were vehement in their disapproval because giving property back to its original owners would have prevented the fledgling entrepreneurial class from taking possession of it. The original owners, the new entrepreneurs argued, were either too old to make use of their property or dead, and their heirs often had no interest in continuing their fathers' trades.[24]

When the Compensation Law passed in April 1991, it did not include reprivatization, but it did include one concession to the ISHP. Compensation for land was total, so peasants who wished to buy their land back with compensation vouchers could do so. This provision was then found to be unconstitutional by the Constitutional Court, which ruled that preferential treatment could not be given to landowners. The final version of the law struck a compromise: land was to be sold at closed auctions where vouchers could be used and the only bidders allowed would be the people who either currently lived in the village or had had landholdings in the area before collectivization (Comisso 1995).[25] This approach provided insurance that people would regain their lands unless there was an agrarian entrepreneur in the village who was able to outbid them.

The Balance Sheet of Privatization

By June 30, 1994, the State Property Agency reported that 47 percent of state property had been "privatized." This calculation was based on a method that counted any property for which the state kept less than half of the shares as if the entire company had been handed over to private owners (see table 9.2). For companies in which the state had a minority interest, the value privatized was calculated in proportion to private interest. Companies that were liquidated or simply closed down were also considered privatized. In addition, the figure ignored cross-ownership. Thus, if the state owned only 49 percent of a company but the rest of the shares were held by other companies in which the state had controlling interest, giving the state a de facto majority, the firm was still counted as one with majority private ownership.

This method, though justifiable, overestimates the success of privatization (table 9.3). Privatization was most successful in food processing, cosmetics, household chemicals, tourism, and domestic and foreign trade. It made little or no headway in mining and heavy industry, industries that had been central to the socialist Great Transformation.

The forms privatization has taken in Hungary were strongly influenced by two groups: enterprise managers and large, private, corporate entrepreneurs. The two are often difficult to distinguish. Many of the private entrepreneurs had been middle- or high-level managers before leaving for the private sector in the 1980s, while many enterprise managers were running part-time private businesses by 1989. Each group exercised its influence only partially through its political organizations. Managers drew most of their power from their ability to resist unwelcome policies

TABLE 9.2. Number of Companies Fully or Partially Privatized and the Method of Their Privatization (February 28, 1995)

Share of State Ownership	Number of Companies
Over 95 percent	354
50 to 95 percent	140
25 to 50 percent	125
Less than 25 percent	176
Total completely or partially privatized	795
Of these privatized	
Through employee-share ownership programs	199
Leased	24

Source: ÁVÜ 1995, 2, 4.

TABLE 9.3. Value of Property Involved in Privatization (June 30, 1994)

	Forints (Billions)
Total assets of companies sold 100 percent	229.30
Total assets of companies with majority private ownership	201.89
Assets of companies with majority state ownership proportionate to state's share	90.74
Other assets sold	88.74
Assets sold in preprivatization	17.05
Assets of firms that were liquidated	315.91
Total	943.63
Total assets to be privatized	2000.00

Source: Hungarian Government 1994.

Note: The total value of all property to be privatized in 1990 is estimated here at 2,000 billion. Thus, the extent of privatization (943.63/2000)*100 = 47.18 percent

individually; private entrepreneurs relied on their presence in political parties to give them political clout. Although small entrepreneurs were similarly represented, and their proportion of the population was much larger, their voice was much weaker.

The path of privatization in Hungary, just as everywhere else in Eastern Europe, has been intensely affected by the social and political legacies of state socialism. Poland, which, like Hungary, developed a strong private sector under state socialism, and whose old political elite, like Hungary's, was able to negotiate its way out of power, resisted reprivatization and mass privatization as the chief means of building its new economy. It is possible that in the end both Hungary and Poland will introduce some form of mass privatization simply because that will be the only way to privatize companies that have not—and never will—attract buyers. What matters most is neither the presence nor the absence of techniques but their timing. Thus, what is essential is sequence and process.

In spite of their many similarities, Poland and Hungary differ in important ways.[26] Much like their similarities, their differences are rooted in the way universal state employment devolved in each country. In Poland, organized workers' strong role in this devolution gives them more leverage in the privatization process than that accorded to their Hungarian counterparts (Levitas 1994; Slay 1994).

New Private Enterprises

Privatization was only one factor in the growth of the private sector. New companies mushroomed. A few large factories were started by foreign multinationals, such as Ford, General Motors, Suzuki, Audi, Coca-Cola, and Pepsi, but the overwhelming majority of the new enterprises were small firms founded by domestic entrepreneurs. A considerable proportion of these new companies had existed as small, full- or part-time private ventures before 1989 (Webster 1992) and changed their legal status after the Enterprise Law took effect. The most popular form of business enterprise was the limited liability company (*korlátolt felelősségű társaság* or KFT). By the end of 1992, the number of KFTs stood at 57,262. The second most popular form was the limited partnership (*betéti társaság* or BT). This form requires no authorized capital, but it lacks the protection of limited liability. By 1992, 41,218 limited partnerships were registered (KSH 1995b, 21, 29).

The growth of licensed individual entrepreneurs was equally spectacular. The number of registered artisans, craftsmen, retailers, and self-employed professionals more than tripled between 1988 and 1993, reaching close to 700,000 (table 9.4). Less than half of this group was self-employed full time, however (Major 1993). Many individuals registered themselves as in business simply to reduce their taxes (by writing off private expenditures as business expenses).

While many licenses were issued to phantom businesses, many real businesses went unlicensed. The unemployed are denied unemployment compensation if they register ownership of a business. Many unemployed people work as labor entrepreneurs anyway—they simply do not bother to report their activities. Thus, it is not surprising that the sudden jump in unemployment from 2 to 8.2 percent during 1991 had no perceptible effect on the steady growth of licensed individual entrepreneurs. In the 1990s, the hidden economy is estimated to have produced between 17 and 30 percent of the GDP (*Figyelő,* March 30, 1995; Árvay and Sik 1994; Ékes 1993).

The small private sector has grown fastest in retail and wholesale trade, catering, tourism, and other services. These areas, which require little capital and typically were neglected in socialist economies, came to dominate trade, services, construction, and agriculture.

The End of Universal State Employment

The collapse of communism formally ended the system of universal state employment. With a rapidly growing private sector and rising unemploy-

TABLE 9.4. Change in Size of Corporate Enterprises throughout the Economy

Corporate Enterprises (limited liability, joint stock companies, cooperatives, etc.)	1990	1991	1992	1993
Number of workers				
0–20	16,465	36,809	52,825	68,219
21–50	4,129	6,169	6,970	7,637
51–300	4,469	5,372	5,773	6,055
300+	2,599	2,396	1,937	1,624
Total number of companies	27,662	50,746	67,505	83,535
Non-corporate enterprises (partnerships, limited partnerships, etc.)		52,136	70,597	98,036
Self-employed (artisans, small traders, professionals, etc.)		510,459	606,207	688,843

Source: KSH 1994a, 109; Baló and Lipovecz 1993, 509, 511; Pichler 1994, 109.

ment (table 9.5), the state abandoned its role as the universal employer.[27] Manpower plans disappeared. Wage policies ceased to be the principal mechanism allocating financial rewards, and wage regulations were phased out. Wages began to be set by the forces of the labor market and by the outcomes of political struggles between employers and newly organized unions. The once all-powerful personnel directors either retired or began studying the latest American textbooks on human resource management. Some started private consulting firms. The state, still the largest employer, had to refashion its role as a boss.

In 1992, a system of civil service was introduced for the 800,000 state employees working in the nonprofit sector, such as those in state administration, health care, education, and scientific and cultural institutions. Civil service workers, called public employees (*közalkalmazottak*), are provided special protections and quite generous benefits. Under the pressure of a large debt, the state has found it increasingly difficult to meet these obligations. Public employees, enjoying relatively good job security but seeing their wages eroding and the funds of their workplace dwindling, have been in the forefront of labor protest. Educated, organized, and focused on a single target, public employees are becoming a strong political force. Other state employees, who work in for-profit enterprises and are subject to the same central regulations as are private employees, are more reluctant to join unions and demonstrations. Their position is precarious. They could lose their jobs as their firms prepare for privatization or they could be dismissed by the new owners. Today, as in past decades, most Hungarian workers try to make it on their own.

About half of the work force is now estimated to be in the private sector. Employees in the private sector are about as well off as are state employees.[28] Wages in foreign-owned private firms are higher than in domestic private companies, and both are higher than what companies eligible for privatization are paying. Reported incomes are the highest in companies that are in the state sector and not eligible for privatization in the near future. These companies, however, include banks and cultural institutions such as Hungarian Radio and Television (TÁRKI 1993, 409). Generally, workers employed in the same type of industries report similar incomes regardless of whether they work for a private or a state company. The only exception is trade: private traders are either very well or very ill paid; their counterparts in state companies fall between these extremes. Fringe benefits provided at the workplace are also comparable in the two sectors (Polonyi 1994, 63). One type of benefit is quickly disappearing, however. In the last decades of socialism, state employees finagled support for their private-sector activities from their companies. They used company facilities, materials, and tools, as well as company time to pursue

TABLE 9.5. Registered Unemployment

	1990 (Jan)	1990 (Dec)	1991 (Dec)	1992 (Dec)	1993 (Dec)	1994 (Dec)	1995 (Nov)
Number of registered unemployed	24,200	79,521	406,124	663,027	632,050	519,592	484,617
All active people, including the registered unemployed	5,496,100[a]	5,404,400[a]	5,202,300[a]	5,015,000[a]	4,768,500[a]		
				4,751,200[b]	4,552,200[b]	4,433,500[b]	4,380,300[c]
Unemployment rates	0.4	1.5	7.8	13.2	13.3		
				14.0	13.9	11.7	11.1

Source: Calculated from KSH 1994a, 24; KSH 1995b, 22; KSH 1995a, 25; and KSH 1994c, 123.

[a]Figures collected through various state organs.

[b]Figures collected by quarterly sample surveys (figures refer to the last quarter of the year).

[c]Figure from a quarterly sample survey conducted in the third quarter of 1995.

their private activities. Now fear of unemployment and the presence of vigilant new owners keep people from helping themselves to company resources. Surveys report that both employers and employees believe labor discipline has become stricter (TÁRKI 1993, 23–24, 284). Paradoxically, universal state employment, originally intended as a tool of social control, in retrospect is now perceived as having provided a shield from exacting bosses.

Overall, real wages are falling. With state-provided benefits and subsidies curtailed, living standards are on the decline for the overwhelming majority. Pensioners see their incomes evaporate as inflation surpasses 20 percent. Regional economic recession, especially in the heavily industrial northeast where unemployment is over 20 percent, has created new pockets of poverty. A small minority, however, is prospering, rapidly catching up with their Western counterparts. Inequalities are on the rise (Róna-Tas 1994).

The Small Transformation

If Lech Wałęşa is right and privatization is like making an aquarium from fish soup, then nationalization must be like making fish soup out of an aquarium. In many respects, the Small Transformation of the early 1990s is the reverse of the Great Transformation of the late 1940s and early 1950s. The socialist Great Transformation achieved an unprecedented concentration of ownership through nationalization. The Small Transformation has aimed at dispersing ownership rights. The Great Transformation targeted banks and large enterprises first; smaller firms were appropriated afterward. During the Small Transformation, this sequence has been running in reverse: the first businesses to return to the private sector were the small companies, and it is in this area that privatization has been most successful. Large firms and banks will be the last to go private. The Great Transformation brought about a period of forced accumulation; the Small Transformation has produced a decline in capital stock.

The early years of state socialism were the years of industry. The fastest development occurred in mining, steel, and machine manufacturing, areas where economies of scale could be exploited and where factory production claimed most of its success. In the 1990s, services and trade have led the way. The Great Transformation created large-scale facilities tooled for mass production. In the Small Transformation, privatization has broken up large industrial companies (see table 9.6). At the same time, tens of thousands of small industrial businesses are being created, most targeting niche markets with customized products. The increasing weight of services and trade further fragments the work force, as companies in these two areas are much smaller than are manufacturing firms (see table 9.7).

The Great Transformation sought to nationalize labor along with capital and land. Labor defied nationalization. Tools, livestock, real estate, and factories all could be divorced from individuals and allocated to the state. Labor could not. It can be disciplined, supervised, exploited, coerced, but never appropriated. Universal state employment was devised to cope with this peculiarity. Labor could never be made to fully surrender its private character, however, and it was labor that led the return of the private sector.

The Great Transformation gave birth to an autarchic, closed economy. Excluding external influences simplified the job of the central planner by keeping most factors that might potentially influence production within the political jurisdiction of the state. The Small Transformation links the fate of postcommunist countries directly to the world economy, thus robbing the state of much of its domestic sovereignty at a time when government is ceding power to its citizens and their associations. Political life necessarily becomes decentered where the International Monetary Fund, the national government, and the city council all appear to exercise the same level of influence over individuals' daily lives.

The fragmentation of the Small Transformation reshapes ideology as well. As it weakens, the state is losing its power to enforce a coherent and explicit system of ideas. Yet people's sense of the unpredictability, instability, and insecurity of daily life makes their desire for powerful ideologies as strong as ever. As the common drumbeat of universal state employment quiets and different groups in society begin to march at different speeds and in varying directions, multiple ideologies develop. In the absence of tightly controlled ideological scholarship to carefully define concepts, Marxist seminars to clear up misunderstanding and doubt, and meticulously coordinated propagandizing to inculcate the fundamentals, the meaning of embourgeoisement will be shaped by television commercials

TABLE 9.6. Change in the Size of Corporate Industrial Enterprises (percentages)

Size of Work Force	1991	1992	1993
Less than 20	57.1	63.8	67.9
21–50	18.5	15.9	14.5
51–300	16.9	14.1	13.0
300 or more	7.5	6.2	4.6
Total number	11,995	14,105	17,170

Source: Calculated from KSH 1994a, 132; and KSH 1995c, 22.

and experiences with the tax authorities, by business courses and standing in line at the unemployment office.

The final chapter focuses on one important aspect of the social change taking place as part of the Small Transformation: the social process by which a new economic elite is developing in the private sector.

TABLE 9.7. Change in the Sectoral Composition of the Labor Force during the Great and Small Transformations

The Great Transformation					
	1949	1951	1953	1955	Change 1949–55
Industry	22.5	23.0	25.9	29.4	+6.9
Construction	2.1	5.6	8.1	5.7	+3.6
Agriculture	64.3	59.4	53.4	51.7	–12.6
Transportation	4.8	5.2	6.0	6.1	+1.3
Trade (retail/wholesale)	6.2	6.8	6.5	7.1	+0.9
The Small Transformation[a]					
	1980	1989	1991	1993	Change 1989–93
Industry	33.3	30.4	29.5	28.7	–1.7
Construction	7.9	7.0	6.6	6.2	–0.8
Agriculture	21.0	18.4	15.6	9.9	–8.5
Transportation post and telecommunications	8.0	8.3	8.5	8.5	+0.2
Trade	9.6	10.8	12.3	15.0	+4.2
Water management	1.5	1.6	1.4	1.3	–0.3
Other material production	0.9	0.9	1.0	0.8	–0.1
Services	17.7	22.6	24.9	29.6	+7.0
Personal and economic services	3.0	4.3	4.5	5.6	+1.3
Health care and social and cultural services	10.9	12.9	15.1	17.7	+4.8

Source: Calculated from KSH 1956, 162; KSH 1990a, 25; and KSH 1994a, 25.

Note: The categories used in the early years of state socialism are somewhat different from the ones used later. They are also less detailed.

[a]The drop in agriculture during the Small Transformation is partly due to the fact that workers in industrial side businesses, as well as the industrial support personnel (tractor mechanics, construction crews) of agricultural cooperatives, were included in agriculture. Once these cooperatives broke up, they were reclassified into industry and construction. Thus, the drop in agriculture is smaller and the decline in industry and construction is larger than these figures indicate.

CHAPTER 10

The Elite of the New Private Sector and the Old *Nomenklatura*

Introduction

Privatization and newly emerging private businesses altered life chances dramatically for many Hungarians. The extent of the changes in the social structure brought about by the Small Transformation can be compared only to those that followed the Great Transformation. In the late 1940s, people could rise from the workbench to the director's chair overnight; in the early 1990s, state-employees working from nine to five could amass business empires in a matter of a few years. The main beneficiaries of the Great Transformation were the Party faithful, people who were willing to give the Party their unconditional loyalty. These cadres were selected in Party personnel offices and carefully groomed, politically and professionally. The chosen were promoted according to plan, and their career steps were closely supervised.

The Great Transformation carried out its institutional overhaul in lockstep with a deliberate revamping of society. Leaving nothing to chance, the Party endeavored to reshape society by means of direct intervention. In attempting to nationalize labor, it reconfigured property, altered the distribution of human capital, and disrupted existing social networks. The Communist leadership was acutely aware of the importance of these efforts. As Mátyás Rákosi, in his opening speech at the Party Congress in 1951, explained:

> The exploiters are defeated, but they are not annihilated. They kept their international base, international capital, to which they belong. They kept a certain part of the means of production, they kept their money, their enormous social connections survived. . . . Their expertise in state, economic, and military management secures a very, very disproportionate weight for them, much larger than their proportion in the population. (MDP 1951, 46)

Human capital was redistributed. Class quotas were set for universities, and loyalists were put on a fast track to close the gaps in their education. Some credentials were abolished, and entire areas of knowledge, deemed anti-Marxist, were nullified. Human capital of a certain kind was difficult to reassign, however. Personal knowledge—knowledge that comes from experience and not from textbooks and courses—cannot be easily explicated and transferred (Polanyi 1962; Murrell 1993a, 1993b).

Social networks were ripped apart. This was the articulated goal of the Party's decision to dispatch aristocrats and the former bourgeoisie to the countryside for hard manual labor during the Great Transformation. But promotion, too, served this purpose. By turning workers into managers, the state cut these individuals loose from their friends and acquaintances and catapulted them into a world where they were suspended on the single, exceedingly thin cord of the Party's generosity. In the wake of collectivization drives that forced peasants off their lands, hostilities billowed across the countryside. Neighbors and relatives turned against one another. Finally, leaving the field to take a job in the factory not only physically uprooted many people, but it also thinned their social networks.

Thus, the social fabric, already frayed from the traumas of World War II, was further shredded by the state's direct efforts to change people's careers and by the indirect effects of its economic policies. Ironically, the ideology that professed collectivistic ideals became the sharp instrument of social atomization: the Great Transformation was a rupture, a sudden and forceful break with the past.

The Small Transformation, by contrast, has been the acceleration of a process of gradual devolution. The beneficiaries of the Small Transformation were not selected by central design. Rather, these people's advantageous positions have emerged as unintended consequences of political struggle and institutional change. In this final chapter, I focus on one important aspect of this ongoing process of social and political transformation: the emergence of new elites.

Theories about the Emerging Elite

Structural Compensation Thesis

The sociological literature presents three competing theses about how a new private-sector elite develops and who benefits most from the emerging new institutions. The first explanation, labeled the structural compensation thesis, draws a polar distinction between an economy coordinated by the state bureaucracy and one in which the law of supply and demand allocates goods and positions (Nee 1989). Since these two institutional structures are radically different, they reward different qualities, and thus they benefit different kinds of people. The post-Communist transformation is a transition between these two structures. Over time, a changing of the guard will occur at the top of the economic hierarchy. As the bureaucratic principle is eclipsed by market mechanisms, cadres will yield to entrepreneurs. The winners of the Small Transformation will be the private entrepreneurs who started their own businesses because they could not succeed in the socialist sector. The losers of the post-Communist transformation will be the Party and state officials, the *nomenklatura,* whose elite positions will disappear as their bureaucratic skills and political loyalties become devalued in the competitive marketplace. The two structures are compensating: losers in one become winners in the other.

We have seen that in the last decades of Hungarian state socialism, the private sector became increasingly attractive for social groups that were dominant in the socialist sector as well. This seems to contradict the structural compensation thesis. Advocates counter that, as long as the economy is dominated by the socialist sector, cadres can parlay their bureaucratic power and influence into private gain simply because they control vast amounts of resources. A Party official of a state company can start his own business partnership and then pressure his state company for sweetheart deals. Thus, in this early phase of the transition, the old elite will not lose but gain. As corruption entices this group to maintain and expand the private sector, however, it will undermine its own power. With the collapse of the old elite's political rule, its economic fortunes will fold as well. This thesis thus describes a process in which losing ground is nonmonotonic over time—the demise of the old elite happens only after a period of gaining strength (Nee 1991).

Technocratic Continuity Thesis

The structural compensation thesis suggests considerable changes at the top of the economic hierarchy. Two other arguments predict a very different scenario, asserting that as the private sector becomes dominant the old elite will survive. The two arguments present two different mechanisms of status preservation. The first one, the technocratic continuity thesis, emphasizes expertise (Szalai 1990, 182). Expertise is transferable because of the structural similarities between state socialist economies and market economies based on private property. This argument points out that, with industrialization, in all state socialist countries education and knowledge gradually became the dominant factors in sorting people into powerful positions (Connor 1979; Simkus 1981; Haller et al. 1990; Blau and Ruan 1990). Large bureaucratic organizations needed competent people. Most people joined the Party in order to promote their own careers. In turn, the Party embraced these individuals for their skills. This technocratic advance, which replaced Reds with experts, did not proceed with the same speed in every Communist country; nevertheless, it has been a clear trend everywhere (Konrád and Szelényi 1991; Wasilewski 1985; Szelényi 1987; Wasilewski 1990; Li and White 1990).

In Hungary, the technocratic elite was especially strong. As earlier chapters have documented, this group increasingly took part in the private sector of the 1980s. At the top, technocrats played an important role in economic reforms. In other countries, these individuals were less able to influence decisions at the highest levels of power. Yet, once the Politburo made its decisions, technocrats in all socialist states were powerful in the phase of implementation. Technocrats have approached the rules of state socialism with the same kind of pragmatism that business people in capitalist economies assume vis à vis the market. Technocrats solve problems; their success depends partially on their ability to accept problems as they are posed. The post-Communist transformation has presented a new set of problems to solve, but technocrats have accumulated human capital that has allowed them to adapt quickly. Thus, they are likely to succeed under the competitive conditions of the new economy, which rewards scarce human capital.

Both the structural compensation and technocratic advance theses depict the post-Communist transformation as a transition between a centralized bureaucratic and a competitive market system. Each structure generates its own specific imperatives, which people must follow. Although the two theses disagree over how much these imperatives differ, both view elite membership as a simple function of one's success in adjusting to new institutional circumstances. People appear as isolated individuals who interface not with each other but with a set of abstract institutions.

A further weakness of both theories is that they build their arguments on ahistorical pictures of the socialist past and the still unknown—and unknowable—capitalist future. They conjure up two static systems and then infer the present as a road linking the two.

Power Conversion Thesis

The power conversion thesis takes a different approach. Its point of departure is an old elite, which it conceives of as being willing to do anything necessary to survive. The question is not how the old elite adapts to new rules but how it shapes the rules incrementally over time to its own advantage and in the process creates a new system (Stark 1990; Staniszkis 1991; Burawoy and Krotov 1992; Wank 1992). The power conversion thesis claims that it is not the human capital of cadres that primarily assures their survival but their political power. The latter can be converted directly into economic assets. We saw evidence of this in Hungary in the 1990s. In anticipation of their demise, Party and state officials scrambled to transform their bureaucratic control over state property into private ownership rights. The theory further predicts that in the future the old elite will try to influence the rules of privatization to assure that the chrysalis of the Communist official will evolve smoothly into the butterfly of the capitalist tycoon.[1]

The power conversion thesis captures important developments in the waning days of state socialism. It runs into difficulty, however, in attempting to explain the ex-cadres' success in maintaining influence once they had been ousted from political office.

The three arguments point to three groups as the primary beneficiaries of the post-Communist transformation. I contend that the theses are not mutually exclusive; they grapple with different and simultaneously existing facets of a complex process. The structural compensation thesis predicts that the new elite of the private sector will be recruited from among those who either left or never joined the socialist sector before the collapse; the technocratic advance argument points to a group of technocrats as the likely new elites; and the power conversion argument singles out Party and state officials as the main beneficiaries of the newly emerging private sector.

My explanation hinges on the nature of the Small Transformation. The Small Transformation has had two countervailing effects. On the one hand, deconcentration of power and the subsequent weakening of the state, as well as the leadership's neoliberal ideology, have precluded any major or direct assault on the life chances of any particular social group.[2] The state is not in a position to systematically reeducate, intrude upon, coerce, uproot, or dislocate its citizenry.

On the other hand, the deconcentration of production brought about tens of thousands of new companies, creating a broad range of new opportunities. Since companies are now considerably smaller, more of them can cluster at the top. Even if the number of enterprises had stayed the same, however, the shift from industry to trade and services, branches with relatively little capital requirements, would have opened new doors for new people (see table 10.1).

But opening new doors does not guarantee success. Both trade and services rely heavily on personal connections and hard-to-teach skills. People who have already accumulated relevant networks and skills have great advantages over newcomers. These initial advantages are then locked in by property rights. Consider this example. Printing is a lucrative business, provided one has a clientele of large corporate buyers. To start a print shop, one needs to have connections to large companies. Once the business takes off and the shop can invest in expensive, high-quality equipment, the initial advantage is transformed into property. Newcomers to the printing business who lack these cumulative advantages will find it more difficult to get in on the ground floor.

Past advantages can be applied to present circumstances, and so the new economy does not compensate for old deprivations. Thus, knowledge and technical skills bring stability for two reasons. Expertise is more than a guarantor of social status. High position also reinforces expertise—not because the new order will reward competence equally or better but because even incompetent people possess local knowledge impossible to replace in the short run.

Finally, the success of cadres in converting their power is directly tied to the social networks that remain, a scaffold standing stable even after the formal organization of the state has been dismantled. The Party is gone, but Party friends and acquaintances remain. The Small Transformation has not turned society upside-down, but society's top has risen higher and its bottom has sunk lower as initial, minor differences continue to gradually expand into larger inequalities.

The New Economic Elite of the Private Sector

Who are the members of the new private-sector elite in Hungary? Our guide to answering this question is a random sample of the leaders of the 3,000 firms, both private and state owned, that reported the largest total sales figures in 1992 (Social Stratification Survey 1993/1993 Elite Sample or SSS–1993/1993SE).[3] Despite the size of their economic activities, many of these firms have no more than a handful of employees and fixed assets of relatively small value.

TABLE 10.1. Segments of the New Economic Elite by Economic Branch in 1993 (percentages)

		Private	
Branch	State	Privatized	Newly Founded Private
Agriculture	14.9	19.3	5.0
Industry	50.3	50.5	41.7
Service/trade	34.8	30.2	53.3
N	161	192	180
$\chi^2 = 30.74403$			
df = 4			

Source: Social Stratification Survey 1993, 1993 Elite Sample.

The analysis below divides the economic elite into leaders of state and private firms. This separation helps demonstrate the extent to which business leaders differ because of the sector in which they operate. Note, however, that the state sector, although less affected by post-Communist reforms than other parts of the economy, still underwent important reorganization. The private sector is further divided into two segments. One was created by privatizing state companies, and the other emerged as privately founded businesses multiplied. I label the first "privatized" and the second "privately founded." This distinction makes it possible to separate the effect of top-down privatization from bottom-up private-sector growth. Although privately founded companies often bought real estate or machinery from state companies, they did not take over these firms' existing organization or employees, as happened in privatization. Since privately founded companies consequently depend less on preexisting internal networks than do privatized ones, we should find that the privately founded sector is the one most open to newcomers.

I also distinguish between managers and manager-owners; the latter include directors who have an ownership stake of any kind in their companies. Among the sample, over a third of the chief executive officers in the privatized and over half in the privately founded sector are owners. In the latter segment, most employee managers work for foreign firms. Especially among privatized companies, owner-managers do not typically hold the majority of shares, but their share is usually sufficient to give them controlling interest. In privately founded domestic businesses, ownership and management are closely tied.

Finally, data for the new economic elite are supplemented with data collected on the same indicators for the population at large (Social Stratification Survey 1993/General Population or SSS–1993/GP).[4] This comparison makes it possible to identify what counts as an asset in becoming part of the economic elite. When an individual's state-socialist past is a factor, the reference is always to the year 1988.

Is private enterprise compensatory? Is the new economic elite predominantly from the ranks of the self-employed private entrepreneurs of state socialism? The proportion of those who were self-employed full time in 1988 is not much different in the new private sector compared with either the state sector or the general population (see table 10.2). It is in part-time private-sector participation that the differences lie. This kind of activity was an excellent springboard for the new economic elite, especially in the privately founded segment. The combination of a state job and a private business was a significant advantage for participants in the newly emerging private sector. The difference is less pronounced between the privatized and the state sector and is more accentuated when we compare heads of state companies with leaders of newly founded businesses. Only among owners in the latter is there a considerable proportion of individuals who were self-employed full time under state socialism. Economic changes since 1989 have not acted as a compensatory mechanism to correct the disadvantages associated with previous self-employment. The majority of the members of the old elite were state employees, possibly engaging in some labor entrepreneurship on the side but not pursuing private business or participating in partnerships or other licensed private activities full time.

Is the newly emerging elite, then, the technocratic group that the technocratic advance thesis depicts? The new private elite is indeed better educated than the average (see table 10.3). In fact, few made it into the elite without a tertiary degree. The self-made, uneducated entrepreneur who climbs high on natural intelligence exists only in myth. There seems to be no difference in education between participants in the two sectors; the private sector apparently does not reward credentials any more than does the state sector.

The majority of the new elite has some kind of technical degree (see table 10.4). Less than half finished law or business school or studied economics. Private companies that hire managers slightly reverse the order of importance of these two degrees. Nevertheless, about one in six of the new entrepreneurs has a degree in the humanities or the social sciences (except economics), areas highly contested by Marxism-Leninism in the past. In this group belong those who have a degree in Marxism.[5] Interestingly, these people are more likely to end up in the elite of the private sector than at the top of state companies. They are especially well represented among owner-managers of private firms. Knowledge and expertise indeed seem linked to stability. Still, there is a complementary, though

TABLE 10.2. Segments of the New Economic Elite and the General Population in Private Business in 1988 (percentages)

		New Elite					
			Private				
Private Sector Participation in 1988	General Population	State Manager	Privatized Manager	Privatized Owner	Newly Founded Manager	Newly Founded Owner
None	92.5	83.2	85.5	78.7	77.5	61.0
Part-time	2.6	10.6	14.5	14.7	20.0	20.0
Full-time	4.9	6.2	0.0	6.7	2.5	19.0
N	3,492	161	117	75	80	100

For population versus private sector, $\chi^2 = 190.04979$, $df = 2$
For state versus private sector, $\chi^2 = 4.15931$, $df = 2$

Source: Social Stratification Survey 1993, General Population Sample and 1993 Elite Sample.

probably weaker, explanation for the importance of degrees. Degrees are conferred by universities, where people spend several years getting to know one another, acquiring social networks in addition to an academic education.

To what extent is the new economic elite comprised of ex-cadres? This group, representing people who were either paid high officials of the state or Party apparatus or those who held high unpaid positions in the Party, are overrepresented in the new elite. Yet their presence is quite modest (see table 10.5). Ex-cadres make up less than 10 percent of the new economic elite. They are more likely to be found in the state sector or the privatized segment of the private sector than at the top of newly created private enterprises. Cadres (as previously defined) comprised a very select group, about 2 percent of the population. (They are discussed in more detail in the next section.) A less restrictive definition of cadres would include Party members in general. Although in 1993 only 8 percent of the now economically active population identified themselves as members of the Communist Party, well over half of the new economic elite previously had been members. In state and privatized companies, two-thirds of the elite were former Party members. As we move into the private sector, the proportion of ex-Party members drops. Cadres show the same pattern. Power is easier to convert in the privatization process than in building a new company. Political power, expertise, and part-time experience with private enterprise

TABLE 10.3. Average Age and Average Number of Years of Education for Segments of the New Economic Elite and the General Population in 1993

Segment of Population	Average Age	Average Years of Education
General Population	43.3889	11.1701
State Manager	49.5217	18.5901
Privatized manager	48.7778	17.8034
Privatized owner	48.4267	18.0267
Newly founded manager	45.6250	18.3375
Newly founded owner	45.8500	18.1300
F		
Age		
Population versus private elite	41.5206***	
State elite versus private elite	11.8682***	
Education		
Population versus private elite		1,271.9389***
State elite versus private elite		4.7529*

Source: Social Stratification Survey 1993, General Population Sample and 1993 Elite Sample.
*.05 > p > .01 **.01 > p > .001 ***p < .001

under socialism are all assets in the new economy, much as they had been in 1988.

Past membership in the Communist Party and advanced education were, however, of little use to individuals who were not part of the proper network. The position from which these assets could be most fully exploited was that of the ex-manager of a socialist company. The bulk of the new economic elite were not those who had ventured into the private sector by 1988, nor were they top Party and state officials. The overwhelming majority of the new private economic elite, about 70 percent, had been directors of socialist companies in 1988 (see table 10.6). This is true for both managers and manager-owners of privatized and privately founded firms. To find former managers leading and owning privatized companies is hardly surprising. Managers had an enormous influence over privatization. Before May 1990, many participated in spontaneous privatization. After a year-long struggle with the new government, they regained control and then took the lead in self-privatization. Some managed to remain at the helm of privatized companies as directors by finding a friendly outside investor, usually a foreigner. Others were able to buy some part of their company with the help of colleagues and selected sub-

TABLE 10.4. Segments within the New Economic Elite and the General Population Holding Degrees in 1988 (percentages)

		New Elite				
			Private			
Degrees Held in 1988	General Population	State Manager	Privatized Manager	Privatized Owner	Newly Founded Manager	Newly Founded Owner
Ideological	2.2	11.2	15.4	17.3	13.8	24.0
Technical	5.2	65.2	65.0	69.3	52.5	66.0
Business	3.3	44.1	38.5	38.7	60.0	41.0
N	3,492	161	117	75	80	100

	χ^2	*df*
Ideological degree		
Population versus private-sector elite	225.35901	1
State elite versus private-sector elite	3.64433	1
Technical degree		
Population versus private-sector elite	1,181.51874	1
State elite versus private-sector elite	0.15388	1
Business degree		
Population versus private-sector elite	830.76950	1
State elite versus private-sector elite	0.00363	1

Source: Social Stratification Survey 1993, General Population Sample and 1993 Elite Sample.
Note: People can hold multiple degrees.

ordinates. No employee buyout program could be successful without including the company director because banks would not loan money without at least some of the directors on board.

It also is not surprising to find managers heading private firms as employees of private owners. Foreign multinationals were especially keen on hiring competent Hungarian managers with proper experience. What is puzzling is the apparent success of managers who started their own businesses. Managers who left their old companies, and thus did not take part in their privatization, often were nevertheless engaged in privatization. What they appropriated when they left their companies were not tangible assets. They "privatized" their old firms' external networks. They took clients. By funneling to their new companies the orders that would have gone to their old employers, they could get off to a secure start. Since their relationships with distributors and suppliers frequently involved personal ties, those relationships also left with the departing managers. So, too, did bank credit, which was tied to lenders' trust in top executives.[6]

Managers also cannibalized the internal networks of their previous companies. They took the best workers by offering them higher pay. Selectively "privatizing" subordinates had a double advantage: the new entrepreneur could be certain about the abilities of his workers, and he was able

TABLE 10.5. State and Party Officials within Segments of the New Economic Elite and the General Population in 1988 (percentages)

		New Elite				
			Private			
Position	General Population	State Manager	Privatized Manager	Privatized Owner	Newly Founded Manager	Newly Founded Owner
State and Party officials	2.1	10.6	13.7	10.7	5.0	7.0
Communist Party members	7.9	65. 4	67.5	66.2	52.5	42.0
N	3,492	161	117	75	80	100

	χ^2	*df*
State and Party officials		
Population versus private-sector elite	66.26783	1
State elite versus private-sector elite	0.16891	1
Communist Party members		
Population versus private-sector elite	732.44488	1
State elite versus private-sector elite	3.15887	1

Source: Social Stratification Survey 1993, General Population Sample and 1993 Elite Sample.

to transplant into his new company an already established authority relationship.

In 1988, the majority of these managers were not chief executives but deputy or assistant directors. They were running a plant or a division of a larger company or they were second or third in line after the chief executive officer.[7] Had there been no political and economic changes, these people would have been promoted to top positions in their socialist companies in due time. The deliberate downsizing of large companies into smaller enterprises allowed these deputy directors to become chief executive officers earlier than would have occurred otherwise.

Comparing state and privatized companies reveals a strong similarity between the two, which holds even when owner-managers are included. The newly founded private sector is somewhat different. Here we find the largest proportion of people who held no high- or second-rank managerial positions. This is the segment most open to newcomers, especially professionals and highly skilled blue-collar workers, people who had joined the private sector after 1982. As one would expect in cases of early promotion, the elite in the private sector is youthful. And, of this group, those running privately founded companies are the youngest.

The Small Transformation thus brought acceleration for some but no profound change in the principles by which the economic elite achieves its success. This continuity is particularly evident in the privatized segment of the private sector, over which political fights were the most fierce. The

TABLE 10.6. Original Occupations of the New Economic Elite and the General Population in Private Business in 1988 (percentages)

		New Elite					
			Private				
Original Occupation in 1988	General Population	State Manager	Privatized Manager	Privatized Owner	Newly Founded Manager	Newly Founded Owner
Top officials	0.2	1.2	0.9	0.0	1.3	0.0
Top managers	0.1	31.1	39.3	30.7	25.0	16.0
Second-rank managers	2.8	41.0	41.9	45.3	45.0	37.0
Full-time self-employed	4.9	6.2	0.0	6.7	2.5	19.0
Other	92.0	20.5	17.9	17.3	26.3	28.0
N	2,439	161	117	75	80	100

For population versus private-sector elite, $\chi^2 = 1{,}927.9801$, $df = 4$
For state elite versus private-sector elite, $\chi^2 = 1.34755$, $df = 4$

Source: Social Stratification Survey 1993, General Population Sample and 1993 Elite Sample.

same kind of people, though not necessarily the same individuals, comprise the new economic elite as once made up the old one.

The fate of the old *nomenklatura* is a question related to but separate from the recruitment and composition of the private-sector elite. This group's experiences are examined in the next section.

The Fate of the Old Communist *Nomenklatura*

What happened to the *nomenklatura* after the 1990 elections has engendered passionate debate. The participation of the old Communist *nomenklatura* in the newly emerging private economy has been especially controversial. The three theses presented at the beginning of this chapter address the future role of this group. The structural compensation thesis suggests that the old elite will disappear. The technocracy argument, on the other hand, implies that most will survive and those who do will be the best qualified. The power conversion argument also expects stability, especially among the most powerful.[8]

I have divided *nomenklatura* members in 1988 into eight groups. The first and most powerful consists of the highest Party officials, those who held leading positions at the national level. The second group includes middle-rank *apparatchiks,* those who ran the county- and city-level offices. The third and the fourth groups contain state bureaucrats at the national level and those at the county and city levels. The fifth group includes leaders of mass organizations, and the sixth contains managers who ran the strategic companies that remained under state control after 1984.[9] In the last two categories are leaders in science, culture, and the media and members of the foreign service.

With an average age of 51 years in 1988, members of the *nomenklatura* were relatively young. Apart from the scientific and cultural elite, which included many elderly academicians, the top Party leadership and *nomenklatura* managers were the oldest group. Leaders of mass organizations were the youngest. Reflecting the growing rift between the more conservative political leadership and the more technocratic state bureaucracy, top state bureaucrats were younger than Party officials. That these young technocrats were on a fast track in 1988 can be surmised from the fact that they were younger than the middle-level state *apparatchiks* (see table 10.7).

By 1993, almost a third of the *nomenklatura* had retired, although only 19.5 percent of this group was over 65, the mandatory retirement age for people in leadership positions. Most retirees were over 60, however. These new pensioners represented the passing of the generation that had started its careers during the Great Transformation. Almost half the top Party officials and managers stepped down, and of these most retired in

1990. The top officials yielded to the results of the April elections and the managers to purges initiated by the new government in the second half of the same year.

Of those who did not retire, only 57.4 percent stayed in the state sector; 18.2 percent remained as top managers or officials. Those with nonmanagerial jobs in the state sector typically worked for banks, for state agencies such as the State Property Agency or the State Property Holding Company, or for nonprofit organizations.

About a tenth found employment in the private sector and another 2.8 percent ran private companies that they did not own. Many were hired by foreign companies. The rest, 29.6 percent, joined the private sector as business owners (see table 10.8).

Those least inclined to exploit new opportunities in the private sector were the cultural and scientific *nomenklatura*. The oldest of all groups, these leaders of scientific institutions, editors of journals, and heads of cultural organizations heavily dependent on government subsidies found the market inhospitable. Those most likely to own business enterprises were the top Party officials and *nomenklatura* managers who had not retired. Members of the foreign service also found it easy to change course. Their knowledge of foreign countries, their contacts, and their fluency in different languages could be put to good use in the private sector.[10] Overall, a fifth of the 1988 *nomenklatura* owned private businesses by 1993, and these

TABLE 10.7. Average Age and Percentage of Those Who Retired by 1993 in the Different Groups of the 1988 *Nomenklatura*

Nomenklatura Groups	Average Age in 1988	Standard Deviation of Age	Percentage over 65 in 1993	Percentage Retired in 1993	*N*
Party officials (national level)	52.5833	11.1586	25.0	45.8	24
Party officials (local level)	49.3333	7.2023	7.6	32.6	132
Central state officials, legislators	48.7476	9.7728	11.7	27.2	206
Local state officials	51.5641	6.4105	7.7	30.8	39
Leaders of mass organizations	44.5556	14.0162	18.2	29.3	99
Nomenklatura managers	52.2059	6.8799	13.7	45.1	102
Science, culture, media	57.7914	9.4638	42.8	27.3	187
Foreign service	51.0000	8.1464	13.0	34.8	23
Total	51.1613	10.3752	19.5	31.5	812

Source: Social Stratification Survey 1993, 1988 Elite Sample.

TABLE 10.8. Forms of Economic Participation by the Different Groups of the 1988 *Nomenklatura*

	State		Private				
Nomenklatura Groups	Employee	Manager	Employee	Manager	Business Owner	Total Percentage	*N*
Party officials (national level)	23.1	0	23.1	0	53.8	100	13
Party officials (local level)	49.4	12.6	5.7	2.3	29.9	100	87
Central state officials, legislators	33.8	18.9	16.2	4.1	27.0	100	148
Local state officials	32.0	40.0	4.0	0	24.0	100	25
Leaders of mass organizations	31.3	21.9	12.5	0	34.4	100	64
Nomenklatura managers	10.7	23.2	3.6	8.9	53.6	100	56
Science, culture, media	59.6	12.5	9.6	0.7	17.6	100	136
Foreign service	13.3	40.0	0	6.7	40.0	100	15
Total	39.2	18.2	10.3	2.8	29.6	100	544

Source: Social Stratification Survey 1993, 1988 Elite Sample.

were sizable enterprises. Their reported average total sales in 1992 was over 300 million forints; the median figure was 31 million.

Nomenklatura entrepreneurs in the 1990s typically act as brokers between market segments in an environment in which information about demand, prices, and availability of supplies is very costly to obtain.[11] Their participation in a surviving network of extensive connections built through the Party organization provides access to precious information. Exploiting their international ties, they often deal in foreign trade, where they act as middlemen between other post-Communist countries, especially the former Soviet Union and some Western partner. "Their international base," to quote Rákosi, survived the collapse of the international Communist movement, and their fluency in Russian makes them eminently suitable brokers between Western corporate culture and Eastern European bureaucracy.

This profile of the *nomenklatura* provides some support for the claims of each of the three theses. Focusing on the early retirees and the relatively large proportion of people in nonmanagerial positions in the state sector confirms that some top cadres did not adapt to the new circumstances. The high educational level of the old elite and the fact that those who were best educated became private entrepreneurs lends some credence to the technocratic advance argument (see table 10.9). Finally, the high proportion of entrepreneurs among the *nomenklatura,* and among top Party cadres in particular, coupled with the volume of their businesses, suggests that power can be converted into property.

The immediate aftermath of the Communist collapse was an especially hostile period for the old *nomenklatura.* More recently, the successor to the Communist Party has been voted back into power and official tirades against ex-cadres have abated. This impressive electoral victory brought back into positions of power many of the old cadres, including *nomenklatura* members. Those members of the old Communist elite who did not accept administrative appointments are finding their old connections even more valuable than they were under the pre-

TABLE 10.9. Average Age and Education of the 1988 *Nomenklatura* Active in 1993 by Forms of Economic Participation

	State		Private			
	Employee	Manager	Employee	Manager	Business Owner	*F*
Average age	54.5	54.1	50.6	49.6	49.8	7.93***
Average years of education	17.8	18.4	17.6	18.2	18.7	4.62**

Source: Social Stratification Survey 1993, 1988 Elite Sample.
*.05 > p > .01 **.01 > p > .001 ***p < .001

vious government. In the summer of 1994, when the new government was formed, the victorious Socialist Party found it difficult to fill certain high-ranking economic jobs in the government. Most of those who had worked in the economic apparatus before 1989 were reluctant to leave their successful private-sector businesses. Returning to government jobs that pay less and are subject to the whims of politics was not an attractive prospect.

Overall, the younger and more dynamic portion of the 1988 *nomenklatura* has fared well in the post-Communist transformation. The older *nomenklatura* members, the pensioners whose early retirement was precipitated by the 1989 collapse, are often beneficiaries of the private sector as well. Their children, highly educated, fluent in foreign languages, and privy to their parents' connections, frequently run private businesses in which the parents either are silent partners or simply partake in the prosperity of their children's businesses as family members. This is a far cry from the power they used to wield, but together with their high government pensions it secures them a comfortable old age.

The positive expectations of the old Communist elite, which made it willing to yield power voluntarily, by and large have been fulfilled. In other Eastern European countries, a similar stability prevails (Böröcz and Róna-Tas 1995; Róna-Tas forthcoming). That outcome, however, could not have been anticipated by Communist elites lacking positive experiences with the private sector under socialism.

Both the recruitment of the new economic elite and the fate of the old *nomenklatura* illustrate that the Small Transformation has brought no reversals of fortune comparable with the ones engineered by the Great Transformation. The rapidly rising private sector only speeded up changes already under way. In the absence of a strong and ruthless central power, precisely the kind the Small Transformation has undermined, the only rules that will be implemented are those that accommodate the interests of powerful players already in place.

Conclusion

The private sector in Hungary evolved as a constantly changing social space. During the Great Transformation, the private sector shrank enormously, since the state's guiding ideology, Marxism-Leninism, saw no future role for private enterprise in the economy. Only activities that were traditional and labor intensive, but also required little organization, survived. The private sector was confined almost entirely to local markets of the consumer economy. The day-to-day economic lives of the population were organized by the fact that the state made the overwhelming majority of the people into its employees.

Still, from the 1960s on, the private sector grew, drawing in increasing numbers of part-time participants. By providing an alternative means of economic advancement, the growth of the private sector eroded the state's power as an employer. In this early period, the private sector was an economy of needs, acting primarily as a vehicle for people worse off in the system of universal state employment to improve their living standards. The social composition of the private sector allowed a still powerful leadership to tighten and loosen its hold over the private sector according to its perceived interests. From 1982, after private partnerships were introduced and the private sector was allowed to leave its ghetto of the consumer economy, the erosion of the social order based on universal state employment worsened. The social character of the private sector changed. It began to involve state employees higher in the hierarchy and eventually drew in even the top elite. With the leadership's loss of faith in the historical vision of Marxism-Leninism, the stage was set for an early and smooth exit from state socialism.

Thus communism tumbled throughout the region because the principal mechanism undergirding its social order, universal state employment, lost its commanding ability to obtain consent and obedience from the population. Though propping up these regimes with naked force was an option, the top leaders, no longer confident in their historical mission, balked. In countries where the private sector penetrated the top echelons of the leadership the loss of self-confidence was aggravated by the conviction of a large portion of the elite that they would be individually better off under a different social system even if they had to give up their political positions. Those elites contested not the exit from communism but the terms of their own farewell.

If communism as a system went under overnight, its social components still linger. Privatization is path dependent insofar as it unfolds in a struggle of players molded by past events and circumstances. The preferred methods of privatization depend on the position of social groups achieved by the time of the collapse. In Hungary and Poland, citizen vouchers and reprivatization were excluded from the array of options because a well-organized group of company managers and a less forceful but still substantial group of private entrepreneurs, both developed in the last decade of communism, wanted to acquire state property.

State employment, though no longer the backbone of social order, is still an institution of political consequence. A large, though decreasing, segment of the population is still employed by the state. Since the collapse, state employees have emerged as a strong political force. Post-Communist states in retreat, beset by economic hardship, are cutting back on state expenditures. The combination of relative job security and declining real wages coupled with worsening working conditions made state employees easy to mobilize. This large social group has one common adversary, the state, which it can now fight not just at the bargaining table or with strikes[12] but with street demonstrations and even at the ballot box. The ex-Communists' return to power in the region within a few years after communism was pronounced dead, another great surprise to many, was due in no small measure to the votes of disgruntled state employees.

The return of the ex-Communists does not mean the return of the Communist social order. The successor parties try to offer social democratic ideas or serve up an unappetizing and muddled blend of nationalism and socialism. With the possible exception of Russia, no ex-Communist wants to resuscitate either the one-party state or the one-nation-one-factory economy. They do not want to, and cannot, reverse the Small Transformation. Though none has renounced privatization, the determination and zeal with which they pursue it varies. In countries with a negotiated exit ex-Communists have been as steadfast in carrying out privatization as their center-right predecessors were.

During the post-Communist Small Transformation, the private sector has developed from two directions. Through privatization it has widened the distribution of property rights, which had been concentrated in the hands of the state. At the same time, privately founded businesses have emerged, many having evolved from private businesses established in the 1980s. Most of these are very small. Even the few that have grown into sizable operations tend to be smaller than the socialist giants that preceded them.

What kind of economic model will emerge from the Small Transformation remains to be seen. It depends on what new institutions will evolve. With the collapse of universal state employment, these small firms could easily become sweatshops linked to the world economy, and small service and trade businesses might come to serve an increasingly impoverished local population. The newly gained flexibility of small businesses could develop into an unrestrained exploitation of underpaid and unprotected workers (Murray 1983; Mattera 1985). At the same time, an ever-increasing segment of these small businesses could sink into the black economy, where the state loses its power to enforce standards of consumer and worker protection and its ability to collect taxes. The risk of this happening is especially large given the private sector's historically antagonistic relationship with the state. The consequences of the state's inability to collect revenues would be especially dire in Hungary, since the population has grown accustomed to the welfare services that complemented their low state salaries.

On the other hand, the Small Transformation may vindicate Proudhon and usher in a new era dominated by small firms engaged in highly skilled artisan production, producing directly for the world market or subcontracting with large, successful companies, such as occurred in Emilia-Romagna in Italy and Baden-Württemberg in Germany (Brusco 1982; Herrigel 1989; Invernizzi and Revelli 1993). For this to happen, however, new forms of cooperation, such as small-firm networks (Perrow 1993), cooperatives, and service-oriented trade associations, must emerge between and among small firms. As long as ties are thought of as individual assets, providing privileged access to resources and information, and not as public goods, such formalization and extension of informal networks is unlikely. It is equally important that the small private sector develop a new, cooperative relationship with the state. On both sides, a greater recognition of and commitment to mutual obligations is needed. The state has to enforce regulations, many of which are externally imposed as a precondition of Hungary's possible future membership in the European Community. The state also must be able to collect taxes and, in return, supply not only welfare benefits but business services as well. Small business loans administered through private banks, information in the form of easily accessible electronic data bases, and foreign representation and promotion all could be provided fully or partially by the state.

Just what kind of postmodern social order will emerge in post-Communist societies it is too early to tell. One of the most important lessons of the Small Transformation is that the future has an immense capacity for surprising us. It is the certainty that we cannot know the future that cradles hope.

Notes

Chapter 1

1. By *institution* I mean a stable pattern of social conduct, which can be described as a set of rules and norms understood as such by participants (Neale 1994).

2. Throughout this book I use the terms *communism, state socialism,* and *socialism* interchangeably. Welfare capitalist countries, such as Sweden, even if governed by leftist parties, are excluded from this category.

3. Totalitarian theory, though mostly discredited by the mid-1970s, was resuscitated by East European dissidents. It was very influential in guiding resistance to the Party-state (Michnik 1985; Havel 1988; Lipset and Bence 1994).

4. Kennedy and Bialecki (1989) wrestle with the same phenomenon of hierarchically organized dependence with the aid of their concept of the system of vassalage.

5. The important difference between China and Eastern Europe was that in China state employment never became universal. The Maoist version of Marxism-Leninism conceived of concentration differently (Schurmann 1966, 76–90).

6. One thoughtful, institutionalist state centered analysis that also gives a short overview of some of the state and society centered literature is Roeder's account of the fall of the Soviet Union (Roeder 1993).

7. The relevance of the Hungarian case for non-European communist countries is much more questionable.

8. Åslund describes these influences, including the Hungarian contribution, on Gorbachev's economic reforms in some detail (1989). See also Szelényi and Szelényi 1994.

9. Since then, access to HSWP papers has become somewhat more restricted, in order, as officials explained to me, to protect the rights of the individuals who produced these materials or whose names appear in them.

Chapter 2

1. For the causal primacy of ideology in the classical version of the socialist system, see Kornai 1992b, 361.

2. Thus, the difference between theory and ideology does not lie in content but in use. There is a long line of neo-Marxist thought that endorses this distinction (see Althusser [1965] 1970, 231–36; and Gramsci [1929–35] 1971, 377).

3. This general theory of social action is similar to the one proposed by the Austrian school of economics (Schumpeter 1934; Hayek 1967; Alchian 1950; Popper [1957] 1986).

4. The institutionalist literature often fails to distinguish between diffuse culture—anything symbolic—and directly and distinctly stated ideology.

5. The strength of large-scale mass production impressed even Marxists like Gramsci, who rejected historical determinism ([1929–35] 1971, 312).

6. For instance, Durkheim claimed that: "The division of labour varies in direct proportion to the volume and density of societies and if it progresses in a continuous manner over the course of social development it is because societies become regularly more dense and generally more voluminous" ([1893] 1984, 205).

7. Few theorists have understood as well as Weber did the difficulties of finding simple laws of history. Nevertheless, he would have had no objection to the idea of increasing concentration as a main trend in history, as illustrated in his statement that the "whole process of rationalization, in the factory and elsewhere, and especially in the bureaucratic state machine, parallels the centralization of the material implements of organization in the hands of the master. This universal phenomenon more and more restricts the importance of charisma and of individually differentiated conduct" ([1922) 1978, 1156).

8. The Second International, though it was dominated by Engelsian and Kautskian Marxism, also included representatives of non-Marxist traditions such as anarchism and Proudhonism.

9. The basic concept of history moved by a single "engine" is an ideological homologue of the factory.

10. Some might prefer to call this dialectic instead of ambivalence. A more detailed discussion of these ambiguities is provided in Burawoy 1985, 85–122.

11. Engels was less optimistic. He recognized the hierarchy of the factory as necessary: "If man, by dint of his knowledge and inventive genius, has subdued the forces of nature, the latter avenge themselves upon him by subjecting him, in so far as he employs them, to a veritable despotism, independent of all social organization. Wanting to abolish authority in large-scale industry is tantamount to wanting to abolish industry itself, to destroy the power loom in order to return to the spinning wheel" (quoted in Marglin 1976, 13).

12. Marx made a distinction between concentration (or accumulation) and centralization of capital. The former meant the introduction of modern large-scale production as gathered in one business enterprise, the latter the accumulation of ownership in the hands of a single capitalist. The first involves capital and labor used in a particular production process; the second addresses the distribution of these assets among capitalists ([1867] 1974, 585–89). Marx contended that "centralisation completes the work of accumulation by enabling industrial capitalists to extend their operations" (588).

13. There are references to socialism scattered throughout Marx's writings, but they do not amount to a detailed exposition of the topic. Originally, socialism for Marx was not a blueprint for a society to be built but rather a theoretical tool with which to dissect capitalism. For instance, the celebrated phrase from the *German Ideology* about how people "will hunt in the morning, fish in the afternoon, rear

cattle in the evening and be a literary critic after dinner, without ever becoming a hunter, a fisherman, a herdsman or a critic" should not be taken as Marx's idea of how labor should be actually performed in socialism (Marx and Engels [1846] 1976, 53). As such, it is ludicrous (see Nove 1983). What it does tell us is that the division of labor lies at the heart of capitalism, and the social system that will supersede capitalism will ultimately have to end the division of labor as we know it. Later, in the "Critique of the Gotha Program," Marx takes a more programmatic approach to socialism. There he recognizes the necessity of setting aside funds for capital accumulation, administration, insurance, and so on. ([1875] 1986, 322). This is an important theoretical shift in Marx's position, which Karl Kautsky would carry further.

14. One may wish to argue that Kautsky, and to a lesser extent Engels, diluted Marxist dialectics and opted for a more mechanistic interpretation of history. To guide action effectively, ideology required this transformation. (Contradictions are useful only when ideology is used to justify action after the fact.) Lidtke argues that the mechanistic, positivistic, and economistic interpretation of Marx was a way of avoiding censorship during the 1880s (1966, 280–81). The fact remains that Marx did not entertain any countervailing force to concentration.

15. Not incidentally, Kautsky made this statement to prove that the liberation of the working class would lead to the liberation of all. Indeed, the concept of the universal class is premised on the idea of a society with one dominant logic of operation, or—to use Marxist parlance—a unified mode of production.

16. Confronted with the labor-repressive policies of the Russian Revolution, Kautsky later shifted his position. By then deposed as the chief ideologue of the already splintered labor movement, Kautsky bitterly attacked the coercive labor regime introduced by the Soviet labor code of 1918 as a threat to democracy ([1919] 1973). He took a cautiously gradualist approach to the appropriation of capitalists (Kautsky [1921] 1983; Steenson 1978; Salvadori 1979).

17. Kropotkin made these points earlier, and with even more passion, in a series of articles beginning in 1888, but he was marginal to the debates in the labor movement (Kropotkin [1899] 1974).

18. Rosa Luxemburg rebutted revisionism by arguing that large-scale capitalist production depended on its noncapitalist classes (small peasants and artisans) and nations. These provided capitalists with markets, raw materials, and cheap labor. Capitalism would destroy itself, as it would devour its noncapitalist environment; all nations would turn capitalist, and all small producers would fall to underpaid factory labor and no longer would be able to buy what capitalists produced ([1900] 1973, [1913] 1972; see also Colletti 1972).

19. In his contribution to the Marxist literature on the historical inevitability of concentration, Lenin described how relations between capitalists interlocked through the large banks. Then he continued:

> But underlying this interlocking, its very base, are the changing social relations of production. When a big enterprise assumes gigantic proportions, and, on the basis of exact computation of mass data, organises according to plan the supply of primary raw materials to the extent of two-thirds, or three-

> fourths, of all that is necessary for tens of millions of people; when the raw materials are transported in a systematic and organised manner to the most suitable places of production, sometimes situated hundreds or thousands of miles from each other; when a single centre directs all the consecutive stages of processing the materials right up to the manufacture of numerous varieties of finished articles; when these products are distributed according to a single plan among tens and hundreds of millions of consumers (the marketing of oil in America and Germany by the American oil trust)—then it becomes evident that we have socialisation of production, and not mere 'interlocking'; that private economic and private property relations constitute a shell which no longer fits its contents, a shell which must inevitably decay if its removal is artificially delayed . . . (Lenin [1916] 1974, 302–3)

20. The most eloquent advocate of Taylorism at that time was Alexei Gastev, who led the influential Central Labor Institute from 1920 until he fell victim to Stalin's Great Purges in the mid-1930s (Bailes 1977). Gastev's wildly utopian vision of society as a single machine was a natural, though highly impractical, extension of Lenin's ideas.

21. The parallel with German state capitalism did not ruffle the Bolsheviks. They had no doubt that increasing centralization and state intervention, the "objective law of historical progress," would operate in both countries. That Germany had been applying some of the same methods as the Bolsheviks had adopted was an indisputable sign that Germany was ripening for the same kind of revolutionary transformation as had taken place in Russia.

22. I am not attempting to prove or disprove the inevitability of the one-nation-one-factory model in the Soviet case. Therefore I set aside the otherwise important question of whether or not the NEP was a viable alternative to centralized planning. My concern is with the ideological origins of socialism in Eastern Europe, and in Hungary in particular. The NEP did not have any direct influence on the original economic and political organization adopted in Eastern Europe after World War II. Indeed, discussion of the NEP era was strongly suppressed in the self-constructed mythology of Soviet Communism. It gained significance only in times when the Soviet-type model came under criticism and when critics were looking for historical precedents with which to legitimate their reform efforts.

23. This is, of course, a recapitulation of Marx and Engels's position in the *Communist Manifesto* of 1848. This text appears in the *History of the Communist Party of the Soviet Union (Short Course),* which was the principal ideological guide after its publication in 1938 in the Soviet Union and after the Communist takeover in Eastern Europe. See also Stalin [1952] 1972. A similar paraphrasing of Marx's position is given by Lenin ([1914) 1974, 64–74).

24. The model charter of the Soviet *kolkhoz,* issued in 1935, allotted a small plot for *kolkhoz* households. These householders could keep personal livestock, poultry, and other small animals in limited numbers, maintain stables for these animals, and possess minor farm implements for working on their plots (Waedekin 1982, 17).

25. Though the Marxist-Leninist vision became a constitutive force only after the communist parties of Eastern Europe took power, many of the ideas discussed previously were in circulation in Eastern European countries before 1945. In Hun-

gary the Social Democratic Party had been in constant intellectual exchange with the international labor movement since its inception. Hungarian Social Democrats were strongly influenced by Marx, Engels, Kautsky, and Hilferding. Most of them shared the vision of concentration as the iron law of history (Solt and Szigeti 1990). While many joined the ranks of the communist parties after 1945, partly out of opportunism and partly because they saw the changes to come as inevitable, many Social Democrats chose to resist Communist designs out of loyalty to their political constituencies.

26. For an explication of the image of the social structure underlying Agrippa's tale, see Ossowski 1963.

27. This tight concept of a functional whole made any deviance inexcusable. The smallest act of disobedience would have consequences of ultimate importance and thus could carry severe penalties.

Chapter 3

1. The actual nationalization was proclaimed a month and a half later on May 11.

2. In September 1945, the Federation of Industrial Employers (GYOSZ) complained that, in theory, such regulations made complete nationalization possible (Pető and Szakács 1985, 53).

3. Another issue that bolstered the HCP's strength concerned Hungarian prisoners of war. Over half a million Hungarian POWs were estimated to be held in the Soviet Union after the war. Many had been taken prisoner not in battle but as soldiers returning home. Some were even civilians. There were few families that did not have a member or an acquaintance in a Soviet POW camp. The Soviet Union used the political significance of the POW issue as a bargaining chip, granting concessions only to the Communists.

4. By then the non-Communist members of the governing coalition were in disarray. In each party, factional infighting raged between the pro- and anti-Communist groups, abetted and manipulated by the Communist Party. The Communists used the police under their command to harass and arrest leaders of the coalition partners hostile to them. In February 1948, they forced the Social Democratic minister of industry to emigrate; thus, at the time of this decision, his Communist deputy was running the ministry (Pető 1988).

5. Beginning in 1949, all functions of the ECC were taken over by the National Planning Office.

6. The new state-owned trading companies were first created in the capital. To supply the countryside, the state took control of the local consumer cooperatives, which had formed before 1945 as voluntary associations. Later, the reach of state-owned trading companies was extended to the rest of the country.

7. During this period, Hungarian statistical data subdivided industry into construction, service industry, and manufacturing (or industry proper). Later, the state sector was further differentiated, but this threefold classification was retained for private small industry (*magánkisipar*).

8. When agricultural and nonagricultural small producers are combined with small shopkeepers, the figures show that in 1949 half of the work force consisted of

self-employed small producers. The proportion of people employed by others (both private and public), had dropped from 58.6 percent in 1930 and 61.2 percent in 1941 to 47.4 percent in 1949.

9. In 1948, workshops that had at least one employee averaged 3.4 persons. According to the 1949 census, 79.7 percent of the industrial small producers had no employees, 11.1 percent had one, and 4.7 had two. The proportion of artisans employing more than six persons was 1.3 percent. These figures may somewhat underestimate employment in small production, because they do not include family members or temporary workers (Nevelő 1973).

10. Data on intergenerational mobility show that over a third of the industrial small producers came from similar backgrounds, that the sons of skilled industrial and white-collar workers were overrepresented, and that the sons of landless and landed peasant fathers were underrepresented. Yet, because of the size of the landed peasantry, the agrarian population still provided one-fifth of this stratum (Andorka 1982, 66–67).

11. This limited concept of labor was reinforced by a widely embraced (albeit now strongly suppressed) anti-Semitism. For historical reasons, Jews in Hungary were overrepresented in nonmanual occupations (McCagg 1972; János 1982, 222–23; Hanák 1984). In the public mind, the merchant, middleman, and banker were pictured in hostile ethnic stereotypes; they were aliens, non-Hungarians, and, most often, Jews.

12. Among industrial small producers, the Social Democrats held the majority of leading positions in organizational bodies, with the Small Holders' Party a distant second. Among the landholding peasantry, the Small Holders' Party had by far the greatest influence, followed by the National Peasant Party.

13. See, for example, the letter sent by President Árpád Szakasits to the National Free Association of Small-tradesmen, responding to this organization's anxious concerns (*Magyar Nemzet,* May 3, 1949).

14. At these elections, in which the leftist bloc led by the Communist Party won 95.5 percent of the vote, one could vote for the leftist bloc or one could tender an unspecific dissenting vote.

15. In certain instances the authorities resorted to more radical forms of elimination. For instance, in 1953 some butchers received severe sentences—including prison terms and the death penalty—for allegedly cheating customers (Berényi 1985, 63).

16. In an unsigned report from the National Planning Board (Országos Terv Hivatal) to Ernő Gerő in 1952, it was acknowledged that the production targets for state firms in the first five-year plan had not taken into account the loss of production from the private sector. A slowdown in the elimination of private artisan production was suggested (PIA/276.116/18/1953, 41).

17. My thinking on collectivization and socialist agriculture in general has been strongly influenced by long discussions with Martha Lampland. Her recent book (1995) is the best historical ethnography of Hungarian socialist agriculture.

18. Respect for private property and fear of the possible consequences of violating property rights were deeply rooted in the peasantry (Lampland 1995, 126–28). In Apátfalva, for instance, in the south of Hungary, many poor peasants did not

dare to apply for land because they felt that the land distributed among them still belonged to its previous owners (Halász 1975, 20).

19. Except for the National Peasant Party (NPP), and to a lesser degree the Social Democrats, all non-Communist parties made their resistance to collectivization the centerpiece of their political programs. But even the National Peasant Party denied that it intended anything more than "private production—cooperative sales," as Péter Veres, the leader of the NPP, put it in August 1947 (quoted in Magyar 1986, 126).

20. The 1944 law was revoked in May 1945 but was essentially reinstated two months later (Pető and Szakács 1985, 49)

21. The golden crown was a unit that measured value of the land in terms of 1853 wheat prices. Good quality land is valued around 25 gold crown per cadastral yoke.

22. For example, on July 3, 1949, the national press denounced three *kulak* saboteurs. One failed to weed his crop, the second cut the wheat early and used it as fodder for livestock, and the last let her cattle graze in her wheat field (*Magyar Nemzet,* July 3, 1949).

23. After swallowing the Social Democratic Party in March 1947, the Hungarian Communist Party became known as the Hungarian Workers' Party.

24. In the United States, the average farm size in 1959 was 117 hectares (Statistical Abstracts 1987, 621). Three average-sized farms in the United States joined together were larger than one average-sized Hungarian *kolkhoz,* which typically would have 72 members.

25. An ideological campaign was fought against "*kétlakiság*" (dual residence), resulting from people's unwillingness to fully renounce their agrarian backgrounds and find exclusive residence in the ranks of the working class (Tóth 1970, 25–33). Miners, with their strong prewar tradition of tending auxiliary plots provided by mining companies, were especially castigated in the ideological propaganda.

26. In 1957, after the 1956 exodus from the cooperatives, there were about 1,200,000 private farms, which meant that almost half of the country's population lived in households with private farms (KSH 1959a).

27. While attempts to collectivize agriculture were made in all the Eastern European Soviet-type societies, their success varied. The least successful was the Polish attempt, which left about 80 percent of the land under private cultivation (Waedekin 1982). Comparative studies of socialist collectivization point to the ethnic and religious homogeneity of the Polish peasantry, demographical factors that increased the rural population beyond the capacities of industry and the cities to absorb them; the lack of positive incentives for the peasants to join the collectives; the role Wladislaw Gomulka played in the Polish Communist Party (United Polish Workers' Party); and the balance of power in the countryside (Orbán 1986; Juhász and Magyar 1984; Torańska 1987).

One of the factors that made collectivization easier in Hungary was that the Hungarian Communists could initially count on the support of the leadership of the National Peasant Party, the party representing mostly the poor peasantry. The Polish Communists did not have such a political convenience.

28. The Trade Union Council estimated that by the fall of 1946 this figure was 106,000 (Baksay 1983, 75).

29. The existence of the B-list was such a sensitive issue that during elections the Communist Party always had to make tactical and temporary concessions. For instance, before the elections of 1949, which secured the final political victory for the Communists, an amnesty was declared for people still employed in their jobs but adversely affected by the "screening procedures" (*igazoló eljárás*) mandated by the B-list. According to one letter to the editor of the *Magyar Nemzet,* the daily paper oriented toward the petty bourgeoisie and the intellectuals, this amnesty was a cause of relief for about 50,000 people (*Magyar Nemzet,* May 13, 1949).

30. Those who returned just two years later had plenty of reason to curse their adventurous decision in the wake of the anti-Yugoslav, anti-Tito hysteria, which branded them as Yugoslav agents.

31. These people were to be sent to do the worst jobs. The Communists reasoned that people responsible for the devastation of the country should bear a special burden in rebuilding it.

32. It is not clear, however, to what extent members of religious orders and inmates in insane asylums were actually subjected to this form of therapy (Belényi 1993, 15).

33. Factory work as character building was invented long before state socialism. The poorhouse in Victorian England operated on this same principle.

34. See, for instance, Rákosi's speech to the central leadership of the Hungarian Workers' Party on May 31, 1949 (Balogh 1986, 63–77).

35. A legal decree by the Council of Ministers was issued on February 16, 1950, effective retroactively as of January 1. This was a general law that made any act harmful to the execution of the plan punishable by up to two years in prison. The Supreme Court in 1951 handed down a decision that "absence from work *without harmful intent* or leave without proper excuse is covered by this law, and *normally* should be punished by corrective-educational labor" (Belényi 1993, 116, emphasis added).

36. In the city of Debrecen in 1951, physical examination of 231 special course candidates found that 39 had some type of heart trouble.

37. In the summer of 1953, five counties issued no licenses at all. Nationwide only 203 of the 2,266 applicants were granted licenses, though by the Party's own calculations the country needed 5,772 more artisans (Tellér 1973, 155).

38. Artisans had lost their houses because their workshops were in their homes and thus the houses were considered capital to be appropriated. Some got their houses back, if the buildings were under a certain size. Because artisans lived in them, those houses were considered as "personal" rather than as private property.

39. Acquiring a business license ceased to be a civil right; licenses were to be granted only if local consumer needs could not be met in other ways. A business license could not be issued to anyone who kept his or her job in the state sector.

40. Artisans were required to pay social security taxes; after ten years they could retire on a pension. In 1967, 12 percent of the artisans paid no taxes for "social reasons," that is, they were handicapped or too old (PIA/288.15/137/1967, 14).

41. In 1960, 3,201 artisans were members of agricultural collectives and kept

their licenses, almost all of them having joined the year before. In the same year, 3,700 (or every fifth artisan who retired his license) joined cooperatives. Agricultural cooperatives also needed the land many artisans in the countryside cultivated to supplement their nonagricultural activities. In 1951, 32 percent of the artisans owned agricultural land; in early 1960, this figure stood at 25 percent.

42. Similar measures were taken in commerce, where the number of companies was cut in half between 1960 and 1965 (Berényi 1985, 157).

43. It was widely believed that reducing the number of companies would make planning easier and that poor cooperation among companies would be replaced with rational coordination within a few large enterprises (Szamuely 1986, 31).

44. In Soviet Russia and Communist China, countries that entered socialism with a less industrialized economy than Hungary's, the Great Transformation was immeasurably more painful.

45. See also Hirschman 1977; Berg 1980; and Heilbroner 1953.

Chapter 4

1. The location of the largest steel town, Dunaújváros, was chosen during the anti-Yugoslav campaign of the late 1940s. Originally planned to be built close to the coal supplies in the Mecsek region and the Yugoslav border, the city was moved north for reasons of military security.

2. There were different workers' organizations controlled by the employer.

3. Railway men had to pass an entrance examination to get into a special training program to become officers. The program provided them with the necessary skills, but it was at least as important that they be trained to obey and keep accurate time schedules. As most of the recruits were young peasants, they had to acquire a completely different notion of time. Peasants lived in a time regime that was regulated by the tasks of agriculture. The feverishly active periods of the summer alternated with the lax months of winter. Work was always in the daytime, and a job lasted as long as it took to finish the task. Time was articulated in terms of tasks rather than tasks being subdivided by an abstract notion of time. The regime at the railways was just the opposite. The constant flow of trains required an even pace of labor day and night. The clock was the taskmaster. Absolute punctuality was a matter of honor. The railway man was as much a slave to the clock as he was to his superiors (Moldova 1978).

4. Socialist state employment bears striking—and not incidental—resemblance to the way Hegel depicted the civil servant in his *Philosophy of Right:*

> What the service of the state really requires is that men shall forgo the selfish and capricious satisfaction of their subjective ends; by this very sacrifice they acquire the right to find their satisfaction in, but only in, the dutiful discharge of their public functions. In this fact, so far as public business is concerned, there lies the link between universal and particular interests which constitutes both the concept of the state and its inner stability. It follows that a man's tenure of his civil service post is *not contractual,* although his appointment involves a consent and an undertaking on both sides . . . the wrong commit-

> ted by . . . the non-performance, or positive misperformance (i.e., through an action contrary to official duty . . .) [of his task], is an infringement of the universal content itself . . . and so is a trespass or even a crime. ([1820] 1967, para. 294, emphasis added)

Hegel's *Philosophy of Right* had a very strong impact on Marx. In Marx's philosophy, Hegel's civil servant is replaced with the factory worker as the constituent of the "universal class."

5. For instance, the Rimamurány-Salgótarján Steelworks had a very similar organization of industrial authority (Szabó 1938).

6. The official interpretation of Article 9 of the Hungarian Constitution of 1949 declared that, since the country's social order was based on work, anyone without a workplace could be considered a criminal. For reasons of tradition, exception was made for women supported by their families unless they were found to be engaged in objectionable practices such as prostitution. The prohibition against "endangering the public by shirking" (*közveszélyes munkakerülés*) was enforced less strictly after 1968, but in 1984 there were still more than 4,000 people convicted of that offense.

7. From the beginning, the general system included exceptions. For instance, in the 1950s and 1960s, agricultural cooperatives worked on a labor-unit system whereby neither workers nor jobs were categorized. Instead, individual tasks, such as hoeing soil of a certain quality, weeding, or cleaning a pigsty were assigned a value in labor units. Each worker in the cooperative accumulated labor units over the year. At the end of the fiscal year, the overall income of the cooperative (less the compulsory state deliveries, other taxes, operating costs, and investments) was distributed in proportion to the labor units each member had collected. This system reflected the low level of specialization in cooperatives; people were rarely assigned to specific tasks permanently. The residual nature of the income paid to the members reflected the fact that the state took no responsibility for providing members with material security. Workers got what was left, and, if little was left, little they got. The system was changed as part of the 1968 economic reforms, and agricultural workers began to receive a regular monthly income from the cooperative.

8. A brochure written for Party activists in 1975 makes this point more concisely: "The question of personnel is essentially the question of power" (Pullai 1975, 11).

9. Even in the 1970s, when Party membership below a certain position was not required, only strongly recommended, managers were expected to represent the Party just as Party members were (Pullai 1975, 10).

10. The term *nomenklatura* is sometimes used to describe the entire system of Party control of personnel decisions from the shop floor to the highest reaches of power.

11. This was explained by one author in the following way:

> Socialism is the society of work, where every able-bodied person must participate in social labor according to his or her capacities and talents. Not only because this is a precondition of economic growth but because labor is a

social need of man and this is the fundamental form in which people get integrated into society. (Molnárné and Orolin 1982, 38; see also Ferge 1982, 216–17)

12. Health care was extended gradually to the entire population. Education was free in that there was no tuition.

13. Sik has demonstrated that in the 1970s, as firms had to find new ways of attracting labor under an inflexible set of wage regulations, they began to increase their welfare budgets (1987).

14. There was a Hungarian version of Monopoly, which was popular before the Communist takeover. Capitaly, as it was called, strictly followed the rules of the original, although it took its street names from Budapest rather than Atlantic City, New Jersey. Capitaly was considered ideologically inappropriate for a long time and was played clandestinely by those fortunate enough to have held onto their old game board, the box of fake money, and the chance and title deed cards.

15. By the 1980s, however, the East German economy had the most concentrated organization in Communist Europe.

16. An extensive overview of economies of scale and company size for developed market economies is given by Scherer 1971. He found no conclusive evidence that concentration increased much overall between the 1930s and the 1960s.

Chapter 5

1. The political, economic, and theoretical considerations leading up to the reforms have been discussed in detail in Berend 1990, 113–67; Szamuely 1982, 1984; Swain 1992, 85–99; Batt 1988; and Révész 1990. The intellectual roots of the reforms, which reach back to Imre Nagy's New Course, are chronicled in Berend 1990 and Szamuely 1986.

2. Of course, in many instances these unrestricted prices were driven by the prices of goods fixed by the National Prices and Materials Office.

3. The renting of small state shops to private individuals was suggested in 1968 but was not introduced until 1981.

4. Animal husbandry is more amenable to factory production than is plant growing, but introducing large-scale production methods into cattle or pig breeding requires expensive investments.

5. This is a reference to China's Great Leap Forward, when Mao Zedong led a campaign to build small foundries in the countryside.

6. Calculating the exact rate of growth is difficult because it was not always clear how to separate the accounts of the side business from those of its parent cooperative. All estimates confirm, however, that in this period side businesses grew very fast (see PIA/288.5/563/1971, 18; or PIA/288.24/1970/56, 159).

7. During the parliamentary debate over the new labor code, it was questioned whether these conditions might abridge the constitutional guarantees of the right to work. The answer that satisfied the legislature was that, while all people have the right to work, they do not necessarily have the right to keep the same job (Radnay 1985, 22).

8. It was very difficult to argue against this, given the labor movement's long history of fighting for shorter workdays.

9. In this debate the epithet "petty bourgeois" became an all-purpose pejorative. Some claimed that this despicable mentality had such consequences as "wavering," "pseudoradicalism" in politics, "ideological subjectivism" (Ovári 1975, 21), the reading of pulp novels (Vitányi 1973, 23), anarchism, utopianism, and liberalism (Ripp 1973). "Petty bourgeois" stood for anything that ran counter to the official orthodoxy. An excellent summary of this debate is given by Berend (1990, 201–31).

10. This is in perfect harmony with the property rights school, which treats property rights as a bundle of entitlements, including the right of use (Pejovic 1990; Furubotn and Pejovic 1974; Alchian 1965).

11. There was an increase in the number of Central Committee members representing the 49 giant firms selected for special treatment (Szalai 1989, 28; Baranyai et al. 1981, 250–59).

12. In Hungary, as in most other socialist countries, decent housing had been unavailable for most people in the precommunist era, and the war also demolished a large part of the existing housing. Yet there were reasons specific to socialist industrialization that made housing shortages particularly severe. Socialist economies overinvested in their industrial base, and about half of the total investment budget was spent in heavy construction (i.e., for building factories, roads, etc.). Resources thus were drained from residential housing. Industrialization itself created an immense demand for housing by relocating a large part of the population from the countryside to the cities.

13. In 1983, every third full-time private artisan worked in this area, compared with 15 percent in 1938 and 1960.

Chapter 6

1. The term *mirrored opposition* is borrowed from David Stark (1986).

2. Using the method of microsimulation based on expert estimates, Éltető and Vita tested different models to estimate the effect of unmeasured income, most of which came from the private sector, on the overall distribution of personal income in 1982 (Éltető and Vita 1987). They found that, even under the least egalitarian assumptions, invisible income increased inequalities in personal income only very modestly.

3. A description of this survey is given in Róna-Tas 1990, 265–73.

4. In the 1981 Social Stratification Survey (SSS–1981), anyone who reported being self-employed full time was included in the full-time private sector.

5. That children of the self-employed followed less and less frequently in their parents' footsteps was partially due to the fact that there was little business property to inherit.

6. This is consistent with some of the Western literature on the self-reported motivation of small entrepreneurs (Boswell 1973, 51).

7. The data in SSS–1981 on part-time private pursuits were gathered by asking a series of questions about regular sources of income.

8. A person who reported participating in household farming and claimed that at least some of the farm's produce was sold that year was classified in SSS–1981 as participating in commercial part-time farming.

9. My analysis does not distinguish between licensed part-time operators and informal moonlighters because SSS–1981 found very few people in the first group (0.7 percent). Part-time license holders were identified by a question asking whether the person operated a licensed part-time business. Informal part-time participation was measured by asking whether people had any regular income from informal activities outside their primary jobs. While licensed activities were most likely to be reported accurately, informal activities were probably underreported. Still, in 1981, when the leadership was already considering major steps to liberalize the private sector, the perceived danger of telling the truth was not as high as one might otherwise expect.

10. A large proportion of social research, including SSS–1981, was conducted in the 1970s and 1980s by contracting for the work of survey interviews, coding, or data entry. Many dissidents unable to find proper state employment because of political persecution made money through such contracts (Rakovski 1978).

11. In SSS–1981, any respondent who reported regular income from part-time labor contracts was included in this group.

12. People were classified as rent collectors in SSS–1981 if they had income either from subletting their residences or from renting their vacation houses. Although these options were both legal, renting was probably underreported. Since one person can do more than one kind of activity, the sum of all these percentages is larger than the percentage of people participating in the private sector.

13. A more complex multivariate statistical analysis can be found in Róna-Tas 1990, 122–227.

14. According to estimates from the late 1980s, about one-third of private-sector earnings were inaccessible through survey questionnaires (Ékes 1987; Kolosi and Róbert 1991). We have no estimates for 1981, but there is reason to believe that at that time reported private-sector earnings were probably somewhat closer to the truth, because personal income tax was introduced only in 1987 for the entire population and the overall size of unreported income, growing slightly in the 1980s, jumped considerably in that year (Lackó 1991).

15. Though their figure is slightly higher, the difference may be due to sampling error.

16. Since income from a state job was reported directly by the person's company in SSS–1981, these income figures can be considered reliable.

17. These calculations are based on income from one's job as reported by the company. The incomes then were averaged over the detailed occupational categories of the first four digits of FEOR, the classification system described in chapter 4. For those in the socialist sector, this code was obtained from their employers; for those with no state employment, it was assigned on the basis of their self-reported occupation. Even using larger categories (the first three digits), the analysis leads to the same conclusion.

18. Those who collect rent are similar to nonparticipant state employees, but they are slightly better educated.

19. In 1965, the Central Committee became concerned over functionaries taking secondary employment in the socialist sector. In the opinion of the Secretariat, this often was simply a form of "money grabbing" (PIA/288.7/228/1965, 29). Subsequent measures prohibited dual employment for functionaries, but this group was not prohibited from making extra money through labor contracts (PIA/288.5/371/1965, 177). Most of these contracts involved lectures in political seminars for cadres or courses at universities in scientific socialism, Marxism-Leninism, and other similar topics.

Chapter 7

1. Sensing danger, defenders of household farming tried to rescue it from the second economy label. They argued that household farming was so thoroughly integrated into the socialist economy as to be a part of it (Radnóti 1979).

2. Typical examples are reports sent by two different departments of the Ministry of Light Industry on private services and artisan production in October 1979 (MF/258i/1979a and MF/258i/1979b). The policy suggestions included letting the private service sector perform repair work covered by manufacturers' warranties, increasing modestly the limit on loans for artisans, improving the supply of materials and parts, and so on. There were some cautious and vague suggestions that the possibilities of new organizational forms should be studied.

3. As Seleny demonstrates (1995), many of these bureaucrats had supported the New Economic Mechanism in 1968 and felt that there could be a return to economic reforms.

4. In a tape-recorded personal interview conducted by Anna Seleny, one of the principal actors emphasized: "At that time, we had no idea what will come out of this, or what will happen later, but it is certain, that it had an important role . . . enterprising and working in organizations outside the state organized sector . . . yes, this came to have a social role, of which we, I believe, did not think in the beginning."

5. Fekete (1990) develops the idea of the "coup" as a method of macroeconomic management in socialist economies.

6. The three-quarters figure was recited often enough so that no one ever questioned its origins. It derived from SSS–1981 by taking the widest possible definition of the "second economy." Thus, families keeping a kitchen garden and families with at least one member who worked overtime at his or her regular job, took a second job in the socialist sector, or received tips in his or her state job were all included (Boros 1984). Keeping to our more restrictive definition of the private sector (i.e., income-producing activity outside state employment), the three-quarters figure boils down to about one-third. Yet, if we add the customers of the private sector as participants, the figure inflates again.

7. "Restructuring" meant not so much a change in the organization of production as a switch from one line of products to another, for example, from iron and steel to chemicals.

8. In official language, the "socially organized sector" is the sector organized by the state.

9. The Ministry of Industry explained this in a directive:

> The objectives of our economic policy must be accomplished primarily within the framework of large-scale production by permanently improving that method. However, we cannot do without forcefully exploring and utilizing the possibilities that are to be found in *the application of socialist economic relations* in small-scale production. (Erdős and Juhász 1983, 51)

10. In January 1981, a new system of contracting applicable to small shops, restaurants, and hotels was introduced. The shops could not employ more than five people, but this number could be expanded to 12 for restaurants and hotels. Individuals and families could win contracts in open auctions.

11. The term *work partnership* (*munkaközösség*) emphasized that these new forms were based on labor and were collective enterprises. This made them sound more in line with socialist ideology.

12. In the literature both the acronyms VGMK and VGM are used.

13. An August 1980 decree of the Economic Committee of the government only suggests that the Minister of Labor should investigate whether private activities linked to state employment is a "meaningful" (*értelmezhető*) concept (MF/1980, 8).

14. The strongest resistance to the private sector came from the Ministries of Education and Health (see, e.g., MF/ME/58.956/1983.XVII; MF/MH/90.560/1982; and MF/SZA/1983). Both ministries felt strongly that in the areas of health and education, private enterprise had to be strictly limited.

15. A description of this survey and a comparison with SSS–1981, used in the previous chapter, is provided in Róna-Tas 1990, 274–78.

16. The "putting-out" system was introduced in 1982. Under it, cooperative would give pigs, cattle, and rabbits to private entrepreneurs, who would raise them on contract (Szelényi 1988, 85; Kovách 1987).

17. In SSS–1986, the comparable proportion would have been 6.6 percent, which shows that the survey somewhat underestimated participation in these forms. There are several reasons why this could occur. First, census figures are from tax registration forms for partnerships and from license registration for part-time artisans. The 1986 survey, on the other hand, asked only whether the respondent had any income from these sources. Another possible reason for the discrepancy is that the activities may have been underreported in the survey. Since these were legal and registered activities, I consider this a less likely explanation. Finally, simple sampling error could have contributed to the discrepancy.

18. This was not to be blamed solely on the VGMKs. A representative survey of 1,000 contracts between VGMKs and their parent firms found that only 27 allowed outside contracting (Csillag 1986, 110).

19. The average full-time GMK member paid a third of his net income in social security taxes. Part-time employees were required to pay only a low flat fee for insurance against work-related injury.

20. The importance of political trust was pointed out by the Ministry of Finance in a memorandum to the Economic Policy Commission as a justification for implementing the Enterprise Law of 1989 (MF/2345/1988).

21. "Small cooperatives" and "small enterprises" were legal categories. Together with the limitation on their size, there were special regulations they had to obey.

22. This cut, originally heralded as a major step toward improving standards of living, was implemented because it had been promised much earlier and the Party had already begun phasing it in by 1980.

23. At a Central Committee meeting, János Kádár reportedly asserted: "We are through with paying the punitive interest on our past mistakes."

24. The fierce debate was displeasing to both hard-liners, who were appalled by the vocal resistance, and reformers, who felt that ideas were being pushed off the agenda by the lengthy discussion.

25. The campaign came on the heels of a similar crackdown in the Soviet Union at the beginning of Gorbachev's rule in 1985.

26. A more complex multivariate statistical analysis is given in Róna-Tas 1990, 228–52.

27. In 1987, Grósz became prime minister and in May of 1988 the first secretary of the HSWP, succeeding Kádár.

28. Just how important connections were was clearly spelled out in a report prepared by the National Organization of Artisans. Most artisans who worked alone or with family for private consumers were at a disadvantage in finding contracts in the socialist sector. As the report put it: "Many [artisans] felt 'on their own skins' the lack of proper personal connections, which had a strong influence on their ability to cooperate with large firms" (MF/MP/Ui–2588/83, 2).

29. The state kept its jurisdiction over certain large firms that it deemed strategically important.

30. This information is drawn from the triennial reports of the Labor Information Center of the State Office of Wages and Labor.

31. See also the joint report of the Ministry of Internal Commerce, the Ministry of Industry, and the Ministry of Finance to the State Planning Board, March 1987 (MF/MIT/MI/1987).

Chapter 8

1. Poland and Hungary influenced events in other Eastern European countries through more than their examples. For instance, Poland and Hungary condemned the Warsaw Pact invasion of Czechoslovakia on the twenty-first anniversary of that event in August 1989. The Czechoslovak leadership, which had been installed by means of the intervention of Polish, Hungarian, and other troops, was furious. In September, in a dramatic gesture, Hungary opened its borders, allowing tens of thousands of East German refugees to pass into West Germany.

2. For the private sector in Poland, see Korbónski 1981; Anonymous 1984; Åslund 1984, 1985; Bloch 1986; Wedel 1986; Zubek 1991; and Kamiński 1991.

3. This survey is described in chapter 10 and in more detail in Szelényi et al. 1995.

4. These included Budaflax, Magyar Optikai Művek (MOM), Videoton, and Ganz-Danubius.

5. Actual bankruptcies remained very rare until 1991.

6. The Ministry of Finance had a long history of political courage. Fiscal concerns also lay behind its public revelations, however. The ministry wanted an orderly sale of state assets in order to patch up the debt-ridden government budget.

7. As a sign of the times, Party bureaucrats chose fanciful names for their private companies. Long gone were names like Red October, Red Star, Progress, Peace, or New Life. Instead, following the lead of Next 2000, these companies sported such Western-sounding names as Allegro, Club Tomaj, Cimbriana, Kelen Tours, and Bács-Touring. Most of these companies were in the tourism business.

8. In 1988, there were 1,374 industrial enterprises in the socialist sector with less than 100 employees; in 1989, this figure had grown to 2,080 (Baló and Lipovecz 1989, 772–73; 1991, 667).

9. The average foreign share was 23.8 percent (Pichler 1994, 19).

10. The successor parties of the HSWP were hoping to capture the presidency by fielding reform Communist Imre Pozsgay as their candidate. Already expecting defeat in the spring elections, they wanted to follow the Polish example, in which the opposition government formed by Solidarity had to share power with President General Jaruzelski.

11. Establishing the true value of privatizable state property is impossible. The figure provided by the SPA and the Ministry of Finance is 1,800 billion forints. This is the book value—purchase price minus depreciation—of fixed assets in material production as of the end of 1988 in the socialist sector. The figure is highly contested, and some give estimates of over 4 trillion. Differences in the calculations vary depending on how one estimates the value of privatizable assets in nonmaterial production (education, health care, culture, financial services, etc.). Estimates also depend on how much one adds for inventory and goodwill. The official figure includes neither the value of the land on which the company is built, nor the worth of investment projects unfinished by 1988, nor the value of patent rights or concessions. Finally, the most peculiar aspect of the official figure is that it ignores inflation—or, rather, discounts assets by the rate of inflation.

In the end, these accounting gymnastics probably tell us very little about how much money privatization can actually earn, since ultimately the value of state assets is decided by the buyers' willingness and ability to pay.

12. Staniszkis, describing Poland, calls this conversion whereby political power is directly transformed into private ownership "political capitalism" (1991).

13. As I showed in chapter 3, company managers were colluding with their workers.

14. There is an immense literature documenting the presence of the private sector in state socialist countries in the late 1970s and 1980s. For the Soviet Union, see Grossman 1977, Katsenelinboigen 1977; Simis 1982; O'Hearn 1980; 1981; Rumer 1981; and Mars and Altman 1983. For elsewhere in Eastern Europe, outside of Hungary and Poland, see Šimečka 1982; Sampson 1983, 1986, 1987; and Łos 1990.

15. Russia stood halfway between the orthodox and reformist communist countries. Perestroika, which granted more autonomy to managers and gave the green light to private partnerships called "cooperatives," came relatively late. Its introduction was sudden and did not result from organic evolution. It was also a much more cautious kind of reform than those undertaken in Hungary and Poland.

Chapter 9

1. The most elaborate statement of this thesis is given by the historian Jenő Szűcs and by István Bibó (Szűcs 1985; Bibó [1972] 1982, [1947] 1982). Both reject the rigid historical determinism of Marxism-Leninism.

2. The slogan of the Third Way was often exploited by the nationalist Right, which had nothing to do with neoliberalism.

3. In 1984(!) in an interview, Valéria Benke, the chief editor of the Party's theoretical journal and a member of the Politburo, explained what she considered the virtues of the *polgár* to be:

> Punctuality, respect for time, expertise, appreciation of expertise, culture. . . . Modesty, moderation, thrift, and entrepreneurial spirit, its best West European type. The several hundred year old mentality of small artisans, and small, then ever larger, commercial firms, which included sober calculation, foresight, reasonable risk taking, a certain responsibility, and fair business practices. These were missing [in our country]; they failed to develop for historical reasons. (Rapcsányi 1984, 23)

4. Some of the many reasons why democracy and a market economy may be in contradiction in the post-Communist transformation are discussed by Przeworski 1991 and Comisso 1991.

5. The educational value of commerce and private enterprise has been extolled for centuries. For an elegant summary, see Hirschman 1977.

6. The state was to forgo a portion of its income from these sales if the buyer was willing to invest these monies in his or her company.

7. During the first years of the transition, Hungary received the largest amount of foreign investment in the region. Between 1988 and the end of 1993, 7 billion U.S. dollars came into the country, which was less than half of the amount Spain received in 1989 (Pichler 1994, 117; Sárközy 1991, 627). Yet only about 2 billion dollars were used for the purchase of state-owned companies (Hungarian Government 1994, 23). The rest were spent on starting new businesses and investing in ones already purchased.

8. Antall was already under pressure from both of his coalition partners on this issue. The ISHP wanted land restitution and the CDPP pressed for a return of church property.

9. In a later debate on company councils, Palotás explained why private entrepreneurs supported recentralization: entrepreneurs can't buy state companies unless the state takes possession of them first (Parliament, October 10, 1990, 2753).

10. By 1993, about one-third of the legislators in the ruling coalition had one or more such lucrative appointments.

11. The Alliance of Young Democrats was the only opposition party that sent a delegate to the supervisory board of the SPA.

12. The bill was very similar to one prepared by the last Communist government, but never brought before the legislature. The Németh government did not feel it had the political muscle to push the bill through.

13. In parliamentary debates, the Socialists stood up for both managers and employees (Parliament, August 27, 1990, 2367, 2374–75).

14. In December 1990, the Second Privatization Program was inaugurated. This time companies that were acting as holding companies and had lost more than 50 percent of their property to spontaneous privatization were put up for sale.

15. In December 1990, the organization representing managers of large companies, the Hungarian Chamber of Commerce, called for more managerial participation in the privatization process and hinted that it was not helping privatization that managers had to endure hostile political campaigns (MGK 1990, 738).

16. Just as citizens began to learn the ways of the stock market, the ballooning budget deficit forced the government to issue bonds at high interest rates, luring investors away from stocks.

17. One catalyst for this decision was the collapse of Eastern European markets beginning in late 1990. The general recession in the region, coupled with the chaos of the transition, pushed many companies to the brink of bankruptcy.

18. In many cases privatization was successful not because of the attractiveness of the companies themselves but because foreign investors wanted to obtain these firms' markets. One example is the confectionery industry, which had a stable domestic market (Vanicsek 1992).

19. This was the so-called *egzisztencia* loan, which was a special privatization loan.

20. Later, compensation was awarded to other groups as well.

21. One HDF member, whose parents were persecuted for being wealthy peasants in the 1950s, presented the following elocution:

> No one expects anyone to risk his life for money, enterprise, factory, automobile or any other object of property. But, if fate demands it, it is our duty to die for land, which sums to the total of the fatherland. (Parliament, February 25, 1991, 6303)

22. Their position was presented by an HDF legislator, an artisan operating his own distillery in the countryside (Parliament, April 8, 1991, 6986–87). The distillery had belonged to his parents and was nationalized; he had managed to repurchase it in 1984.

23. On August 1, 1990, its presidium declared that it "definitely condemns any form of free property rearrangement that requires no payment and considers it to be extremely dangerous for and undermining of the foundations of the economy" (quoted in VOSZ 1990, 740).

24. This was pointed out by AFD legislator Pál Juhász among others (Parliament, May 23, 1990, 286; Juhász 1991).

25. In about a third of the auctions buyers reached agreements beforehand and no bidding took place (Privinfo 93/14, 18).

26. For a comparison of the roles the Hungarian and Polish intelligentsias played, see Kennedy 1992.

27. A recent decrease in the number of registered unemployed is partially due to the fact that after a while many people fall out of the system.

28. According to a different estimate, in 1994 this proportion was between 41 and 44 percent (Laky 1995, 102.)

Chapter 10

1. The metaphor is from Jadwiga Staniszkis.

2. Attempts to take revenge on the old Communist elite have failed. Even if the center-right government had been willing to pass punitive legislation on Communist cadres, this would have affected only a handful who could have been charged with criminal misconduct. In the end, a handful of old Communists were tried for ordering troops to shoot at civilians during the 1956 revolution.

3. This definition omits economic policymakers and investors, who own and don't manage. The managers were interviewed in 1993. The sampling method and the technical details of surveying the new and the old elite, as well as the population, are described in Szelényi et al. 1995.

4. The comparison group is comprised of people between the ages of 23 and 65 in 1993.

5. Under state socialism, one could—and often had to—acquire a tertiary degree in Marxism-Leninism. To get this degree, one had to take courses in scientific socialism, Marxist political economy, the history of the labor movement, dialectical materialism, historical materialism, and a host of other ideological subjects.

6. The State Property Agency explained the importance of these personal assets in a 1993 brochure extolling the virtues of management buyouts (Mészáros 1993).

7. Tamás Kolosi has coined the phrase "the revolution of department heads" to describe this phenomenon (1991).

8. The *nomenklatura* sample was drawn from the '*nomenklatura* list' of the Party's Central Committee. This list reflects the most important positions controlled by the Party leadership. In 1988, 3,500 people were in these positions in Hungary. One thousand of them were selected by stratified random sampling.

9. It is important to recall that by 1988 most companies, including many large ones, were not headed by *nomenklatura* directors.

10. This subsample is nonrepresentative, since those who stayed in the foreign service and lived outside the country were undersampled. The post-1990 government appointed its own cadre and recalled most of the foreign service *nomenklatura,* but it kept some of those who were posted in less important places and whose local knowledge was deemed irreplaceable.

11. See also Staniszkis 1991, 39 and McAuley 1991, 98.

12. In the post-Communist world almost all known strikes have been by state employees.

References

Separate listings of Databases, Archival Documents, and Newspapers and Periodicals follow these published sources.

ÁBMH. 1983. A munkabér és az anyagi ösztönzés (Wage and economic incentives). Budapest: Állami Bér- és Munkaügyi Hivatal Munkaügyi Kutató Intézete.

Alchian, Armen A. 1950. "Uncertainty, Evolution, and Economic Theory." *Journal of Political Economy* 58:211–22.

———. 1965. "Some Economics of Property Rights." *Il Politico* 30 (4): 816–29.

Alchian, Armen A., and Harold Demsetz. 1973. "The Property Rights Paradigm." *American Journal of Economic History* 23/1:16–27.

Althusser, Louis. [1965] 1970. *For Marx.* New York: Vintage.

Andorka, Rudolf. 1982. *A társadalmi mobilitás változásai Magyarországon* (Changes in social mobility in Hungary). Budapest: Gondolat.

Anonymous. 1984. "Polonian Enterprises and Private Enterprise in Poland: The Reality of the Green Light." *Studium Papers* 8 (4).

Antal, László, Lajos Bokros, István Csillag, László Lengyel, and György Matolcsy. "Fordulat és reform 1987" (Turning point and reform, 1987). *Medvetánc* 2 (supplement): 2–130.

Arato, Andrew. 1981. "Civil Society against the State." *Telos* 47:23–47.

Arendt, Hannah. [1951] 1973. *The Origins of Totalitarianism.* New York: Harcourt, Brace.

Arthur, W. Brian. 1990. "Positive Feedbacks in the Economy." *Scientific American* 262 (2): 92–99.

Árvay, János, and Endre Sik. 1994. "A rejtett gazdaság nagysága" (The size of the hidden economy). Pp. 112–19 in *A magánszektor fejlődése Magyarországon 1990–1993. Összefoglaló kutatási beszámoló az Állami Vagyonügynökség számára.* (Development of the private sector in Hungary, 1990–1993: Summary report for the State Property Agency). Budapest: TÁRKI.

Åslund, Anders. 1984. "The Functioning of Private Enterprise in Poland." *Soviet Studies* 36:427–44.

———. 1985. *Private Enterprise in Eastern Europe: The Non-Agricultural Private Sector in Poland and the GDR, 1945–1983.* New York: St. Martin's.

———. 1989. *Gorbachev's Struggle for Economic Reform.* Ithaca, NY: Cornell University Press.

———. 1994. "Lessons of the First Four Years of Systemic Change in Eastern Europe." *Journal of Comparative Economics* 19:22–38.

Avineri, Shlomo. 1972. *Hegel's Theory of the Modern State.* Cambridge: Cambridge University Press.

ÁVÜ. 1990. *Első Privatizációs Program, 1990* (First Privatization Program, 1990). Budapest: Állami Vagyonügynökség.

———. 1991. *Évi jelentés* (Annual report by the State Property Agency). Budapest: Állami Vagyonügynökség.

———. 1995. *Privatizációs Monitor, 1995, február 28* (Privatization Monitor, February 28, 1995). Budapest: Állami Vagyonügynökség.

Bailes, Kendall E. 1977. "Alexei Gastev and the Soviet Controversy over Taylorism, 1918–24." *Soviet Studies* 29 (3): 373–94.

Baksay, Zoltán. 1983. *A munkaerőhelyzet alakulása és a munkanélküliség felszámolása Magyarországon, 1945–1949* (Development of the labor force and the elimination of unemployment in Hungary, 1945–1949). Budapest: Akadémiai Kiadó.

Baló, György, and Iván Lipovecz, eds. 1988. *Tények Könyve '89* (The book of facts '89). Budapest: Computerworld Informatika Kft.

———. 1990. *Tények Könyve '90* (The book of facts '90). Budapest: Ráció.

———. 1991. *Tények Könyve '91* (The book of facts '91). Budapest: Ráció.

———. 1993. *Tények Könyve '93* (The book of facts '93). Debrecen: Greger Media.

Balogh, Sándor, ed. 1975. *Parlamenti és pártharcok Magyarországon, 1945–1947* (Parliamentary and Party struggles in Hungary, 1945–1947). Budapest: Kossuth.

———. 1986. *Nehéz esztendők krónikája, 1949–1953: Dokumentumok* (The chronicle of difficult years, 1949–1953: Documents). Budapest: Gondolat.

Baranyai, Tibor, et al., eds. 1981. *Pártmunkások kézikönyve* (Handbook for Party activitists). Budapest: Kossuth.

Barla Szabó, Ödön. 1981. "Gazdaságpolitika és gazdasági fejlődés az MDP KV 1953. júniusi ülése után" (Economic policy and economic development after the June meeting of the Hungarian Workers' Party's central leadership). *Párttörténeti Közlemények* 2:1–53.

Bartlett, David. 1991. "The Political Economy of Privatization: Property Reform and Democracy in Hungary." *East European Politics and Societies* 6 (1): 73–118.

———. 1995. "Losing the Political Initiative: The Impact of Financial Liberalization in Hungary." Pp.114–50 in *The Waning of the Communist State: Economic Origins of Political Decline in China and Hungary,* edited by Andrew G. Walder. Berkeley and Los Angeles: University of California Press.

Batt, Judy. 1988. *Economic Reform and Political Change in Eastern Europe: A Comparison of the Czechoslovak and Hungarian Experiences.* London: Macmillan.

Bauer, Tamás. 1981. *Tervgazdaság, beruházás, ciklusok* (Planned Economy, Investments, Cycles). Budapest: Közgazdasági és Jogi.

Békefi, Mihály. 1984. "A lakossági személygépkocsi állomány fenntartása" (Maintenance of passenger vehicles). Manuscript.

Belényi, Gyula. 1993. *A sztálini iparosítás emberi ára, 1948–1956* (The human cost of Stalinist industrialization, 1948–1956). Szeged: JATE Press.

Belyó, Pál, and Béla Dexler. 1985. *Nem szervezett (elsősorban illegális) keretek között végzett szolgáltatások* (Not socially organized [primarily illegal] services). Manuscript.

Berend, Iván T. 1983. *Gazdasági útkeresés 1956–1965* (Economic quest, 1956–1965). Budapest: Magvetö.

———. 1988. "A magyar reform sorsfordulója az 1970-es években" (Turning point in the fate of Hungarian reform in the 1970s). *Valóság* 31 (1): 1–26.

———. 1990. *The Hungarian Economic Reforms, 1953–1988*. Cambridge: Cambridge University Press.

Berényi, József, ed. 1985. *A belkereskedelem négy évtizede, 1945–1985* (Four decades of domestic trade, 1945–1985). Budapest: Közgazdasági és Jogi Kiadó.

Berg, Maxine. 1980. *The Machinery Question and the Making of Political Economy*. Cambridge: Cambridge University Press.

Bernstein, Eduard. [1909] 1961. *Evolutionary Socialism: A Criticism and Affirmation*. New York: Schocken.

Bibó, István. [1945] 1982. "A magyar demokrácia válsága" (The crisis of Hungarian democracy). Pp. 39–80 in *Bibó István összegyűjtött munkái* (István Bibó's collected works), edited by István Kemény and Mátyás Sárközy. Bern: EPMSZ.

———. [1947] 1982. "A magyar társadalomfejlődés és az 1945. évi változás értelme" (Hungarian societal development and the meaning of the change in the year 1945). Pp. 351–62 in *Bibó István összegyűjtött munkái* (István Bibó's collected works), edited by István Kemény and Mátyás Sárközy. Bern: EPMSZ.

———. [1972] 1982. "Az európai társadalomfejlődés értelme" (The meaning of European societal development). Pp. 560–635 in *Bibó István összegyűjtött munkái* (István Bibó's collected works), edited by István Kemény and Mátyás Sárközy. Bern: EPMSZ.

Bizám, Lenke. 1974. "Mitől kispolgár?" (What makes the petty bourgeois?) *Társadalmi Szemle* 29 (7): 44–49.

Blau, Peter M., and Danching Ruan. 1990. "Inequality of Opportunity in Urban China and America." Pp. 3–32 in *Research in Social Stratification and Mobility*, vol. 9, edited by Arne L. Kalleberg. Greenwich, CT: JAI.

Bloch, Andrzej. 1986. "The Private Sector in Poland." *Telos* 66:128–32.

Blumstock, Robert. 1977. "Public Opinion in Hungary." Pp. 132–66 in *Public Opinion in European Socialist Systems*, edited by W. D. Connor and Z. Y. Gitelman. New York: Praeger.

Böröcz, József. 1993. "Simulating the Great Transformation: Property Change under Prolonged Informality in Hungary." *Archives Européennes de Sociologie* 34:81–106.

Böröcz, József, and Ákos Róna-Tas. 1995. "Small Leap Forward: Emergence of New Economic Elites." *Theory and Society* 24 (5): 751–81.

Boros, Anna. 1984. *Családi megélhetési stratégiák a két gazdaságban* (Economic family strategies in the two economies). Budapest: Social Research Institute.

Boswell, Jonathan. 1973. *The Rise and Fall of Small Firms.* London: George Allen and Unwin.

Brada, Josef C. 1993. "The Transformation from Communism to Capitalism: How Far? How Fast?" *Post-Soviet Affairs* 9 (2): 87–110.

Brezinski, Horst. 1985. "The Second Economy in the Soviet Union and Its Implications for Economic Policy." Pp. 362–77 in *The Economics of the Shadow Economy,* edited by Wulf Gaertner and Alois Wenig. Berlin: Springer.

Brusco, Sebastiano. 1982. "The Emilian Model: Productive Decentralization and Social Integration." *Cambridge Journal of Economics.* 6, 2(June): 167–84.

Bruszt, László. 1990. "Hungary's Negotiated Revolution." *Social Research* 57 (2): 365–87.

Bukharin, Nikolai I. [1920] 1971. *The Economics of the Transformation Period.* New York: Bergman.

Bukharin, Nikolai I., and Evgeniy Preobrazhensky. [1919] 1966. *The ABC of Communism: A Popular Explanation of the Program of the Communist Party of Russia.* Ann Arbor: University of Michigan Press.

Burawoy, Michael. 1985. *The Politics of Production: Factory Regime under Capitalism and Socialism.* London: Verso.

Burawoy, Michael, and Pavel Krotov. 1992. "The Soviet Transition from Socialism to Capitalism." *American Sociological Review* 57:16–38.

Burawoy, Michael, and János Lukács. 1992. *The Radiant Past: Ideology and Reality in Hungary's Road to Capitalism.* Chicago: University of Chicago Press.

Chandler, Alfred D., Jr. 1984. "The Emergence of Managerial Capitalism." *Business History Review* 54:473–503.

Chirot, Daniel. 1991. "What Happened in Eastern Europe in 1989?" Pp. 3–32 in *The Crisis of Leninism and the Decline of the Left: The Revolutions of 1989.* Seattle: University of Washington Press.

Colletti, Lucio. 1972. "Bernstein and the Marxism of the Second International." Pp. 45–142 in *From Rousseau to Lenin: Studies in Ideology and Society,* edited by Lucio Colletti. New York: Monthly Review Press.

Comisso, Ellen. 1991. "Property Rights, Liberalism, and the Transition from 'Actually Existing' Socialism." *East European Politics and Societies* 5 (1): 162–88.

———. 1995. "Legacies of the Past or New Institutions: The Struggle over Restitution in Hungary." *Comparative Political Studies* 28 (2): 200–238.

Connor, Walter D. 1979. *Socialism, Politics, and Equality: Hierarchy and Change in Eastern Europe and the USSR.* New York: Columbia University Press.

Cserhalmi, Imre. 1983. *Történelmi kulcsátvétel* (Historic transfer of "housekeys") Budapest: Kossuth.

Cserkúti, Ferenc. 1975. "A közös és a háztáji" (The collective and the household farm). *Népszabadság* (June 4).

Csillag, István. 1986. "A kisvállalkozás Magyarországon" (Small enterprise in Hungary). *Gazdaság* 4:95–111.

Darvas, Péter. 1984. "Oktatás és tervgazdálkodás 1949–1953" (Education and the planned economy, 1949–1953). *Medvetánc* 83 (4)/84 (1): 59–82.

David, Eduard. 1903. *Sozialismus und Landwirtschaft.* 2 vols. Berlin: Verlag der Sozialistischen Monatshefte.

Denzau, Arthur T., and Douglass C. North. 1994. "Shared Mental Models: Ideologies and Institutions." *Kyklos* 47 (1): 3–31.

Djilas, Milovan. 1957. *The New Class: An Analysis of the Communist System.* New York: Praeger.

Domański, S. Ryszard. 1994. "The Quest for Ownership: Why It Was So Easy to Break Communism and Why It Is So Difficult to Find Consensus: A Response to the Surprise Literature." *Eastern European Economics* 32 (2): 71–94.

Donáth, Ferenc. 1977. *Reform és forradalom* (Reform and revolution). Budapest: Akadémiai.

Draper, Theodore. 1992. "Who Killed Soviet Communism?" *New York Review of Books* (June 11): 7–14.

Durkheim, Émile. [1893] 1984. *The Division of Labor in Society.* New York: Free Press.

Ehrlich, Éva. 1985. "The Size Structure of Manufacturing Establishments and Enterprises: An International Comparison." *Journal of Comparative Economics* 9:267–95.

Ékes, Ildikó. 1987. "A gazdaság rejtett szférája: A láthatatlan jövedelmek" (The hidden sphere of the economy: Invisible incomes). Ph.D. diss. Hungarian Academy of Sciences, Budapest.

———. 1993. *Rejtett gazdaság:—Láthatatlan jövedelmek* (Hidden economy: Invisible incomes). Budapest: Ékes.

Éltető, Ödön, and László Vita. 1987. "A láthatatlan jövedelmek és a jövedelem egyenlőtlenség" (Invisible incomes and income inequality). *Statisztikai Szemle* 65 (8): 979–89.

Engels, Frederick. [1886] 1986. "Ludwig Feuerbach and the End of Classical German Philosophy." Pp. 594–632 in *Karl Marx and Frederick Engels: Selected Works.* New York: International.

Erdélyi, Sándor. 1979. "A másodlagos elosztásról" (About secondary distribution). *Valóság* 12:38–52.

Erdős, Ákos, and András Juhász, eds. 1983. *Vállalkozók zsebkönyve* (Pocketbook for entrepreneurs). Budapest: Alkotó Ifjuság Egyesülés.

Fábián, Tamás. 1986. "Az ipar új tisztikara 1948–1949-ben" (The new captains of industry in 1948–1949). Budapest, University of Economics. Manuscript.

Falussy, Béla, and István Harcsa. 1987. *Időmérleg* (Time budget). Budapest: KSH.

Fazekas, Károly, and János Köllő. 1985. "Munkaerőpiaci kampányok a hetvenes években" (Labor-market campaigns in the 1970s). *Közgazdasági Szemle* 32 (5): 545–59.

Fekete, Judit. 1987. "Kríziskezelésünk krízise" (The crisis of our crisis management). Ph.D. diss. Hungarian Academy of Sciences, Budapest.

———. 1990. "'Coup' As a Method of Management: Crisis Management Methods in Hungary in the Eighties." *Acta Oeconomica* 42 (1–2): 55–72.

Filtzer, Donald. 1986. *Soviet Workers and Stalinist Industrialization: The Formation of Modern Soviet Production Relations, 1928–1941.* London: Pluto.

Foucault, Michel. 1979. *Discipline and Punish: The Birth of the Prison.* New York: Vintage.

Frentzel-Zagórska, Janina. 1990. "Civil Society in Poland and Hungary." *Soviet Studies* 42 (4): 759–77.

Frey, Mária. 1979. "A termelés ingadozásának okai és hatása a munkaerőszükségletre" (Causes of fluctuation in production and its influence on labor demand) *Munkaügyi Szemle* 23 (12): 21–28.

Friedrich, Carl J. 1954. "The Unique Character of Totalitarian Society." Pp. 47–60 in *Totalitarianism,* edited by Carl J. Friedrich. Cambridge: Harvard University Press.

Friedrich, Carl J., and Zbigniew Brzezinski. 1956. *Totalitarian Dictatorship and Autocracy.* Cambridge: Harvard University Press.

Friedrich, Carl J., Michael Curtis, and Benjamin R. Barber. 1969. *Totalitarianism in Perspective.* New York: Praeger.

Furubotn, Eirik G., and Svetozar Pejovic, eds. 1974. *Property Rights and Economic Theory: Some Basic Issues.* Cambridge, MA: Ballinger.

Gábor, R. István. 1979. "A második (másodlagos) gazdaság" (The second [secondary] economy). *Valóság* 1:22–36.

———. 1989. "Second Economy and Socialism: The Hungarian Experience." Pp. 339–60 in *The Underground Economies: Tax Evasion and Information Distortion,* edited by Edgar L. Feige. Cambridge: Cambridge University Press.

Gábor, R. István, and Péter Galasi. 1981a. "The Labour Market in Hungary since 1968." Pp. 41–53 in *Hungary: A Decade of Economic Reform,* edited by P. G. Hare, H. K. Radice, and N. Swain. London: George Allen and Unwin.

———. 1981b. *A "második" gazdaság* (The "Second" Economy). Budapest: Közgazdasági és Jogi Kiadó.

Gábor, R. István, and Tamás Horváth. 1987. "Bukás és visszavonulás a magánkisiparban" (Bankruptcy and retreat in the small private sector). *Közgazdasági Szemle* 34 (4): 404–19.

Galasi, Péter, and György Sziráczky. 1983. "Gazdasági fejlődés és munkaerőpiac Magyarországon, 1968–1982: Az 'aranykortól' a válságig" (Economic development and the labor market in Hungary, 1968–1982: From "golden age" to crisis). Manuscript.

Garton Ash, Timothy. 1989. "Does Central Europe Exist?" Pp. 179–213 in *The Uses of Adversity.* New York: Random House.

Gerő, András. 1993. *A magyar polgárosodás* (Hungarian embourgeoisement). Budapest: Atlantisz.

Gerschenkron, Alexander. 1960. "Problems and Patterns of Russian Economic Development. Pp. 42–71 in *The Transformation of Russian Society: Aspects of Social Change since 1981,* edited by Cyril E. Black. Cambridge: Harvard University Press.

———. 1962. "Some Aspects of Industrialization in Bulgaria, 1878–1939." Pp.

198–234 in *Economic Backwardness in Historical Perspective: A Book of Essays,* edited by Alexander Gerschenkron. Cambridge: Harvard University Press.

Gervai, Béla. 1960. *A kisipar fejlődése, helyzete és szerepe a népi demokráciában* (The development, position, and role of small artisans in the people's democracy). Budapest: Kisiparosok Országos Szervezete.

Gonda, Irén. 1979. "Kistermelés, kistermelők" (Small production, small producers). *Valóság* 12:65–73.

Gramsci, Antonio. [1929–35] 1971. *Selections from the Prison Notebooks,* edited and translated by Quintin Hoare and Geoffrey Nowell Smith. New York: International.

Grossman, Gregory. 1977. "The 'Second Economy' of the USSR." *Problems of Communism* 26 (5): 25–40.

Gyekiczky, Tamás. 1984. "Törvényesen elítéltetett" (Legally convicted). *Kritika* 3:20–21.

Gyurgyák, János, ed. 1991. *Polgárosodás Magyarországon* (Embourgeoisement in Hungary). Budapest: Századvég.

Habuda, Miklós. 1980. "A Magyar Dolgozók Pártja munkáspolitikájának néhány kérdése a Központi Vezetőség 1953. júniusi határozata után" (Some questions of the Hungarian Workers' Party's workers' policies after the 1953 decree of the central leadership). *Párttörténeti Közlemények* 1: 23–55.

Halász, Péter. 1975. *A termelőszövetkezeti mozgalom története Apátfalván* (The history of the agricultural cooperative movement in the village of Apátfalva). Budapest: Akadémiai Kiadó.

Haller, Max, Tamás Kolosi, and Péter Róbert. 1990. "Social Mobility in Austria, Czechoslovakia, and Hungary." Pp. 153–98 in *Class Structure in Europe: New Findings from East-West Comparisons of Social Structure and Mobility,* edited by Max Haller. Armonk: M. E. Sharp.

Hanák, Péter. 1984. "A lezáratlan per" (Case unclosed). Pp. 355–79 in *Zsidókérdés, asszimiláció, antiszemitizmus* (Jewish question, assimilation, anti-Semitism), edited by P. Hanák. Budapest: Gondolat.

Hankiss, Elemér. 1988. "The Second Society: Is There an Alternative Social Model Emerging in Contemporary Hungary?" *Social Research* 55:13–42.

———. 1990. *East European Alternatives.* Oxford: Clarendon.

Hann, C. M. 1990. "Second Economy and Civil Society." In *Market Economy and Civil Society in Hungary,* edited by C. M. Hann. London: Frank Cass.

Hannah, Leslie, and J. A. Kay. 1977. *Concentration in Modern Industry: Theory, Measurement, and the U.K. Exprience.* London: Macmillan.

Hare, Paul, Hugo Radice, and Nigel Swain, eds. 1981. *Hungary: A Decade of Economic Reform.* London: George Allen and Unwin.

Havel, Václav. 1988. *Living in Truth.* London: Faber.

Hayek, F. A. 1967. *Studies in Philosophy, Politics, and Economics.* London: Routledge and Kegan Paul.

Hegedűs, András, and Mária Márkus. 1979. "The Small Entrpreneur and Socialism." *Acta Oeconomica* 22 (3–4): 267–89.

Hegel, G. F. W. [1821] 1967. *Hegel's Philosophy of Right,* translated and with notes by T. M. Knox. Oxford: Oxford University Press.

———. [1840] 1956. *The Philosophy of History,* translated by J. Sibree. New York: Dover.

Heilbroner, Robert L. 1953. *The Worldly Philosophers.* New York: Simon and Schuster.

Herrigel, Gary B. 1989. "Industrial Order and the Politics of Industrial Change: Mechanical Engineering in the Federal Republic of Germany." Pp. 185–220 in *Industry and Politics in West Germany: Toward the Third Republic,* edited by Peter Katzenstein. Ithaca, NY: Cornell University Press.

Héthy, Lajos. 1980. "A 'második gazdaság': A gazdaság és a társadalom" (The "second economy": Economy and society). *Társadalmi Szemle* 11:40–47.

Héthy, Lajos, and Csaba Makó. 1978. *Munkások, érdekek, érdekegyeztetés* (Workers, interests, bargaining). Budapest: Gondolat.

Hilferding, Rudolf. [1910] 1981. *Finance Capital: A Study in the Latest Phase of Capitalist Development.* London: Routledge and Kegan Paul.

Hirschman, Albert O. 1970. *Exit, Voice, and Loyalty: Responses to Decline in Firms, Organizations and States.* Cambridge: Harvard University Press.

———. 1977. *The Passions and the Interests: Political Arguments for Capitalism before Its Triumph.* Princeton: Princeton University Press.

Hirst, Paul. 1991. "The State, Civil Society, and the Collapse of Soviet Communism." *Economy and Society* 20 (2): 217–41.

Hirst, Paul, and Jonathan Zeitlin. 1991. "Flexible Specialization versus Post-Fordism: Theory, Evidence, and Policy Implications." *Economy and Society* 20 (1): 1–56.

Howard, M. C., and J. E. King. 1989. *A History of Marxian Economics,* Vol. 1: 1883–1929. Princeton: Princeton University Press.

Hungarian Government. 1994. "Beszámoló az Állami Vagyonügynökség, az Állami Vagyonkezelő Rt. és a Kincstári Vagyonkezelő Szervezet 1990–94 közötti tevékenységéről és a három szervezet pénzügyi helyzetéről 1994 nyarán" (Report on the activities and financial situation of the State Property Agency, the State Property Management Company, and the Property Management Organization of the Treasury in the summer of 1994). Document issued for the legislature on November 11, 1994. Mimeo.

Invernizzi, B., and Riccardo Revelli. 1993. "Small Firms and the Italian Economy: Structural Changes and Evidence of Turbulence." Pp. 123–54 in *Small Firms and Entrepreneurship: An East-West Perspective,* edited by Zoltan J. Acs and David B. Audretsch. Cambridge: Cambridge University Press.

János, Andrew C. 1982. *The Politics of Backwardness in Hungary, 1825–1945.* Princeton: Princeton University Press.

Jasny, Naum. 1949. *The Socialized Agriculture of the USSR: Plans and Performance.* Stanford: Stanford University Press.

Juhász, György. 1982. "A Magyar Szocialista Munkáspárt káderpolitikája. A személyzeti munka pártirányítása" (The cadre policies of the Hungarian Socialist Workers' Party: Party guidance of personnel work). In *A személyzeti munka kézikönyve* (The manual of personnel work), edited by Miklós Gazdag. Budapest: Kossuth.

Juhász, Pál. 1979. "Adatok és hipotézisek a mezőgazdasági szövetkezetek állandó dolgozóinak rétegződéséről" (Data and hypotheses concerning the stratification of the permanent workers of agricultural cooperatives). *Társadalomtudományi Közlemények* 2:117–39.

———. 1988. "Zsákutcában van-e a magyar mezőgazdaság?" (Is Hungarian agriculture on a dead-end street?). *Medvetánc* 1:197–211.

———. 1991. "Agrárkérdés a gazdasági és politikai válság nyomása alatt" (The agrarian question under pressure from the economic and political crisis). Pp. 332–36 in *Magyarország Politikai Évkönyve* (Hungary's political yearbook), edited by Sándor Kurtán, Péter Sándor, and László Vass. Budapest: Ökonómia.

Juhász, Pál, and Bálint Magyar. 1984. "Néhány megjegyzés a lengyel és a magyar mezőgazdasági kistermelő helyzetéről a hetvenes években (Some comments on the situation of Polish and Hungarian small producers in the 1970s). *Medvetánc* 2–3:181–208.

Kádár, János. 1987. *Művei* (Works). Vol. 1. Budapest: Kossuth.

Kamiński, Bartlomiej. 1991. *The Collapse of State Socialism: The Case of Poland.* Princeton: Princeton University Press.

Kaplan, Frederick I. 1968. *Bolshevik Ideology and the Ethics of Soviet Labour, 1917–1920: The Formative Years.* London: Peter Owen.

Katsenelinboigen, Aron. 1978. *Studies in Soviet Economic Planning.* White Plains, NY: M. E. Sharpe.

———. 1977. Coloured Markets in the Soviet Union. *Soviet Studies* 29 (1): 62–85.

Kautsky, Karl. [1891] 1910. *Class Struggle (Erfurt Program),* translated by William E. Bohn. Chicago: Charles Kerr.

———. [1899] 1966. *Die Agrarfrage: Eine Übersicht über die Tendenzen der modernen Landwirtschaft und die Agrarpolitik der Sozialdemokratie.* Hannover: Verlag J. H. W. Dietz.

———. [1919] 1973. *Terrorism and Communism.* Westport, CT: Hyperion.

———. [1921] 1983. "Capitalism and Socialism." Pp. 127–36 in *Karl Kautsky: Selected Political Writings,* edited by Patrick Goode. New York: Macmillan.

Keane, John, ed. 1988. *Civil Society and the State.* Verso: London.

Kenedi, János. 1982. *Do It Yourself!* London: Pluto.

Kennedy, Michael D. 1992. "The Intelligentsia in the Constitution of Civil Societies and Post-Communist Regimes in Hungary and Poland." *Theory and Society* 21:29–76.

Kennedy, Michael D., and Ireneusz Bialecki. 1989. "Power and the Logic of Distribution in Poland." *East European Politics and Societies* 3 (2): 300–328.

Kocsis, Györgyi. 1992. "Privatizáció '91" (Privatization '91). Pp. 587–91 in *Tények könyve '92* (Book of facts '92), edited by György Baló and Iván Lipovecz. Budapest: Ráció.

Kolakowski, Leszek. 1978. *Main Currents of Marxism.* Vols. 1–3. Oxford: Oxford University Press.

Köllő, János, and Péter Pete. 1980. "Az ördögszekér és utasai" (The devil's carriage and its passengers). *Valóság* 4:88–94.

Kolosi, Tamás. 1991. *A reális szocializmus összeomlásának társadalmi okai* (The sociological reasons for the collapse of real socialism). *Valóság* 9:11–16.

Kolosi, Tamás, and Péter Róbert. 1991. *A rendszerváltás társadalmi hatásai* (The social effects of the regime transition). Budapest: TÁRKI.

Konrád, György. 1993. *91–93*. Budapest: Pesti Szalon.

Konrád, George, and Iván Szelényi. 1979. *The Intellectuals on the Road to Class Power*. Brighton, England: Harvester Press.

———. 1991. "Intellectuals and Domination in Post-Communist Societies." Pp. 337–61 in *Social Theory for a Changing Society*, edited by Pierre Bourdieu and James S. Coleman. Boulder, CO: Westview.

Kopátsy, Sándor. 1983. *Hiánycikk: A vállalkozás* (A good in short supply: Entrepreneurship). Budapest: Közgazdasági és Jogi Kiadó.

Korbónski, Andrzej. 1981. "The Second Economy in Poland." *Journal of International Affairs* 35 (1): 1–14.

Kornai, János. 1980. *Economics of Shortage*. Amsterdam: North-Holland.

———. 1992a. "The Affinity between Ownership and Coordination Mechanisms: The Common Experience of Reform in Socialist Countries." Pp 97–116 in *Constructing Capitalism: The Reemergence of Civil Society and Liberal Economy in the Post-Communist World*, edited by Kazimierz Z. Poznanski. Boulder, CO: Westview.

———. 1992b. *The Socialist System: The Political Economy of Communism*. Princeton: Princeton University Press.

Kovách, Imre. 1987. "A mezőgazdasági kisárutermelés üzemformái" (The types of agricultural small-commodity production). *Szociológia* 4:513–53.

——— ed. 1991. *Előadások a polgárosodásról*. Vol. 1: *Rendiség és polgárosodás* (Lectures on embourgeoisement. Vol. 1: Estate and embourgeoisement). Budapest: MTA Politikai Tudományok Intézete.

Kovách, Imre, and Kuczi Tibor. 1983. "Kisárutermelők gazdálkodástörténetének kohorszonkénti elemzése" (A cohort analysis of the business history of small producers). *Szociológia* 3:273–87.

Kovács, M. Mária, and Antal Örkény. 1981. "Szakérettségisek" (People with a special secondary school diploma). *Mozgó Világ* 5:102–9.

———. 1991. *Káderek* (Cadres). Budapest: ELTE.

Kövér, György. 1982. *Iparosodás agrárországban* (Industrialization in agrarian country). Budapest: Gondolat.

Kovrig, Bennett. 1979. *Communism in Hungary: From Kun to Kádár*. Stanford: Hoover Institution Press.

Kropotkin, Peter. [1899] 1974. *Fields, Factories, and Workshops Tomorrow*. London: George Allen and Unwin.

KSH. 1956. *Magyar Statisztikai Zsebkönyv, 1956* (Hungarian statistical handbook, 1956). Budapest: Központi Statisztikai Hivatal.

———. 1959a. *Az egyénileg gazdálkodó parasztság jövedelem szerinti rétegződése 1957–ben. 11 551 parasztgazdaság adatai* (Income stratification of the private peasantry in 1957: Data from 11,551 peasant farms). Budapest: Központi Statisztikai Hivatal.

———. 1959b. *Magyar Statisztikai Évkönyv, 1959* (Hungarian statistical yearbook, 1959). Budapest: Központi Statisztikai Hivatal.

———. 1961. *A magyar magánkisipar: Statisztikai adatgyűjtemény, 1938–1960* (Hungarian private small production: Statistical compendium, 1938–1960). Budapest: Központi Statisztikai Hivatal.

———. 1967. *Az ipar koncentrációja* (The concentration of industry). Statisztikai Időszaki Közlemények, 98. Budapest: Központi Statisztikai Hivatal.

———. 1971. *Az ipari centralizáció nemzetközi összehasonlításban* (Industrial concentration in international comparison). Budapest: Központi Statisztikai Hivatal.

———. 1979. *Lakásépítés és megszűnés, 1979* (Housing construction and liquidation, 1979). Budapest: Központi Statisztikai Hivatal.

———. 1981a. *Magyar Statisztikai Zsebkönyv* (Hungarian statistical pocketbook). Budapest: Központi Statisztikai Hivatal.

———. 1981b. *Mezőgazdasági adattár IV. Értékesítés, felvásárlás, árak* (Agricultural compendium 4: Selling, purchasing, prices). Budapest: Központi Statisztikai Hivatal.

———. 1984. *A kisszervezetek 1983-ban és 1984 I. félévében* (Small-scale organizations in 1983 and the first half of 1984). Budapest: Központi Statisztikai Hivatal.

———. 1985a. *Foglalkoztatottság és kereseti arányok, 1982, 1983, 1984* (Employment and income differences, 1982, 1983, 1984). Budapest: Központi Statisztikai Hivatal.

———. 1985b. *Magyar Statisztikai Zsebkönyv, 1984* (Hungarian statistical handbook, 1984). Budapest: Központi Statisztikai Hivatal.

———. 1987. *Statisztikai Zsebkönyv, 1986* (Statistical Pocketbook, 1986). Budapest: Központi Statisztikai Hivatal.

———. 1989. *Piaci szereplők a magyar gazdaságban, 1982–1989. A kisvállalkozások szerepe, fejlődése* (Market actors in the Hungarian economy, 1982–1989: The role and development of small ventures). Budapest: Központi Statisztikai Hivatal.

———. 1990a. *Magyar Statisztikai Zsebkönyv, 1989* (Hungarian statistical handbook, 1989). Budapest: Központi Statisztikai Hivatal.

———. 1990b. *The Situation, Working Conditions, and Possibilities of Further Development of Small Ventures in Hungary.* Budapest: Központi Statisztikai Hivatal.

———. 1994a. *Magyar Statisztikai Zsebkönyv, 1993* (Hungarian statistical handbook, 1993). Budapest: Központi Statisztikai Hivatal.

———. 1994b. *Gazdaságstatisztikai Évkönyv, 1992* (Yearbook of economic statistics, 1992). Budapest: Központi Statisztikai Hivatal.

———. 1995a. *Magyar Statisztikai Zsebkönyv, 1994* (Hungarian statistical handbook, 1994). Budapest: Központi Statisztikai Hivatal.

———. 1995b. *Statisztikai Havi Közlemények '95/11* (Monthly bulletin of statistics '95/11). Budapest: Központi Statisztikai Hivatal.

———. 1995c. *Gazdaságstatisztikai Évkönyv,1994* (Yearbook of economic statistics, 1992). Budapest: Központi Statisztikai Hivatal.

Kuczi, Tibor. 1984. "A legális kisipar" (Legalized small production). In *Gazdaság és Rétegződés* (Economy and stratification), edited by I. Kovách. Budapest: Social Science Institute of Central Committee of the Hungarian Workers' Party.

Kuczi, Tibor, and Ágnes Vajda. 1990. *A kisvállalkozók társadalmi összetétele* (The social composition of small entrepreneurs). Budapest: Munkaügyi Kutató Intézet.

Kuran, Timur. 1991. "Now Out of Never: The Element of Surprise in the East European Revolutions of 1989." *World Politics* 44:7–48.

———. 1995. "The Inevitability of Future Revolutionary Surprises." *American Journal of Sociology* 100 (6): 1528–51.

Lackó, Mária. 1991. *Az illegális gazdaság aránya Magyarországon 1970 és 1989 között* (The proportion of the illegal economy in Hungary between 1970 and 1989). Budapest: Economics Institute.

Laky, Teréz. 1984. "Small Enterprises in Hungary: Myth and Reality." *Acta Oeconomica* 32 (1–2): 39–63.

———. 1995. *Munkaerőpiaci helyzetjelentés. 1995 április* (Labor-market report, April 1995). Budapest: Munkaügyi Kutatóintézet.

Lampland, Martha. 1987. "Working through History: Ideologies of Work and Agricultural Production in a Hungarian Village, 1918–1983." Ph.D. diss. University of Chicago, Department of Anthropology.

———. 1991. "Pigs, Party Secretaries, and Private Lives in Hungary." *American Ethnologist* 18 (3): 459–79.

———. 1995. *The Object of Labor: Commodification of Agrarian Life in Socialist Hungary.* Chicago: University of Chicago Press.

Lengyel, György. N.d. "Szakszerűsödés és szakmásodás: A gazdasági vezetés professzionalizációja." Budapest University of Economics, Department of Sociology. Manuscript.

Lengyel, László. 1987. "Adalékok a Fordulat és reform történetéhez" (Contributions to the history of turning point and reform). *Medvetánc* 2:131–64.

Lenin, Vladimir I. [1914] 1974. "Karl Marx." Pp. 43–91 in *Collected Works,* vol. 21. Moscow: Progress.

———. [1916] 1974. "Imperialism: The Highest Stage of Capitalism." Pp. 185–304 in *Collected Works,* vol. 22. Moscow: Progress.

———. [1917] 1971. *State and Revolution.* New York: International.

———. [1918] 1974a. "The Immediate Tasks of the Soviet Government." Pp. 225–78 in *Collected Works,* vol. 27. Moscow: Progress.

———. [1918] 1974b. "'Left-Wing' Childishness and the Petty Bourgeois Mentality." Pp. 325–54 in *Collected Works,* vol. 27. Moscow: Progress.

Levitas, Anthony. 1994. "Rethinking Reform: Lessons from Polish Privatization." Pp. 99–114 in *Changing Political Economies: Privatization in Post-Communist and Reforming Communists States,* edited by Vedat Milor. Boulder, CO: Lynne Rienner.

Li Cheng and Lynn White. 1990. "Elite Transformation and Modern Change in

Mainland China and Taiwan: Empirical Data and the Theory of Technocracy." *China Quarterly* 121:1–35.

Lidtke, Vernon L. 1966. *The Outlawed Party: Social Democracy in Germany, 1878–1890.* Princeton: Princeton University Press.

Lipset, Seymour Martin, and György Bence. 1994. "Anticipations of the Failure of Communism." *Theory and Society* 23: 169–210.

Lipton, David, and Jeffrey Sachs. 1990. "Creating a Market Economy in Eastern Europe: The Case of Poland." *Brookings Papers on Economic Activity* 1:75–133.

Lörincz, Ernő. 1974. *A munkaviszonyok szabályozása Magyarországon a kapitalizmus kezdeteitől az első világháború végéig* (Regulation of labor relations from the beginnings of capitalism until the end of World War I). Budapest: Akadémiai Kiadó.

Łos, Maria, ed. 1990. *The Second Economy in Marxist States.* London: Macmillan.

Luxemburg, Rosa. [1900] 1973. *Reform or Revolution.* New York: Pathfinder.

———. [1913] 1972. *The Accumulation of Capital: An Anti-critique.* New York: Monthly Review Press.

Magyar, Bálint. 1982–83. "A szövetkezetek és az állami szektor a lengyel mezőgazdaságban" (Cooperatives and the state sector in Polish agriculture). *Medvetánc* 4 (1): 225–44.

———. 1986. *Dunaapáti, 1944–1958* (The village of Dunaapáti, 1944–1958). 3 vols. Budapest: Művelődéskutató Intézet, Szövetkezeti Kutató Intézet.

Major, Tibor. 1993. *Kisiparosok létszámalakulása az egyéni vállalkozók számának tükrében* (Change in the number of artisans reflected in the number of individual entrepreneurs). Budapest: IPOSZ.

Makó, Csaba, and Tamás Gyekiczky. 1987. "Szociológiai szempontok a munkafegyelem problémáinak elemzéséhez" (Sociological aspects of labor discipline). *Közgazdasági Szemle* 34 (5): 562–76.

Manchin, Róbert. 1988. "Individual Economic Strategies and Social Consciousness." *Social Research* 55, no. 1–2 (Spring-Summer): 77–95.

Manchin, Róbert, and Iván Szelényi. 1987. "Social Policy under State Socialism." In *Stagnation and Renewal in Social Policy,* edited by G. Esping-Anderson, L. Rainwater, and M. Rein. White Plains, NY: M.E. Sharpe.

Marcuse, Herbert. 1960. *Reason and Revolution: Hegel and the Rise of Social Theory.* Boston: Beacon.

Marglin, S. A. 1976. "What Do Bosses Do?" Pp. 13–54 in *The Division of Labour: The Labour Process and Class-Struggle in Modern Capitalism,* edited by A. Gorz. Atlantic Highlands, NJ: Humanities.

Mars, Gerald, and Yochanan Altman. 1983. "The Cultural Bases of Soviet Georgia's Second Economy." *Soviet Studies* 35 (4): 546–60.

Marx, Karl. [1844] 1967. "Economic and Philosophical Manuscripts." Pp. 283–337 in *Writings of the Young Marx on Philosophy and Society,* edited by L. D. Easton and K. H. Guddat. Garden City, NY: Doubleday.

———. [1847] 1963. *The Poverty of Philosophy.* New York: International.

———. [1867] 1974. *Capital,* vol. 1. Moscow: Progress.

———. [1875] 1986. "Marginal Notes to the Program of the German Workers'

Party." Pp. 319–35 in *Karl Marx and Frederick Engels: Selected Works.* New York: International.

Marx, Karl and Friedrich Engels. [1846] 1976. *German Ideology.* Moscow: Progress.

———. [1848] 1986. "The Communist Manifesto." Pp. 31–63 in *Karl Marx and Frederick Engels: Selected Works.* New York: International.

Matolcsy, György. 1989. "Spontán bűvészet" (Spontaneous magic). *HVG* 10 (28): 70–72.

Mattera, Philip. 1985. *Off the Books: The Rise of the Underground Economy.* London: Pluto.

McAuley, Alastair. 1991. "The Economic Transition in Eastern Europe: Employment, Income Distribution, and the Social Security Net." *Oxford Review of Economic Policy* 7:93–105.

McCagg, William O. 1972. *Jewish Nobles and Geniuses in Modern Hungary.* New York: Columbia University Press.

McIntyre, Robert J. 1988. *Bulgaria: Politics, Economics, and Society.* London: Pinter.

MDP. 1951. *Az MDP II. kongresszusának jegyzőkönyve* (The documents of the Hungarian Workers' Party's Second Congress). Budapest: Szikra.

Mészáros, László. 1993. *Privatizáció vezetői kivásárlással* (Privatization with management buyout). Budapest: Állami Vagyonügynökség.

MGK. 1990. "A Magyar Gazdasági Kamara küldöttgyűlésének állásfoglalása" (The position of the congress of the Hungarian Chamber of Commerce). Pp. 731–38 in *Magyarország Politikai Évkönyve* (Hungary's political yearbook), edited by Sándor Kurtán, Péter Sándor, and László Vass. Budapest: Ökonómia.

Michnik, Adam. 1985. *Letters from Prison and Other Essays.* Berkeley: University of California Press.

Mihályi, Péter. 1993. "Hungary: A Unique Approach to Privatization—Past, Present, and Future." Pp. 84–117 in *Hungary: An Economy in Transition,* edited by István P. Székely and David M. G. Newbery. Cambridge: Cambridge University Press.

Mód, Aladár. 1946. *A magyar ipar jövője* (The future of Hungarian industry). Budapest: Szikra.

Moldova, György. 1978. *Akit a mozdony füstje megcsapott*. . . (Who was hit by the smoke of the locomotive . . .). Budapest: Szépirodalmi.

Molnárné, Venyige Júlia, and Zsuzsa Orolin. 1982. *Szociálpolitika és gazdaság.* (Social policy and economy). Budapest: Közgazdasági és Jogi Könyvkiadó.

MSZMP. 1974. *A Magyar Szocialista Munkáspárt határozatai és dokumentumai 1967–1970* (The resolutions and documents of the Hungarian Socialist Workers' Party, 1967–1970). Budapest: Kossuth.

———. 1983. *A Magyar Szocialista Munkáspárt határozatai és dokumentumai 1975–1980* (The resolutions and documents of the Hungarian Socialist Workers' Party, 1975–1980). Budapest: Kossuth.

Murray, Fergus. 1983. "The Decentralization of Production: The Decline of the Mass Collective Worker? *Capital and Class,* no. 19 (Spring): 74–99.

Murrell, Peter. 1993a. "Evolutionary and Radical Approaches to Economic Reform." Pp. 215–31 in *Stabilization and Privatization in Poland: An Economic Evaluation of the Shock Therapy Program,* edited by Kazimierz Z. Poznanski. Boston: Kluwer.

———. 1993b. "What Is Shock Therapy? What Did It Do in Poland and Russia?" *Post-Soviet Affairs* 9 (2): 111–40.

Murrell, Peter, and Mancur Olson. 1991. "The Devolution of Centrally Planned Economies." *Journal of Comparative Economics* 15:239–65.

Neale, Walter C. 1994. "Institutions." Pp. 402–6 in *The Elgar Companion to Institutional and Evolutionary Economics,* edited by Geoffrey M. Hodgson, Warren J. Samuels, and Marc R. Tool. Brookfield, VT: Edward Elgar.

Nee, Victor. 1989. "A Theory of Market Transition: From Redistribution to Markets in State Socialism." *American Sociological Review* 54:663–81.

———. 1991. "Social Inequalities in Reforming State Socialism: Between Redistribution and Markets in China." *American Sociological Review* 56:267–82.

Nee, Victor, and Peng Lian. 1994. "Sleeping with the Enemy: A Dynamic Model of Declining Political Commitment in State Socialism." *Theory and Society* 23:253–96.

Nee, Victor, and David Stark, eds. 1989. *Remaking the Economic Institutions of Socialism: China and Eastern Europe.* Stanford: Stanford University Press.

Németh, Károly. 1975. *A gazdasági épitőmunka feladatai* (The tasks of economic construction). Budapest: Kossuth.

Nevelő, Irén. 1973. "A magyar kisiparosság társadalmi és politikai arculatának néhány jellemző vonása a felszabadulás után" (Some characteristic features of the sociopolitical profile of small tradesmen and artisans after World War II). *Történelmi Szemle* 16 (1–2): 110–40.

North, Douglass C. 1977. "Markets and Other Allocation Systems in History: The Challenge of Karl Polanyi." *Journal of European Economic History,* 3:703–16.

———. 1990. *Institutions, Institutional Change, and Economic Performance.* Cambridge: Cambridge University Press.

Nove, Alec. 1982. *An Economic History of the U.S.S.R.* Harmondsworth: Penguin.

———. 1983. *The Economics of Feasible Socialism.* London: George Allen and Unwin.

Nyitrai, Ferencné. 1969. "Munkaerő-helyzet az iparban" (The labor situation in industry). *Gazdaság* 3 (1): 21–32.

Obláth, Gábor. 1993. "Hungary's Foreign Debt: Controversies and Macroeconomic Problems." Pp. 193–223 in *Hungary: An Economy in Transition,* edited by István P. Székely and David M. G. Newbery. Cambridge: Cambridge University Press.

O'Driscoll, Gerald P., Jr., and Mario J. Rizzo. 1985. *The Economics of Time and Ignorance,* with contribution by Roger W. Garrison. New York: Blackwell.

Offe, Claus. 1995. "Designing Institutions for East European Transitions." Pp. 47–66 in *Strategic Choice and Path-Dependency in Post-Socialism. Institutional Dynamics in the Transformation Process,* edited by Jerzy Hausner, Bob Jessop and Klaus Nielsen. Brookfield, VT: Edgar Elgar.

O'Hearn, Dennis. 1980. "The Consumer Second Economy: Size and Effect." *Soviet Studies* 32 (2): 218–34.

———. 1981. "The Second Economy in Consumer Goods and Services." *Critique* 15:93–110.

Olson, Mancur. 1982. *The Rise and Decline of Nations: Economic Growth, Stagflation, and Social Rigidities.* New Haven: Yale University Press.

Orbán, Sándor. 1986. "A termelőszövetkezeti átszervezés másfél évtizede az európai szocialista országokban, 1948–1962" (Two and a half decades of collectivization in the European socialist countries, 1948–1962). *Párttörténeti Közlemények* 4:3–33.

Oros, Iván. 1983. "A mezőgazdasági kistermelés" (Agricultural small production). *Statisztikai Szemle* 12:1216–37.

Oros, Iván, and Miklós Schindele. 1985. "A háztáji és kisegitő gazdaságokban végzett emberi munka" (Human labor in household and auxiliary farms). *Statisztikai Szemle* 63 (10): 965–87.

Ossowski, Stanislaw. 1963. *Class Structure in the Social Consciousness.* London: Routledge and Kegan Paul.

Ostrovityanov, K. V. et al. 1955. *Politikai gazdaságtan tankönyv* (Textbook of political economy). Budapest: Szikra.

Óvári, Miklós. 1975. "Ideológiai helyzetünk és feladataink" (Our ideological situation and our tasks). *Társadalmi Szemle* 12:15–28.

Parliament. Minutes of the Hungarian Parliament. Various Years.

Pejovic, Svetozar. 1990. *The Economics of Property Rights: Towards a Theory of Comparative Systems.* Boston: Kluwer.

Pelikán, P. 1992. "The Dynamics of Economic Systems; or, How to Transform a Failed Socialist Economy." *Journal of Evolutionary Economics* 2:39–63.

Perrow, Charles. 1993. "Small Firm Networks." Pp. 377–402 in *Explorations in Economic Sociology,* edited by Richard Swedberg. New York: Russell Sage.

Pető, Iván. 1988. "Bársonyszékfoglalás" (Taking the driver's seat). *HVG* 460:54–56.

Pető, Iván, and Sándor Szakács. 1985. *A hazai gazdaság négy évtizedének története, 1945–1985.* Vol. 1: Az újjáépítés és a tervutasításos irányítás időszaka (History of the four decades of the national economy, 1945–1985. Vol. 1: The reconstruction and command economy period). Budapest: Közgazdasági és Jogi.

Pichler, Ferenc, ed. 1994. *A privatizáció története* (The history of privatization). Budapest: Állami Vagyonügynökség.

Piore, Michael J., and Charles F. Sabel. 1984. *The Second Industrial Divide: Possibilities for Prosperity.* New York: Basic Books.

Polanyi, Karl. [1944] 1957. *The Great Transformation: The Political and Economic Origins of Our Time,* introduction by R. M. MacIver. Boston: Beacon Press.

Polanyi, Michael. 1962. *Personal Knowledge: Towards a Post-Critical Philosophy.* Chicago: University of Chicago Press.

Polonyi, Gábor. 1994. *A magánszektorban foglalkoztatottak társadalmi-szociális jellemzőiről* (On the social characteristics of those employed in the private sector). Budapest: TÁRKI.

Popper, Karl. [1957] 1986. *The Poverty of Historicism.* London: Routledge.

Powell, W. Walter, and Paul J. DiMaggio, eds. 1991. *The New Institutionalism in Organizational Analysis.* Chicago: University of Chicago Press.

Poznanski, Kazimierz Z. 1992. "Property Rights Perspective on Evolution of Communist-Type Economies." Pp. 71–96 in *Constructing Capitalism: The Reemergence of Civil Society and Liberal Economy in the Post-Communist World,* edited by Kazimierz Z. Poznanski. Boulder, CO: Westview.

———. 1993. "An Interpretation of Communist Decay: The Role of Evolutionary Mechanisms." *Communist and Post-Communist Studies* 26 (1): 3–24.

——— ed. 1995. *The Evolutionary Transition to Capitalism.* Boulder, CO: Westview.

Pozsonyi, Pál. 1987. "A szervezeti struktúra alakulása a magyar iparban" (The development of organizational structure in Hungarian industry). Karl Marx University of Economics, Budapest. Manuscript.

Preobrazhensky, Evgeniy. [1926] 1965. *The New Economics.* Oxford: Clarendon.

Proudhon, Pierre-Joseph. [1840] 1970. *What Is Property? An Inquiry into the Principle of Right and of Government.* New York: Dover.

———. [1846] 1972. *System of Economical Contradictions; or, the Philosophy of Misery.* New York: Arno.

Przeworski, Adam. 1991. *Democracy and the Market: Political and Economic Reforms in Eastern Europe and Latin America.* Cambridge: Cambridge University Press.

Pullai, Árpád. 1975. *A pártélet, a pártmunka időszerű kérdései* (Current problems of Party life and Party work). Budapest: Kossuth.

Pünkösti, Árpád. 1988. *Kiválasztottak* (The chosen). Budapest: Gondolat.

Radnay, József. 1985. "Négy évtized a magyar munkajogban" (Four decades of Hungarian labor law). *Munkaügyi Szemle* 29 (April): 16–23.

Radnóti, Huba. 1979. "A háztáji gazdálkodás és a 'második' gazdaság" (Household farming and the "second" economy). *Valóság* 3:92–94.

Rákosi, Mátyás. 1947. *A magyar demokráciáért* (For Hungarian democracy). 2d ed. Budapest: Szikra.

Rakovski, Marc. 1978. *Towards an East European Marxism.* London: Allison and Busby.

Rapcsányi, László. 1984. "Interjú Benke Valériával" (Interview with Valéria Benke). *Valóság* 10:14–26.

Rau, Zbigniew, ed. 1991. *The Reemergence of Civil Society in Eastern Europe and the Soviet Union.* Boulder, CO: Westview.

Rév, István. 1987. "The Advantages of Being Atomized: How the Hungarian Peasant Coped with Collectivization." *Dissent* 34: 335–50.

Révész, Gábor. 1990. *Perestroika in Eastern Europe: Hungary's Economic Transformation, 1945–1988.* Boulder, CO: Westview.

Richter, Anna. 1990. *Ellenzéki Kerekasztal: Portrévázlatok* (Opposition Roundtable: Portrait sketches). Budapest: Ötlet Kft.

Ripp, Géza. 1973. "A kispolgári ideológia szélsőségei" (The extremes of petty bourgeois ideology). *Népszabadság* (July 5).

Roeder, Philip G. 1993. *Red Sunset. The Failure of Soviet Politics.* Princeton: Princeton University Press.

Róna-Tas, Ákos. 1990. "The Social Origins of the End of Socialism: The Second Economy in Hungary." Ph.D. diss., University of Michigan, Ann Arbor, Department of Sociology.

———. 1994. "The First Shall Be Last? Entrepreneurship and Communist Cadres in the Transition." *American Journal of Sociology* 100 (1): 40–69.

———. 1995. "The Second Economy as a Subversive Force: The Erosion of Party Power in Hungary." Pp. 61–84 in *The Waning of the Communist State: Economic Origins of Political Decline in China and Hungary,* edited by Andrew G. Walder. Berkeley and Los Angeles: University of California Press.

———. Forthcoming. "Social Engineering and Historical Legacies: Privatization and the Business Elite in Hungary and the Czech Republic." In *Legacies of the Past vs. Liberalization Imperatives: Comparative Perspectives on Eastern Europe,* Beverly Crawford and Arend Lijphard. Thousand Oaks, CA: Sage.

Rumer, Boris. 1981. "The 'Second' Agriculture in the USSR." *Soviet Studies,* 33 (4): 560–72.

Rupp, Kálmán. 1983. *Entrepreneurs in Red: Structure and Organizational Innovation in the Centrally Planned Economy.* Albany: State University of New York Press.

Sabel, Charles F., and David Stark. 1982. "Planning, Politics, and Shop-Floor Power: Hidden Forms of Bargaining in Soviet-Imposed State-Socialist Societies." *Politics and Society* 11 (4): 439–75.

Salvadori, Massimo. 1979. *Karl Kautsky and the Socialist Revolution, 1880–1838.* London: NLB.

Sampson, Steven L. 1983. "Is Romania the Next Poland?" *Critique* 16:139–44.

———. 1986. "The Informal Sector in Eastern Europe." *Telos* 66:44–66.

———. 1987. "The Second Economy of the Soviet Union and Eastern Europe." *Annals of the American Association of Political and Social Science* 493 (September): 120–36.

Sárközy, Tamás. 1991. "Privatizáció" (Privatization). Pp. 621–28 in *Tények könyve '91* (Book of facts '91), edited by György Baló and Iván Lipovecz. Budapest: Ráció.

Schackle, G. L. S. 1972. *Epistemics and Economics: A Critique of Economic Doctrines.* Cambridge: Cambridge University Press.

Scherer, F. M. 1971. *Industrial Market Structure and Economic Preformance.* Chicago: Rand McNally.

Schotter, Andrew. 1981. *The Economic Theory of Social Institutions.* Cambridge: Cambridge University Press.

Schumpeter, Joseph. 1934. *Theory of Economic Development.* Cambridge: Harvard University Press.

Schurmann, Franz. 1966. *Ideology and Organization in Communist China.* Berkeley: University of California Press.

Schwarz, Solomon M. 1951. *Labour in the Soviet Union.* New York: Praeger.

Seleny, Anna. 1994. "Constructing the Discourse of Transformation: Hungary, 1979–1982." *East European Politics and Societies* 8 (3): 439–66.

———. 1995. "Property Rights and Political Power: The Cumulative Process of Political Change in Hungary." Pp. 27–60 in *The Waning of the Communist State: Economic Origins of Political Decline in China and Hungary,* edited by Andrew G. Walder. Berkeley: University of California Press.

Selucky, Radoslav. 1979. *Marxism, Socialism, Freedom: Towards a General Democratic Theory of Labour-Managed Systems.* London: Macmillan.

Sik, Endre. 1987. "New Trends in the Hungarian Welfare System." Manuscript.

———. 1994. "From the Multicoloured to the Black and White Economy: The Hungarian Second Economy and the Transformation." *International Journal of Urban and Regional Research* 18 (1): 46–70.

Šimečka, Milan. 1984. *The Restoration of Order: The Normalization of Czechoslovakia.* London: Verso.

Simis, Konstantin. 1982. *USSR: The Corrupt Society.* New York: Simon and Schuster.

Simkus, A. Albert. 1981. "Comparative Stratification and Mobility." *International Journal of Comparative Sociology* 22 (3–4): 213–36.

Simon, Herbert A. 1957. *Models of Man.* New York: Wiley.

Simon, Péter. 1979. "A párt agrárpolitikája a szocializmus alapjai lerakásának időszakában" (The agrarian policies of the Party in the period of laying the foundations of socialism). In *Agrárpolitika és átalakulás Magyarországon, 1944–1962* (Agrarian policies and transformation in Hungary, 1944–1962), edited by S. Balogh and F. Pölöskei. Budapest: Akadémiai.

———. 1981. *The Sciences of the Artificial.* Cambridge: M.I.T. Press.

Skilling, H. Gordon, ed. 1988. "Parallel Polis; or, an Independent Society in Central and Eastern Europe: An Inqury." *Social Research* 55, no. 1–2: 211–46.

S. Kosztricz, Anna., et al., eds. 1993. *A Magyar Szocialista Munkáspárt Központi Bizottságának 1989 évi jegyzőkönyvei* (The Minutes of the Central Committee of the Hungarian Socialist Workers' Party from 1989). Vols. 1–2. Budapest: Magyar Országos Levéltár.

Slay, Ben. 1994. *The Polish Economy: Crisis, Reform, and Transformation.* Princeton: Princeton University Press.

Solt, Katalin, and Endre Szigeti. 1990. *A magyar szociáldemokraták közgazdasági nézetei, 1890–1945* (The economic views of the Hungarian Social Democrats, 1890–1945). Budapest: Akadémiai Kiadó.

Soós, Attila Károly. 1986. *Terv, kampány, pénz* (Plan, campaign, money). Budapest: Jogi és Közgazdasági Kiadó.

Spulber, Nicolas. 1957. *The Economics of Communist Eastern Europe.* New York: Wiley.

Stalin, Josip V. [1938] 1972. "Dialectical and Historical Materialism." Pp. 300–333 in *The Essential Stalin: Major Theoretical Writings, 1905–1952,* edited by Bruce Franklin. New York: Doubleday.

———. [1952] 1972. "Economic Problems of Socialism in the USSR." Pp. 445–81 in *The Essential Stalin: Major Theoretical Writings, 1905–1952,* edited by Bruce Franklin. New York: Doubleday.

Staniszkis, Jadwiga. 1991. *The Dynamics of the Breakthrough in Eastern Europe: The Polish Experience.* Berkeley: University of California Press.

Stark, David. 1986. "Rethinking Internal Labor Markets: New Insights from a Comparative Perspective." *American Sociological Review* 51:492–504.

———. 1989. "Coexisting Organizational Forms in Hungary's Emerging Mixed Economy." Pp. 137–68 in *Remaking of the Economic Institutions of Socialism: China and Eastern Europe,* edited by Victor Nee and David Stark. Stanford: Stanford University Press.

———. 1990. "Privatization in Hungary: From Plan to Market or from Plan to Clan?" *East European Politics and Societies* 4 (3): 351–92.

———. 1994. "Path Dependence and Privatization Strategies in East-Central Europe." Pp. 115–46 in *Changing Political Economies: Privatization in Post-Communist and Reforming Communist States,* edited by Vedat Milor. Boulder, CO: Lynne Rienner.

———. 1996. "Recombinant Property in East European Capitalism." *American Journal of Sociology* 101 (4): 993–1027.

Statistical Abstracts of the United States. 1987. 107th ed. Washington, DC: U.S. Department of Commerce.

Steenson, Gary P. 1978. *Karl Kautsky, 1854–1938: Marxism in the Classical Years.* Pittsburgh: University of Pittsburgh Press.

Swain, Nigel. 1992. *Hungary: The Rise and Fall of Feasible Socialism.* London: Verso.

Szabó, Kálmán. 1967. "A munka áruvonásai a szocializmusban" (Commodity features of labor in socialism). *Közgazdasági Szemle* 14/4:401–16.

Szabó, Zoltán. 1938. *Cifra nyomorúság: A Cserhát, Mátra, Bükk földje és népe* (Adorned misery: The land and the people of the Cserhát, Mátra, Bükk). Budapest: Cserépfalvi.

Szalai, Erzsébet. 1989. *Gazdasági mechanizmus, reformtörekvések és nagyvállalati érdekek* (Economic mechanism, reform efforts, and large enterprise interests). Budapest: Közgazdasági és Jogi.

———. 1990. *Gazdaság és hatalom* (Economics and power). Budapest: Aula.

———. 1994a. *A civil társadalomtól a politikai társadalom felé: Munkástanácsok, 1989–1993* (From civil society to political society: Workers' councils, 1989–1993). Budapest: T-Twins.

———. 1994b. *Útelágazás: Hatalom és értelmiség az államszocializmus után* (Fork in the road: Power and intellectuals after state socialism). Budapest: Pesti Szalon.

Szamel, Lajos. 1989. *A korrupció, a protekció, és a többi . . .* (Corruption, pulling strings, and the rest . . .). Budapest: Kossuth.

Szamuely, László. 1982. "The First Wave of the Mechanism Debate in Hungary (1954–1957)." *Acta Oeconomica* 1 (2): 1–24.

———. 1984. "The Second Wave of the Economic Mechanism Debate and the 1968 Reform in Hungary." *Acta Oeconomica* 1 (2): 43–67.

———. 1986. "Negyedszázados vita a szocialista gazdaság mechanizmusáról

Magyarországon" (A quarter-century debate about the mechanism of the socialist economy in Hungary). Pp. 9–56 in *A magyar közgazdasági gondolat fejlődése, 1954–1978* (The development of Hungarian economic thought, 1954–1978), edited by L. Szamuely. Budapest: Közgazdasági és Jogi.

Székács, Anna. 1987. *A kisüzemi szervezetek működéséről* (The operation of small-scale organizations). Internal study for the Ministry of Finance, Budapest, April 15, 1987.

Szelényi, Iván. 1982. "The Intelligentsia in the Class Structure of State-Socialist Societies." In *Marxist Inquiries*, edited by M. Burawoy and T. Skocpol. *American Journal of Sociology* 88 (supplement): S287–327.

———. 1983. *Urban Inequalities under State Socialism.* Oxford: Oxford University Press.

———. 1988. *Socialist Entrepreneurs: Embourgeoisement in Rural Hungary.* Madison: Wisconsin University Press.

Szelényi, Iván, and Eric Kostello. 1996. "The Market Transition Debate: Toward a Synthesis?" *American Journal of Sociology* 101 (4): 1082–96.

Szelényi, Iván, and Balázs Szelényi. 1994. "Why Socialism Failed: Toward a Theory of System Breakdown: Causes of Disintegration of East European State Socialism." *Theory and Society* 23:211–31.

Szelényi, Iván, and Szonja Szelényi. 1995. "Circulation or Reproduction of Elites during Post-Communist Transformation in Eastern Europe: Introduction." *Theory and Society* 24 (5): 615–38.

Szelényi, Szonja. 1987. "Social Inequality and Party Membership: Patterns of Recruitment into the Hungarian Socialist Workers' Party." *American Sociological Review* 52 (5): 559–73.

Sziráczki, György. 1989. "Internal Subcontracting in Hungarian Enterprises." In *Alternatives to Capitalism*, edited by J. Elster and K. O. Moene. Cambridge: Cambridge University Press.

Szmicsek, Sándor. 1986. "Bérrendszer, vgm és belső vállalkozás" (Wage-system, VGM, and internal enterprising). *Társadalmi Szemle* 11:62–71.

Szpirulisz, Ildikó. 1972. *A vasutas dolgozók társadalmi helyzete* (The social conditions of railroad workers). Budapest: Kossuth.

Szűcs, Jenő. 1985. *Le trois Europes.* Paris: Harmattan.

TÁRKI. 1993. *Privatizáció: A vizsgálat dokumentációja és alapmegoszlásai* (Privatization: The documentation and basic frequencies of the research project). Budapest: TÁRKI.

Teichová, Alice. 1988. *The Czechoslovak Economy: 1918–1980.* London: Routledge.

Tellér, Gyula. 1973. *A magyar kisipari szövetkezetek története, 1945–1962* (The history of the Hungarian small producers' cooperatives, 1945–1962). Budapest: Szövetkezeti Kutató Intézet.

Ternovszky, Ferenc. 1987. "Műhelyzet: VGMK-esettanulmány" (The state of affairs: A case study of a VGMK). *Heti Világgazdaság* 9 (42): 53–54.

Tímár, János, ed. 1981. *Munkagazdaságtan* (Labor economics). Budapest: Közgazdasági és Jogi Könyvkiadó.

———. 1985. "A társadalmi újratermelés idôalapja" (The labor time basis of social reproduction). Budapest, Karl Marx University of Economics. Manuscript.

———. 1988. *Idő és munkaidő* (Time and labor time). Budapest: Közgazdasági és Jogi Könyvkiadó.

Torańska, Teresa. 1987. *Them: Stalin's Polish Puppets.* New York: Harper and Row.

Tóth, A. Ernö. 1970. *Háztáji gazdaság, foglalkoztatottság, és jövedelem* (Household farming, employment, and income). Budapest: Economics Research Institute of the Hungarian Academy of Sciences.

Tsebelis, George. 1990. *Nested Games. Rational Choice in Comparative Politics.* Berkeley and Los Angeles: University of California Press.

Tugan-Baranovsky, Mikhail I. [1907] 1970. *The Russian Factory in the Nineteenth Century.* Homewood, IL.: American Economic Association.

T. Varga, György, and István Szakadát. 1992. "Íme, a nómenklatúrák!" (Here are the nomenklaturas!). *Társadalmi Szemle* 3:73–95.

Vági, Gábor. 1980. "A másodlagos elosztásról" (About secondary distribution). *Valóság* 3:98–103.

Vanicsek, Mária. 1992. "Édes privatizációnk. A cukoripar privatizációjának tanulságai" (Our sweet privatization: Lessons of the confectionery industry's privatization). Pp.71–77 in *A privatizáció tapasztalatai Magyarországon* (The experience of privatization in Hungary), edited by Tamás Mellár. Budapest: Privatizációs Kutató Intézet.

Vitányi, Iván. 1973. "Kispolgáriság és kultúra" (The petty bourgeois way of life and culture). *Társadalmi Szemle* 7:19–25.

VOSZ. 1990. "A VOSZ elnökségének állásfoglalása a tulajdonrendezésről, a privatizációhoz kapcsolodó kedvezményekről" (The position of the presidium of the National Organization of Entrepreneurs on property arrangements and preferential treatment in privatization). Pp. 740–42 in *Magyarország Politikai Évkönyve* (Hungary's political yearbook), edited by Sándor Kurtán, Péter Sándor and László Vass. Budapest: Ökonómia.

Waedekin, Karl-Eugen. 1982. *Agrarian Policies in Communist Europe: A Critical Introduction.* London: Allenheld, Osmun.

Walder, Andrew G. 1986. *Communist Neo-Traditionalism: Work and Authority in Chinese Industry.* Berkeley: University of California Press.

———. 1994. "The Decline of Communist Power: Elements of a Theory of Institutional Change." *Theory and Society* 23:297–323.

Wank, David. 1992. "Symbiotic Alliance of Entrepreneurs and Officials: The Logics of Private Sector Expansion in a South China City." Paper presented at the conference on "The Political Consequences of Departures from Central Planning," August 25, 1992, Harriman, NY.

Wasilewski, Jacek. 1985. "Social Process of Regional Power Elite Recruitment." *Sisyphus* 4:205–24.

———. 1990. "The Patterns of Bureaucratic Elite Recruitment in Poland in the 1970s and 1980s." *Soviet Studies* 42:743–57.

Weber, Max. [1922] 1978. *Economy and Society,* edited by G. Roth and C. Wittich. 2 vols. Berkeley and Los Angeles: University of California Press.

Webster, Leila. 1992. "Private Sector Manufacturing in Hungary: A Survey of Firms." Industry Series Papers, no. 67. Washington, DC: World Bank.

Wedel, Janine. 1986. *The Private Poland.* New York: Facts on File.

Wright, Eric Olin. 1985. *Classes.* London: Verso.

Závada, Pál. 1986. *Kulákprés: Dokumentumok és kommentárok egy parasztgazdaság történetéhez* (Kulak squeeze: Documents and commentaries on the history of a peasant farm). Budapest: Művelődéskutató Intézet.

Zloch-Christy, Iliana. 1987. *Debt Problems of Eastern Europe.* Cambridge: Cambridge University Press.

Zsuffa, Ervin. 1975. "A háztáji és kisegítő gazdaságok biztonságáért" (For the security of the auxiliary and household farms). *Pártélet* (March): 59–61.

Zubek, Voytek. 1991. "The Polish Communist Elite and the Petty Entrepreneurs." *East European Quarterly* 25 (3): 339–64.

Databases of Survey Data

Social Stratification Survey 1981.

Social Stratification Survey 1986.

Social Stratification Survey 1993.

All three databases—with the exception of the elite samples of SSS-93—are available with English language documentation from TÁRKI, Budapest.

Archival Documents

MF	Ministry of Finance
ML	Ministry of Labor
PIA	Party Institute Archives
SOWL	State Office of Wage and Labor

MF/1–00107/1987. Jelentés a Gazdaságpolitikai Bizottság részére a kiegészítő és kisegítő tevékenységek helyzetéről. Pénzügyminiszter, Ipari Miniszter és Mezőgazdasági és Élelmezésügyi Miniszter. Április.

MF/1980. A Gazdasági Bizottság 10009/1980. számú határozata a kisüzemi termelés és kisegítő tevékenységek továbbfejlesztéséről.

MF/2345/1988. Előterjesztés a Gazdaságpolitikai Bizottság részére a kisüzemi gazdálkodás helyzetéről. PM Jogi Főosztály.

MF/2448/1979. Előterjesztés az Állami Tervbizottság részére. Tárgy: A kisipar szolgáltató tevékenységének fejlesztése. Könnyűipari Minisztérium.

MF/258i/1979a. Előterjesztés az Állami Tervbizottság részére. Tárgy: A kisipari szolgáltató tevékenységének fejlesztése.

MF/258i/1979b. Jelentés a kisipar V. ötéves tervi feladatai teljesítésének helyzetéről, a kisiparra vonatkozó új közgazdasági és jogi szabályozás tapasztalatairól, javaslat a VI. ötéves terv fő célkitűzéseire.

MF/HI/1984. Levél dr. Hetényi István elvtárs, pénzügyminiszternek. 03.16: Hazafias Népfront Országos Tanácsának Titkára.

MF/MH/58.956/1983.XVII. A Művelődésügyi Minisztérium Államtitkárának

jelentése az új kisüzemi szervezeti formák működésének eddig tapasztalatairól.
MF/MH/90.560/1982. Az Egészségügyi Miniszter állásfoglalása egyes humán szolgáltatások magánkezdeményezésen alapuló szervezetek utján való ellátásáról.
MF/MIT/MI/1987. Előterjesztés az Állami Tervbizottág részére. Javaslat a magánkisvállalkozások fejlődését előmozdító intézkedésekre. Székács Anna iratai.
MF/MP/Ui–2588/83. Levél dr. Medgyessy Péter elvtársnak, miniszterhelyettes. 08.29: Kisiparosok Országos Szervezete, Országos Központ, Elnökhelyettes.
MF/MP/Ui.2596/83. Tájékoztató az új kisüzemi formák működésének Borsod megyei tapasztalatairól. 08.31, 1983. MSZMP Borsod-Abaúj-Zemplén Megyei Bizottsága. Medgyessy Péternek.
MF/MP/Ui.2598/83. Levél dr. Meggyessy Péter elvtársnak, miniszterhelyettes, Pénzügyminisztérium. 09.01, 1983. Szakszervezetek Országos Tanácsa, Főtitkárhelyettes.
MF/MP/Ui–2817/83. Levél Medgyessy Péternek. 1983. Művelődésügyi Minisztérium.
MF/SZA/1983. Megjegyzések a "kisvállalkozási formák elterjesztésének lehetősége az egészségügyi és szociálpolitikai ágazatban" c. anyaghoz. Székács Anna iratai.
ML/2718/82.Ui–7/1982. Állásfoglalás. Munkajogi Önálló Osztály, Munkaügyi Minisztérium.
PIA/276.94/111/1949. Jegyzőkönyv a Kisipari Pártbizottság 1949 július 14-én tartott értekezletéről. Csatolt feljegyzések.
PIA/276.94/121/1949. A kisiparosság mai helyzete. Államgazdasági Osztály.
PIA/276.94/142/1949. A kisipar 5 éves terve. Államgazdasági Osztály.
PIA/276.94/142/1950. Marosán György feljegyzése a kisipar helyzetéről.
PIA/276.116/18/1953. Az ötéves terv mezőgazdasági és kézművesipari termelési keretszámainak mérlegelése. Országos Terv Hivatal.
PIA/288-/5/945/PB/1985. Jelentés a kiegészítő és kisegítő gazdasági tevékenységek helyzetéről. MSZMP Központi Bizottsága.
PIA/288/22/1970/18. Jelentés. Csongrád megyei bizottság Propaganda és Művelődési Osztálya.
PIA/288.15/76/1964. Előterjesztés a munkaerőhelyzetről és a munkaerőgazdálkodás feladatairól. Államgazdasági Osztály.
PIA/288.15/137/1967. Feljegyzés a Gazdaságpolitikai Bizottság 1967 december 13–i (18.) üléséről.
PIA/288.15/183/1970. Előterjesztés az MSZMP Gazdaságpolitikai Bizottsága részére. Tárgy: a magánszemélyek gépjármű használata. Közlekedési és Postaügyi Miniszter. A GPB válasza.
PIA/288.22/1970/2. Információs jelentés. MSZMP Bács-Kiskun megyei bizottság.
PIA/288.22/1970/17. Információs jelentés. Szakszervezetek Országos Tanácsa.
PIA/288.22/1970/18. Jelentés a népgazdaság fejlesztésének 1969. évi tapasztalatai és az 1970. évi feladatai c. téma feldolgozásáról. MSZMP Budapesti Bizottság Propaganda és Művelődési Osztály.
PIA/288.22/1970/19a. Jelentés az Oktatási Igazgatóság által 1969/70-es oktatási

évben szerzett pártiskolai és egyéb továbbképző tanfolyamok tapasztalatairól. Heves megyei bizottság oktatási igazgatósága.
PIA/288.22/1970/19b. Jelentés a pártiskola 1969/70 évi munkájáról. Vas megyei bizottság oktatási igazgatósága.
PIA/288.22/1970/34. Információs jelentés. MSZMP Egyesült Izzó üzemi pártszervezete.
PIA/288.22/1970/35a. Információs jelentés. Csepel Vas- és Fémüvek.
PIA/288.22/1970/35b. Információs jelentés. MSZMP Videoton PB.
PIA/288.24/1970/56. Jelentés a mezőgazdasági termelőszövetkezetek kiegészítő tevékenységéről.
PIA/288.24/1970/57/1970. Jelentés a termelőszövetkezeti melléküzemek vizsgálatáról.
PIA/288.5/200/1960. Előterjesztés a Politikai Bizottsághoz a népgazdaságban tapasztalt feszültségek okairól. Államgazdasagi Osztály.
PIA/288.5/223/1961. Tájékoztató a Politikai Bizottság részére a mezőgazdaság szocialista átszervezésével kapcsolatos néhány gazdaságpolitikai kérdésről. Államgazdasági Osztály.
PIA/288.5/327/1964. Jegyzőkönyv a Politikai Bizottság 1964 február 18-án megtartott üléséről.
PIA/288.5/352/1964. Jegyzőkönyv a Politikai Bizottság 1964. november 27-i üléséről.
PIA/288.5/371/1965. Javaslat a Titkárságnak az 1965. március 2-i titkársági határozat kiegészítésére. MSZMP KB.
PIA/288.5/375/1965. Jegyzőkönyv a Politikai Bizottság 1965. szeptember 21-én tartott üléséről.
PIA/288.5/377/1965. Jegyzőkönyv a Politikai Bizottság 1965 október 12-én tartott üléséről.
PIA/288.5/381/1965. Jegyzőkönyv a Politikai Bizottság 1965 december 3-i üléséről.
PIA/288.5/384/1966a. Jegyzőkönyv a Politikai Bizottság 1966. január 4-én megtartott üléséről.
PIA/288.5/384/1966b. Jelentés a Politikai Bizottság részére a termelőszövetkezeti mozgalom helyzetéről és irányelvek megszilárdításuk néhány feladatára. KB Mezőgazdasági Osztálya.
PIA/288.5/394/1966. A Politikai Bizottság állásfoglalása a gazdasági mechanizmus reformjáról.
PIA/288.5/406/1966. Jegyzőkönyv a Politikai Bizottság 1966. október 4-i üléséről.
PIA/288.5/426/1967. Gazdaságpolitikai irányelvek az új mechanizmus bevezetésének időszkában. A Politikai Bizottság 1967 június 6-án tartott ülésére.
PIA/288.5/563/1971. A Politikai Bizottság 1971. szeptember 7-i határozata a termelőszövetkezetek nem mezőgazdasági jellegű tevékenysége állami szabályozásának alapelveiről.
PIA/288.5/621/1973. A Központi Bizottság irányelvei a munkásosztály szerepének erősítésére, helyzetének javítására. A Politikai Bizottság által kiküldött munkabizottság.

PIA/288.5/684/1976. Jegyzőkönyv a Politikai Bizottság 1976. február 10-én megtartott üléséről.

PIA/288.5/687/1976. Jelentés a Politikai Bizottságnak a mezőgazdaságban a gazdasági együttmüködés formái fejlődéséről, javaslat az agráripari egyesülések alapelveire. KB Ipari, Mezőgazdasági és Közlekedési Osztály.

PIA/288.5/694/1976. Irányelvek a szövetkezetek kongresszusán résztvevő kommunisták részére. KB Ipari, Mezőgazdasági és Közlekedési Osztály.

PIA/288.5/793/1980a. Előterjesztés a Politikai Bizottságnak a másodlagos gazdaság szerepéről és fejlesztésének lehetőségéről. MSZMP KB Gazdaságpolitikai Osztály.

PIA/288.5/793/1980b. Határozat (a másodlagos gazdaság szerepéről és fejlesztésének lehetőségéről) MSZMP KB.

PIA/288.5/996/1987. Jelentés a Politikai Bizottságnak a kiegészítő és kisegítő gazdasági tevékenységek helyzetéről. MSZMP KB.

PIA/288.7/228/1965. A Titkárság 1965. március 2-i határozata a pártmunkások másodállás és mellékfoglalkozás vállalásainak rendezéséről. MSZMP KB.

PIA/288.f.5/945/PB/1985. Jelentés a kiegészítő és kisegítő gazdasági tevékenységek helyzetéről. MSZMP Központi Bizottsága.

PIA/BB.1/VB–1986/2. Jelentés az önálló gazdasági munkaközösségek, az ipari-szolgáltató szövetkezeti szakcsoportok és a szerződéses üzemeltetés fővárosi tapasztalatairól. MSZMP Budapesti Bizottsága, Gazdaságpolitikai Osztály.

PIA/BB/1.f./1984–89/330. Tájékoztató a kiegészítő, kisegítő gazdaság fejlődésének helyzetéről. MSZMP Budapesti Bizottsága, Gazdaságpolitikai Osztály.

PIA/BB/1.f./1984–89/v./110. Jelentés a leányvállalatoknál, kisszövetkezeteknél és egyéb vállalkozási formáknál dolgozó párttagok és pártszervezetek helyzetéről, munkájuk tapasztalatairól. MSZMP Budapesti Bizottsága.

PIA/BB/1.f/1984–89/GPO/8. A vállalati gazdasági munkaközösségek helyzete a XV. Kerületi pártszervezetek hatáskörébe tartozó egységeknél. MSZMP XV. ker. Bizottsága.

SOWL 1986. Javaslat a munkafegyelem javítására teendő intézkedésekre, a munkaidőalap védelmére. Előterjesztés a Gazdaságpolitikai Bizottság részére. Január.

SOWL/1976–1/1982. V/21. Észrevételek a kisgazdaságok, a kisüzemi termelés tapasztalatairól a GPB részére készitett jelentés tervezethez. November 30: Állami Bér- és Munkaügyi Hivatal.

SOWL/2741–1/1987.V/5. Tájékoztató a Minisztertanács részére a munkaidő jobb kihasználására, a munkafegyelem javítására hozott 3253/1986. Mt.h. számú határozat végrehajtásáról.

SOWL/79–1/1985.V/31. A munkaidőalap védelmét szolgáló átfogó cselekvési program. Állami Bér- és Munkaügyi Hivatal Foglalkoztatáspolitikai és Területi Főosztály.

Newspapers and Periodicals

Figyelő (economic weekly)
HVG (economic weekly)

Magyar Nemzet (daily newspaper)
Népszabadság (daily newspaper)
168 óra (weekly political paper)
Pártélet (journal of the internal affairs of the Hungarian Socialist Workers' Party)
Privinfo (monthly information bulletin of the State Property Agency).
Társadalmi Szemle (theoretical journal of the Hungarian Socialist Workers' Party)
Új Írás (literary monthly)

Index